About the Author

Anne lived and worked in Algeria, Greece, Jamaica, Jordan, Kenya, Pakistan, Tanzania and Turkey. She now lives with her husband John in the Scottish Borders.

Dedication

This book is dedicated to all who have ever made a
home in foreign parts.

Anne Prentice

BORN UNDER A WANDERING STAR:

Memoirs of Forty-Five Years on the Overseas Circuit

AUSTIN MACAULEY
PUBLISHERS LTD.

A CIP catalogue record for this title is available from the British Library.

ISBN 9781785540462 (Paperback)
ISBN 9781785540479 (Hardback)
ISBN 9781785540486 (E-Book)

www.austinmacauley.com

First Published (2016)
Austin Macauley Publishers Ltd.
25 Canada Square
Canary Wharf
London
E14 5LQ

Acknowledgments

I must thank Patricia Mosel for invaluable advice on the content and style of the manuscript; also Robert Sears for ongoing help with computer skills, Christine Sears for selecting a manageable number of photos from the many available, and lastly my husband John for patiently putting up with my preoccupation over several years.

Anne Prentice

Contents

Chapter 1 A Born Traveller 13

Chapter 2 Never on Tuesdays 34

Chapter 3 A Byzantine Joke 47

Chapter 4 Island in the Sun 65

Chapter 5 Small Island 78

Chapter 6 The Die is Cast 93

Chapter 7 Biggest is Best 103

Chapter 8 Bradford, Bolton and Burnley 115

Chapter 9 Families 131

Chapter 10 Reflections in a Palmerie 158

Chapter 11 Sahara 187

Chapter 12 The Two-Year Tourists 205

Chapter 13 The Land of Hamna 228

Chapter 14 The Damned Dam 252

Chapter 15 The Lake on the Roof of the World 273

Chapter 16 Land of Milk and Honey 297

Chapter 17 Living in An Antique Land 321

Chapter 18 Byzantium 352

Chapter 19 Byzantium Revisited 366

Chapter 1

A Born Traveller

Birth is unremembered. This is just as well perhaps since Anne will discover, many years later when she delivers her children, that newborns may arrive in the world looking like victims of a mugging; pushed, pulled, pummelled, punched, reddened and bruised. Her earliest memories, in 1936, are of a train to Liverpool dockside bound for... India. Father is posted to the Royal Bombay Sappers and Miners while Mother returns to the land of her birth, the realm of her awakening to young womanhood and her courting; now the sixth generation of her family to be posted to India. Grandfathers and grandmothers come to Liverpool from the Home Counties to see off the family.

Is there a tear in the eye of the maternal Grandmother? She had spent the first thirty years of her married life in India going out in 1904 from a Fife farming family as the bride of a civil engineer in the Indian Civil Service. She lived to the hilt, riding, hunting, tennis, shooting: she even shot a crocodile. Or thought she had. Tied nose to tail, put in a sack and slung in the boot of the car, the crocodile regained consciousness slowly. By the time it was unloaded and emptied out onto the drive it was ready to move; and did, in circles.

Sometimes grandmother accompanied her husband on his tours of inspection: six weeks away round the district in Bombay Presidency. Twelve miles a day by bullock cart staying at Government rest houses or *Dak* (Post) bungalows. In the first cart sat grandfather and grandmother in upholstered armchairs fireside style, swathed in goggles, veils, gauntlets, hats, scarves, overall capes and dust covers. Behind came the food cart and the kitchen accessories, followed by the servants' cart and their food. Then came the furniture cart carrying the office and bathroom equipment, and finally the bullocks' fodder cart: in all a five-strong bullockade.

India, a magic place, land of Rudyard Kipling and Kim, The Grand Trunk Road and the Great Game! Princes and peacocks, of course, but also heat, dust, disease such as cholera, typhoid, dysentery, malaria and squalor and decay. The British Raj was not all dress parades and blanco, tennis parties, polo and pig-sticking. It was also mind-blowing boredom (Home leave came once every three or four years) and ruinous routine; it was also family exile and parental rupture since children were summarily sent 'Home' to school in Britain.

The India of this record is culled from old photo albums, and grandparents', and parents' reminiscences. Half a century later all the frustrations and disappointments have been exorcised. Perceptions reveal a hierarchy of eminence among both the expatriates and the galaxies of Indian staff, comforting for those who did not infringe any of the unwritten rules. Grandfather had followed his father into the Indian Civil Service: not into the Administration among the 'Heaven-Born' but into the Public Works Department, Roads and Bridges. He was not among the third class, the *Box Wallahs* or commercial people. Busy with his engineering career and his inspections which often incorporated a shooting safari, probably for the pot, the *sahib* was well occupied.

Not so the *memsahib*.

Grandmother received an excellent education at Dollar Academy where she first met her future husband. Pretty, practical and pragmatic, she had no thought of early marriage. She travelled. In France and in Switzerland she lived *en famille* teaching English to assorted youngsters. In the late nineteenth century she was a Governess; nowadays she would be a TEFL teacher.

At the age of 27, she married her school friend and sailed to India. 'How did the bride react?' Was she intrigued by all the strange sights, smells, people, climates, colours and cultures or did she quake at the immense task of adapting to such an alien environment? There is no record. She certainly learned to speak some Hindustani. What else did she do to relieve the ennui spawned by a posse of servants already well versed in every idiosyncrasy of her new husband? There would be Bearer or butler, a Cook, a Boy to run around the Cook, a Sweeper to bring the water for the bathtub and empty the thunderbox, a *Syce* or groom to look after the horses. In addition there would be a *Mali* or gardener to water the plants, the plaited mats hanging around the verandah, platoons of pot plants and, indeed, the house walls themselves to cool them down in the hot weather. Some *memsahibs* became so adjusted to frequent postings that they kept their entire garden in tubs, jerry cans, pots and pails so that it could be transported with them to the next posting. And when, a year later, Grandmother was delivered of a daughter in Poona (Pune) an *Ayah* or nursemaid was added to the ménage. There would also, of course be the services of the *Dhobi* who washed, starched and ironed, and of the *Dhirzi* who came upon command to cut, fit and sew or mend, clothes, curtains or sheets. Any garment could be copied; shirts, trousers, dresses, skirts and divided skirts, gave him no problem. Seated cross-legged on the verandah before a creaking sewing machine, the *Dhirzi* could deliver a new garment in a day if bullied, in two days if not. It is probable that Grandmother did not indulge in extra-marital affairs, drink or ill-health and thereby qualify for an early cabin in a Home-bound ship. Perhaps she taught; children of expatriate neighbours, servants and their families, anyone. Or assisted in community work, charity coffee (tea) mornings with bring-and-buy or make-and-bake stalls. No one knows.

How did she manage her household in a hot climate in the days before fridges? There were glass butter dishes cooled by standing in water-filled earthenware containers and larder cupboards surrounded by charcoal casings continually sprayed with water, evaporation being a powerful coolant in communities without electricity. Muslin-covered cages were placed over food and beaded net covers over milk jugs and sugar bowls. Table legs stood in tins of water to deter ants. Everyone automatically knocked their boots and shoes on the floor before upending them to tip out a lurking scorpion, slept under mosquito nets and wore slippers to the bathroom lest snakes had slithered up the drain hole.

What did the grandparents eat? They may not have had much choice. A cook was a necessity, cooking being done over one or more wood fires in an adjacent shed. Cook suggested the daily menu, bargaining for the ingredients in the bazaar, and if cook added his commission it is probably no more than the *memsahib* would have had to pay the merchants in the bazaar. For dinner parties, likely menus would start with soup – mulligatawny or Julienne – then maybe cutlets or meat rissoles (known as 'russells pups' on one station) or curry. This would be followed by trifle, pineapple or banana fritters or fruit salad. Lastly, a savoury such as sardines or anchovies or Gentleman's Relish on toast fingers would be offered, these items drawn from the precious 'Home' imports cupboard. Beer and spirits, made locally, were available and served. Game, when they were on tour, was a welcome change; guinea fowl, jungle cock, duck, deer meat and wild pig were enjoyed while on safari but game does not keep long in a world without refrigerators so did not appear on the dinner party table. Dairy products were difficult to obtain. Milk was likely to be from buffalo rather than cow since the buffalo is tubercular-free. It was normal for a *memsahib* to command the *Dudhwallah*, or milkman, to milk his animal at her verandah steps before her eyes lest he be tempted to omit washing the udder before milking or add a measure of water to the can.

Father's family was Army and Establishment. Grandpa was in the Highland Light Infantry and did well for himself by marrying the Colonel's daughter. He served in Aldershot, Ireland (stationed at Mullingar), Flanders Field in the 1st World War and later in Edinburgh. Looking further back beyond Father's mother, the Colonel's daughter, there was a China posting at the time of the Boxer Rebellion in 1900. Upon retirement, Grandpa was appointed an officer of the Scottish Curling Club and for some years wintered in Adelboden attending to Scottish curling interests in Switzerland.

Father joined the Royal Engineers. He loved the Army, its order, discipline and sport. There were sporting opportunities on offer far above his means; rugger, athletics (he hurdled for the Army), rowing, squash, skiing, polo, sailing, he did them all. If the Army did not offer city salaries he did not mind. He had half a day's pay for half a day's work and all the sporting facilities, Army quarters and, latterly, a batman available to him. When, later, his granddaughter was to join the Army for much the same reasons, go to Sandhurst, get a Commission in the Gunners, he would have turned in his grave. Women were, of course, for the home.

Mother had bullied her parents into letting her attend Art courses at the *École des Beaux Artes* in Paris. There she lodged with a school friend, Jean Leadbetter who was studying at the *Conservatoire de Musique*, in a pension carefully chaperoned by two mademoiselles, known in their absence as 'Pip' and 'Squeak'. But art alone had no future and eventually Mother sailed to join her parents in India, one of the 'fishing fleet' which arrived each season to join relations, have a ball and catch a husband. Looking through the old photo albums she had much fun, and plenty of swains.

Father and Mother met in India and were married in London; Father limped, hirpling with the help of a stick, up the aisle having just had a knee job done on an old rugger injury. Anne's amnesic birth occurred in Hertford hospital three years later in 1933.

***

And so to Bombay by P&O aged three, goes Anne. By which time there is an unsolicited addition to the family, brother Colin of one and a half years. The ship is massive, inspiring in its panoramas of planked pavements and playgrounds; its shops, hairdressers, restaurants and endless cabined, carpeted corridors of tiny homes, each with its numbered front door. Do they enter by the Gateway of India? No, of course not, that is for Viceroys and visiting royalty. They arrive at Bombay docks in plebeian style.

One cannot say whether they travel POSH, that is Port Out, Starboard Home but they take with them Nanny. Not because Mother wants a nanny (she does secretly) but because the Army accorded officers of Father's rank free passage for a nanny. The Army saw nannies as a way of providing suitable brides for NCOs: better by far than having them 'go native'. In years to come this will be an image to flash upon the inward eye in connection with the French Army 'drumhead' marriages in the early days of the French colonisation in Algeria in the 1840s. The Army advertised in Rousillon and Languedoc for suitable strong peasant daughters and offered to send them to Algeria with 10FF in their pocket and a gold wedding ring in a sealed envelope. Many went.

Of India in Anne's early childhood there is scant memory. Photos show a serious child with two huge bows in her hair, in party dress, in fancy dress, sitting in child baskets on porters' backs on an outing in the hills; in *topi* on a pony or bicycle. Sometimes there is a move from Bombay to Rawalpindi in the Punjab. There are expeditions to Murree and Changlagalli in the Himalayan foothills but the family does not summer in the hill stations. Damage limitation to the oppressive mounting heat and humidity which precedes the onset of the monsoon in July, is by ceiling fans, water-sprayed walls, wet woven matting on deep verandahs and long, long midday siestas. Then comes the intoxicating relief of the first showers, exploding baked dust and exhaling its pungent aroma. Alas the onset of the monsoon brings its own problems. Water drips from the ceiling and a bowl is placed and another and another until every available vessel is in use. Eventually, Father leads his team of surveyors, all wearing gumboots and wielding umbrellas, through the house and soon repairs are under way. Thump, thump, thump... for three days with heartbeat rhythm that signals a migraine, mud is beaten onto the flat roof. It happens every year.

Towards the end of the India posting, war breaks out in Europe and home leave at the end of 1939 suddenly becomes a mobilisation of servicemen stationed in India. Father's unit entrains at 'Pindi for Karachi, four days distant. Mercifully, it is mid-December, the cool season. From Karachi a convoy of five troopships sets out. Apart from stringent blackout regulations, families manage a fun Christmas on board ship. At the children's fancy dress party, Anne is Miss Muffet with spider on shoulder made from Mother's ball of sock knitting wool, stuck with pipe cleaner legs, pipe cleaners being in ready supply since Mother is a heavy smoker from a long cigarette holder. Five year old Colin is to go as Doc, one of Snow White's seven Dwarves. Mother descends on him and envelops him in Father's shirt, stuffing a pillow up the shirtfront and securing a bright scarf tight around child, pillow and shirt.

"Why?" wails Colin.

"Because you are Doc."

"I don't want to be Doc." The cry is heartfelt.

"Oh yes you do. Now put this on." Mother holds up a cardboard and cotton wool contraption, which she drapes over Colin's face and hooks behind his ears. "That is Doc's specs and beard," she explains optimistically.

"I won't!" shouts Colin.

"Yes, darling, you must. You might win the prize." The cabin suddenly resembles a bull-fighting arena. Colin bunches his body and hurls himself at Mother, fists flying, feet flailing. She ducks, awaiting the return of the bull calf. Colin, looking like the cow with the crumpled horn, the cardboard specs sticking high above his brow, roars revenge but his voice is muffled by a mouthful of cotton wool. Flinging handfuls of cotton wool about the cabin, Colin launches himself floorwards, kicking and bawling. Mother unfurls like a bracken frond, cautiously, as in a late cold spring. She gives in graciously.

"Right. Go without the specs and beard. Come on. We're late." She scoops up Colin, airlifting him to the ballroom, thrusts him with a face like thunder into a parade of pirates and fairies where he wins, as the Dwarf Grumpy.

Five troopships dock at Marseilles, twelve French trains being commandeered to carry the servicemen and their families across France since the Atlantic passage is considered too risky, destination unknown; perhaps Dieppe, possibly Calais but unlikely. The trains are not the best and frequent faults cause delays. At a dim, blue-lit, blacked out platform like a movie-town prison corridor, the first night is fractured by the raucous ranting of furious French railwaymen. They argue with passengers about one of the trains' dining cars whose brake is binding so that the train slows down in a series of kangaroo leaps accompanied by tumbling children and luggage. Cracked limbs and broken mirrors later, the passengers insist that the dining car be disconnected. The railwaymen, already late, are afraid of further delays which will jeopardise their promised bonus.

Soon agonised shrieks of released steam couplings', wounded groans, crashes of shunting wagons and warning whistles of explosion as scheduled *rapides* scream through the station in a shower of scarlet sparks, rend the night. Anne lies on her bunk, petrified as a hare in its form. So this is war! There is a war on, everyone says so and now she knows what war is.

Eventually truculent train drivers shunt the faulty diner to the rear but remain obdurate about allowing passengers time to get refreshments at stations. Passengers have to wait for halts, have to race down the platform with trays and carry back their rations. Without warning, the trains will move on and there is a dash for doors, children being swung up steep steps and fathers vaulting in after them. Anne's recurring nightmare remains one of running after a train which does not stop long enough for boarding. Two more days of altercation, complaint and frustration end at... Cherbourg. Here, commandeered ferries load everyone and everything: destination and ETA both subject to random rumour and whispered puffery until dreary delays eventually deliver the ferries to Southampton at 8 o'clock on New Year's Eve, 1939. It is snowing. At midnight, the weary family steps off a local train in Hampshire into Grandfather's arms. He drives with dipped headlights the short distance home, sweeping into the black hole of the garage, the nightmare journey over.

The car headlights illuminate garage walls hung with a tiger's head, its glass eyes glinting dangerously, and a dozen antlered bison, sambur and deer skulls; Grandfather's Indian hunting trophies. While memory of that first sight remains as a heart-stopping shock, years of residence in the grandparents' home breeds familiarity with the trophies which will inspire rainy day games. A special thrill is a hall-wide slide on a tiger skin, arms around the stuffed head; adrenalin-raising since there is a spank-worthy ban on this activity. Less stimulating will be the disposal of these trophies twenty years later when a widowed Grandmother moves into a small apartment. A leopard skin goes to a regimental band in Aldershot, another to the Salvation Army; a local repertory theatre is persuaded to give storage space to some native spears and spiked turtle shell shields but the bulk of the skulls and heads are buried in the garden. The tiger skin moulders in Mother's attic for another twenty years before being sold on with her house to the owner of a pet shop.

War remains for another four and a half years after the midwinter journey. Mother learns the hard way to cook with rationed, dried, egg powder and little meat except rabbit. They pick pounds of rose hips for the Government to be processed into vitamin C-rich syrup for the nation's children. And later, at boarding school, Anne spends Saturday mornings pulling charlock weed out of local farmers' wheat fields. The autumn half-term is always dedicated to potato-picking; a week of hard labour in all weathers but most of the girls love it, shouting popular ballads as they travel from school to the farms in commandeered furniture vans.

Peace when it comes seems no different from war: they are still rationed; 60 grams of butter, 60 grams of sweets per week, bread units, clothes coupons: such desirable units and coupons can make marvellous gifts and no doubt coupons and rationed items fuel a flourishing black market. So be it.

***

She is sent to an all-girls boarding school situated on the top of the Chiltern Hills, a bracing blustery settlement with huge horizons to the back of beyond. The expansive environment incubates a latent travel bug now developing into a disease. Always a bit of a loner, naturally inclined to the solo mode, Anne could lie on the springy, scented turf and perceive, hung between Heaven and the Here, cloudscapes from the uttermost parts of the earth. Banks of cauliflower cumulus are the Himalayas, windy mackerel cirrus the Sahara and nimbo-cumulus with coming curtains of rain, are the terrible tearing territory of Tierra del Fuego. The school's stated aim is to turn out good wives and mothers. Confidence building is not on the curriculum, whereas deportment is. "Anne, if it's your bosom on the table pull it up; if it's your belly pull it in," roars the games mistress across the dining hall. Charm is not a subject and coquetry is frowned upon. Sex education is taboo but elocution is highly recommended.

A stocktaking of her suitable skills are mostly on the debit side; lack of confidence, no sense of direction, totally un-streetwise and without any vocational interest except a desire to travel. On the credit side, there is a prediction of three respectable Higher School Certificate passes, in English, History and Geography plus an optional extra in Art. But the destination is marriage, the brain having been programmed consciously and subconsciously since birth. Romantic love and erotic pleasures are confined to fiction.

So far so good, but where does that leave her? Number one task is to find a husband but in the meantime there must be something more to life. Indeed. There are four immediate options, namely nursing, teaching, secretarial duties or a variation on one of these themes. Radiotherapy is recommended and, following an interview, a training post at the Middlesex Hospital in London is offered. She is just seventeen.

Of doubtful value on the skills credit side is a naïve belief that if she is good to God and goes sometimes to church, God will be good to her. She discovers the maidens' prayer to St Catherine:

"A husband, sweet St. Catherine; handsome, sweet St. Catherine; rich, sweet St. Catherine; soon, sweet St. Catherine."

Alas, she does not know personally any saints on whom she can call. At this point, the school's headmistress, with perspicacious divination, comes on line. Is she a saint? She does not look like one, being a dumpy disciplinarian, daughter of Duty, wrinkled, sporting long grey whiskers on her cheeks and chin. But one cannot judge by looks.

"What about going to university?" University! No one in the family has ever been to university. Military Staff College, The 'Shop at Woolwich, Engineering College for the Indian Civil Service, yes; even Mother's Beaux Artes in Paris for two frolicsome years. But university, no!

"You should get to university on the strength of your Higher Schools Certificate," she predicts. "What about Edinburgh where I graduated?" she prompts. "You could read History," she pauses, "or Geography."

The idea tantalises: as mould in bread it spreads its tentacles through the system. Yes, this is what is wanted above all.

"What will you read?" The saint, in a second interview, continues remorselessly. "History is an excellent foundation for life." What she means is that a degree in History would furnish one with employment, probably in teaching, and thereafter fit one for life in the community or in wider society; in other words, marriage.

But the gymnastics of language, etymological exercise, the fine-tuning of paraphrase and précis and the primitive power of metaphor and onomatopoeia vault among the pericranium's parallel bars. "I prefer English."

"Ah!" sighs the saint, pausing long enough to encompass the career choice of a lifetime. "English is a very difficult and highly competitive subject. There's a lot of comparative literature to do. You may or may not get into the English Department."

The Higher Certificate syllabus has not mentioned comparative literature and Anne is not yet equipped to be a loser. "Geography then." Yes. There are visions of mountains and rivers, sites and situations, people and populations: the where and why of the world. And travel!

So to Edinburgh University aged seventeen and a half. Mentally she is still in cotton socks and gym slips but there she finds a mixed world of men and women. Mercifully sheltered socially in a women's hall of residence, she makes a few good friends, goes to dances, on skiing holidays and class excursions. Meanwhile nothing touches the core woman. Amnesia wraps the four university years. But a degree, MA Honours Geography, is recorded in the 1954 lists: a beautiful, vellum inscribed in Latin contained in a red canister entitles her to call herself a *Magistrum in Artibus Liberalibus*!

One event remains in the memory. Her pesky desire to travel languishes undernourished during the university years, money the main problem. In the final year, a hall of residence friend, an MA Honours Fine Art student named Ann Powell, desperate to travel, hatches a plot. What about a University Expedition, an official one blessed by the University and financially assisted with a travel bursary? Where? "Well, Greece of course; good old Byzantine Greece" volunteers Ann Powell whose Head of Fine Art Department is the eminent Byzantologist, Professor David Talbot Rice.

Why not Greece? A geographer can work anywhere. Anne seeks an appointment with the Head of the Geography Department, Professor Alan Grant Ogilvie.

"Greece!" he muses, his eyes focusing on something several thousand miles away. "And what" he erupts "Is the purpose of this expedition?"

"Do some research, collect some data, record it all then write it up when we get home."

Meanwhile, Ann has a recommendation from her Professor that Thessaloniki in north Greece would yield interesting study. Taking the idea of Thessaloniki to Anne's Professor Ogilvie in the Geography Department, the familiar distant gaze returns. Unbeknownst to Anne, Alan

Grant Ogilvie is an inherent terrestrial space traveller, researching and writing about Morocco, the USA, the Andes and, more extensively, the Balkans. Serving in the British Army during the Gallipoli Campaign in 1915, stationed temporarily in Thessaloniki and later fighting in the Turkish Dardanelles, his geographer's eye and enquiring mind ranged across the landscapes interpreting topography, land use and political patterns. He had later been invited by the Naval Intelligence Division of the Admiralty to write *Greece* and edit the Balkans edition of their *Geographical Handbook*. Minutes later, Professor Ogilvie promises Anne an introduction to the Geography Department of Salonika University.

Ann in the Fine Art Department is joined by another Fine Art student from their third year, Mimi from Manchester, and also by two final year Norwegian students from the Department of Architecture, Finn and Bengt. The University stipulates that they must have a member of staff on the expedition and Alan Carr from the College of Art is persuaded to join them.

Hoorah! They are almost there. Many letters later they achieve University of Edinburgh Expedition status, permission to stay at a University of Salonika student hostel, the patronage of the Duke of Edinburgh, some reels of free film from the National Geographic Society and a very basic travel bursary towards their return rail fare to Salonika.

***

The train to Salonika is the Orient Express, no less; *wagons-couloir, wagons-lit, wagons-restaurant* and *wagons-poste* coupled together and labelled 'Vienna', 'Skopje', 'Salonika' and 'Istanbul'. But this is not Agatha Christie's Orient Express. Rather, the Edinburgh University Expedition carries its own food and drink for the 36 hour journey, sits up all night, talks tumultuously, plays cards and arrives haggard, unwashed, bristly, tense and terse to the point of monosyllables; they could pass as a posse of druggies. (They have almost bisected Europe but only travelled half the distance of Septimus Severus, a first century AD Roman Governor who was born in modern Libya and died in Britain's York. This observation is offered merely as a measure of awe at the enormity of the ancient Roman Empire in relation to modern Europe. True, the journey time bears no comparison but it is possible the culture shock is of similar magnitude.) Having been flung from Scotland to Salonika they, the Edinburgh University Expedition, are at their most impressionable: blinding Mediterranean July light on tired eyes, psychedelic patterns in black and white, *a la* Bridget Riley the artist who played compositional games with zebra stripes in the 1960s. An enthusiastic welcome springs from Greek students in the University hostel, and indeed from staff members who had been apprised on the academic grapevine of their arrival. Professors David Talbot Rice and now the late Alan Ogilvie are manifestly more eminent than their respective undergraduates have hitherto appreciated. The Greek support for their studies in fine art, architecture and geography is both overwhelming and humbling. Has the travel project snowballed, seized the controls of the space machine and flung them unequipped into a maelstrom? They hope they are worthy of such interest.

Their Greek student colleagues not only persevere in teaching them rudimentary colloquial Greek but also in persuading Edinburgh to march with Salonika in an *Enosis* rally. *Enosis*, Greek for 'unity', represents a movement pursuing the unity of Cyprus with Greece. At this moment in time Cyprus, a British colony, and Greece, an independent kingdom, demand that Britain should release Cyprus and thereby allow it to become part of Greece. Both populations are Greek speakers, both lands having once been part of Byzantium and its Eastern Orthodox Church. It could be assumed, as Lawrence Durrel explains in his book,

Bitter Lemons of Cyprus[1], that Byzantium 'is the true parent of Modern Greece' and of Cyprus since in Byzantium, government and religion knew no geographical or racial bounds. Historically, however, there are differences. The Orthodox Church in Cyprus was appropriated by the Roman Catholic Church of the West in the Middle Ages and later restored to Orthodoxy, more revered than ever before, by the Ottoman Turks. Meanwhile rebellion and liberation from the Ottoman Empire started in Greece in 1821 where, aided and abetted by Lord Byron, the new Greece assumed a Hellenic moniker rather than a Byzantine one. Cyprus, which remained in Ottoman hands until the end of World War I when it was given to Britain, remained a bastion of orthodoxy, a true child of Byzantium. And it could be argued that the minority of Turks in Cyprus are descendants of peasants from Byzantine Anatolia who were obliged to convert from Christian Orthodoxy to Islam. *Enosis*, perhaps a myopic myth born of anxiety about the emerging size and strength of modern Turkey, is to prove itself a heartfelt root and branch movement in both Greece and Cyprus. At this moment in time however, in the summer of 1954, the *Enosis* student parades and demonstrations are jolly affairs, genially watched by police.

Edinburgh University Expedition to Salonika has less weighty concerns than the deep divisions of Cyprus. The students turn out in the cool of the day, after the water bowsers have sprinkled the hot streets, for the evening promenade. To background music of surging traffic and sounding trams, the city's youth stroll along the waterfront. Glamorous girls sashay along in balloon petticoats encased in pastel cotton print; lovingly, optimistically starched and ironed by mothers or aunties; sugared almonds pirouetting in spindle sandals, lightly laughing with their swains. Young blades, in carefully casual cambric, nonchalantly unbuttoned to the waist revealing tantalising glimpses of

---

[1] Durrell, Lawrence, *Bitter Lemons of Cyprus,* Faber and Faber 1957

hirsute chest: men like gods, macho by birthright with libido bred from babyhood. This is the marriage mart. Heavily chaperoned in groups of no less than three young people, there is nothing promiscuous, not a see-through bodice or slit skirt. Nevertheless, it is achingly, stirringly erotic, this strutting and preening display on the recognised road to the altar.

The Edinburgh students climb the hill, Salonika's Acropolis, to the Vlatadon Monastery at the summit. Father Pantagrios receives them in his spacious volume-lined study where a graceful vase holds three peacock feathers. This man of the cloth, in black clerical robe and with a stovepipe hat framing a genial face, has a skull reposing on his desk. Well, the clergy are in the business of life and death; it is appropriate.

"My *memento mori,*" grins the Father, "from my days as a medical student." He caresses the bald pate tenderly. "Now I am priest, doctor to the poor of this city and breeder of peacocks."

Peacocks! In the early Christian Church peacocks, symbol in Western Art of incorruptibility, are generally represented in confronting pairs. It is said that Father Pantagrios dispersed his flock in 1941 in an attempt to save some from falling into the hands of the occupying German Army cooks. On making enquiries at the end of the war, he discovered two birds remained alive.

"By great good fortune, they were a male and a female. Now I have thirty-five" he muses serenely on the indestructibility of his peacocks.

But what of the work these Edinburgh students are supposed to be doing? Anne is taken under the wing of a young lecturer in Salonika University Department of Forestry. Inspired by George's enthusiasm for his subject she ingests a deepening perception of the plight of Greek forests. The country has lived on its trees for generations; timber for fuel and construction, cutting, burning and clearing for cultivation or to improve grazing value, daily donkey loads of new-cut branches being carried miles for animal fodder, and millions of goats wandering in wooded country where they browse on young trees; these are sights so commonplace that they quickly become the norm. Greece is a country of small lowland plains sharply delineated by large tracts of mountain range and high inter-montaine plateaux. Vistas of limestone rock sparsely bristled with grey-green scrub, pale hills that bedazzle – bald as skulls, mountains stripped to the buff and small precious plains spotted with fruit trees, fig, almond or walnut, to provide midday shade for farming families. Only around a village can any woodland be found; usually shelterbelts, shade trees, orchards and cemetery cypress. The quantities of soil being washed in to the sea is appalling, soon there will be little left of this historic country.

The circumstances of deforestation are legion. There is indication from ancient Greek literature, place names, fossil remains and other such evidence that Greece was once well wooded. But centuries of occupation, revolution, war and civil war have made unbearable demands on the forest cover. Add to that a poor thin soil, steep gradients, extreme climate and sheer inaccessibility to all but villagers and their donkeys. It is a daunting prospect – this vision of reforestation that George unrolls before Anne.

"We will go and visit a Government Forest Nursery. You'll see the sort of work they are doing" he enthuses. "You know, the most obvious physical disadvantage to reforestation is climate. Our hot summers coincide with the dry season, unfortunately. And the planting season is far too short; the soil is not moist enough until November and killing frosts occur in December. There is only a six week planting season in autumn and another in spring from mid March until the end of April." George has the gift of inspiring his listeners with more than bare facts; it all comes across as live. They tour the nurseries inspecting a range of different species, pour over YPEM's (acronym for the Government Forest Service) statistics, reports and photographs.

"So you see, we can adapt our planting techniques. The soil is usually shallow and stony; right, place a stone to provide shade for the seedling, or a sod of earth even." George explains that this technique was preferred to planting the seedling in a depression of earth, a saucer to catch the rainwater, since the microclimate temperature in the bowl can rise, baking the seedling's roots. Even so, the Forest Service expects no more than a 30-50% rate of success in the southern islands and peninsulas.

And what about the rape and pillage of the bare soil, the ruination of farmland and roads to sheet and gully erosion caused by torrential rain on steep slopes? For generations, the earth has been abused and mismanaged by overstocking and by persistent burning to improve its grazing value until roots are damaged and the underlying limestone detrimentally altered. On the basis of one hectare per animal, two million goats is the maximum number but there are four million goats in Greece, all germane to the problem of re-forestation. There is a learned article here to be written, polished into immortal prose and submitted to an academic journal.

George's gift for inspiration does not stop at forestry. His eyes are laser beams singeing sleeping senses. During the evening promenade on George's arm, and later as stars lighten the indigo sky, Anne experiences a spontaneous primeval prompting; a kick-start to the fires of youth, a tingling in the loins which ripples to a sea swell, welling down to break on the beach in a solace of surf. So this is what life is really about. Awake the dormant woman.

"So, what now?" quizzes Father. The new woman is back home to the old game of Tinker, Tailor, Soldier, Sailor; Teacher, Secretary or Nursing Profession. The learned paper on re-forestation in Greece she submitted to a highbrow journal, *The Scottish Geographical Magazine,* is accepted for publication. Walking on air, she contemplates a career in journalism.

In the interim, the sudden summons to travel comes. The wheels of academia have turned. Professor Alan Ogilvie died in 1954 and some of his team of Readers and Lecturers moved on. One, Dr Robert Common, accepted a post in the Geography Department of Glasgow University and in the interval between Edinburgh and Glasgow, ventures into a six month sabbatical, travelling to Salonika to undertake study on the Vardar River delta. The late Professor Ogilvie, one of the British experts on Greece and present at the 1919 Versailles Peace Conference held by The League of Nations, was unable to return to the Balkans after his war service in Salonika in 1915. Since then much has changed. As Victoria Clark explains it,[2] modern Greece, emerging from Ottoman rule and, cherishing old dreams of Byzantium, had thought to take advantage of the Ottoman defeat and reclaim her heritage. The Greek army regained Istanbul in 1922 and, not content, marched on to Ankara where it was decisively defeated by Kemal Ataturk's recently reformed Turkish army. In Greek minds, this event was to live on as the *Katastroph* and will be significant in subsequent outbreaks of violence between Greeks and Turks. In 1922, The League of Nations, deciding to separate Greek from Turk, arbitrarily moved half a million Greeks from Turkey to Greece and a quarter of a million Turks from Greece to Turkey. A huge influx of Greek refugees from Asia Minor, were settled on the Vardar delta near Salonika. After extensive reclamation of delta swamps and lagoons occurred in the 1930s, it is now thought that a survey of current land utilisation would bring Professor Ogilvie's own work up to date.

"It has been suggested that you take part in this research project," explains Dr Robert Common now of the Geography Department in Glasgow University. "We can

[2] Clark, Victoria *Why Angels Fall: A Journey Through Orthodox Europe from Byzantium to Kosovo,* Macmillan, 2000, Picador 2001.

get you a Carnegie Grant-in-Aid-of-Research. It will mean about four months' field work in Greece and a period of study at Glasgow University thereafter."

So it is arranged. Bob Common is taking his wife, Cathy and their two children, Jennifer aged five and Bobby at two and a half. He is buying a second-hand car to be shipped from Marseilles to Piraeus. Correspondence with the British Consul in Salonika reveals the chance to housewarm his American counterpart's luxury apartment during the latter's home leave. The British Consul fails to mention the two outsized black poodles that go with the loan of the flat. Nevertheless it is all falling into place like a dream.

While Bob Common and family drive to Marseilles, Anne will go ahead by train to Montpellier University where Professor Marres of the Geography Department will brief her about the reclamation of the Rhone River delta from barren marsh to productive risiculture, a sequence thought to bear suitable comparison with the development of the Vardar delta. It is mid March 1955.

Chapter 2

Never on Tuesdays

'Voyageurs sont informes que le pourboire n'est pas compris!' Such is the notice in the station restaurant at the *Gare de Lyons*. What clarity! After travelling from London to Paris by train and ferry, fielding complaints in concert from taxi drivers and porters about the paucity of her tip. But Anne, a postgraduate student on a Carnegie Grant-in-Aid-of-Research, cannot afford to tip graciously.

Now for the detachment and curiosity of a born traveller. Overnight, sitting in a full third-class carriage, speeding south through France, conversation flows. The musical lilt of French intonation and inflexion is somnolent; sleep-a-little, sleep-a-lot, sleep—a-little, sleep-a-lot sing the train wheels.

Arriving next morning at Montpellier University and finding Professor Marres absent, sick, she is grateful to find herself apparently expected. A chair is offered while the Geography Department staff of one disappears to phone around for accommodation. In the hour that passes, Anne, tired and in need of a wash, experiences firstly relief and elation and secondly a loathing for the whole venture.

"I have arranged your accommodation and your course in Phonetics for Foreign Students," informs the lecturer. She almost acquiesces. Accommodation has been found in the *Chemin de Nazareth*.

"Is it possible to have a bath?" Anne begs the landlady.

"Ah no. Not possible. There are public baths in the town."

Oh well, c'est la vie. "What a delightful garden you have; it is enchanting." Anne lavishes praise.

"Yes. You must see round it. Let me show you." In the course of the promenade round the garden the landlady melts, offering the use of a tenant's bathroom. It has a half-length but deep bath and Ascot heater. Bliss. No door, no lock; just a yellow plastic curtain between bathroom and kitchen but in she goes, then her hair, then her undies.

On the morrow M. Marres, now recovered, helpfully offers a potted geography and history of the Camargue – delta of the Rhone – supplies a list of names and addresses to be visited, pats Anne's hand and sends her to the Office of the Director of *La Reserve Zoologique et Botanique de Camargue*.

So to one of the world's wild places armed with a permit of entry. From Arles at Tête du Rhone, the bus, bound for Les Saintes Maries, crosses a swirling turgid tide beating up river. Brilliant green wheat separates wide stretches of sandy moor; ditches and roads are lined with tall marsh grasses, slender plumed courtiers bowing to passing royalty. Vineyards pruned to the quick, a forest of sea polyps; paddy pans of yesteryear's rice with stubble half burnt. Then the marshes proper, the road at times being a narrow isthmus between shallow lagoons where the reeds whisper their secrets to the infant ripples who pass them on to the gulls. The Camargue is benign; two small boats in the reeds beguile, a *chasseur* and his dog slip across the road. But in its savage Mistral mood when new rice plants may be uprooted and dashed against the balk of their paddy pan and the air is opaque with an aqueous gale, then an angry deity can swallow an intruder in its saline water wastes.

Les Saints Maries de la Mer is a typical tourist resort, now out of season, on a Mediterranean Sea which, cold and corrugated, is disappointingly similar to the North Sea in Scotland. Groins protect the drifting sand and giant boulders protect the sea wall. In May, the town awakes for the Festival of St Mary Jacobe, sister of the Virgin and St. Mary Salome, mother of James and John, who are alleged to have landed here when fleeing persecution in AD40. Processions, flags, bunting, souvenirs, singing and dancing commemorate the Saints Maries in practice but in principal, it is Saint Sarah of the Gypsies who draws the crowds. Her effigy stays under wraps in the crypt since in the eyes of the Roman Catholic Church, she is not a saint, until once and once only during the Festival St. Sarah, bejewelled and crowned, is borne aloft around the town, happy highlight of the whole event.

Entry to the Camargue Reserve proves a problem: the gate is found to be nowhere near Les Saintes Maries. Passed like a parcel from hotel to taxi to Reserve Custodian's cottage, Anne is sat down to family *dejeuner* with the astonished Guardian and his wife. He frowns repeatedly at the permit of entry on the lunch table.

"Can you ride?"

The question, shot from the hip, takes Anne aback.

"Can you wear my wife's breeches?"

A quick glance at Madame's backside and a nod. "With a belt perhaps."

Anne is escorted upstairs, where Madame finds breeches and belt before going out to ready the horse, not beautiful but sure-footed in the marshes, a white horse of the Camargue. A flock of pink flamingos, duck, geese, heron and a herd of black bulls bred for arenas in Arles and Nimes, are going about their business beneath a dramatic sky of thunderous cloud and piercing spears of sun. Some words of a Wordsworth sonnet come to mind: 'The world is too much with us: late and soon. Getting and spending, we lay waste our powers: Little we see in Nature that is ours." It is magical. Boundless, trackless, the marshes of the Camargue diminish the ego to a vanishing point of absorption in Nature. She sees no wild Camargue horses but is content to be riding a tame one.

For several days now, Anne has travelled with more or less detachment, casting herself only in the present and with no time to doubt, to assess her precarious self-confidence in the light of these happenings. The time has come to try and telephone Bob Common, now in Marseilles, for tomorrow is D-day for *SS Corinthia* bound for Piraeus. Alas, telephone communication fails to find the Common family and at the agreed rendezvous in Marseilles station where she expects to meet them, nobody. Fighting a sense of panic, angry with herself for undertaking a return to Salonika, she calls in at the station Information Office and the Enquiry Office before taking a taxi to the docks. There she spots the Commons' car, a 1937 Morris 8; a bull-nosed, armour-plated little job, no tin can but of heavy metal, later to be granted the sobriquet of 'Hercules'. Hoorah! She is adopted by their porter, restored to resolution and takes off to a small dock workers' restaurant for a superb beefsteak and salad.

Soon the Common family appear and all board the ship, *S S Corinthia*. After a day at sea, the passengers prove to be amazingly cosmopolitan: Iraqis, Lebanese, Egyptians and Syrians, a sprinkling of Swedes, Dutch, Austrian, Spanish, Greeks and a large party of middle-aged British from a Society of Biblical studies going to the Holy Land. Why do these people travel? Not for holiday, that is clear; many are people whose tickets will have cost them perhaps a month's salary. They have little luggage, mostly a number of small bags and parcels done up with string. Many are students, homesick and unhappy, going on holiday from their further education courses in the hallowed halls of Europe. Others are erstwhile refugee families going back to the old country, drawn by ties of blood, culture and nostalgia. One such Lebanese paterfamilias accompanied by six beautiful and perfectly behaved young children, admits to a further six older children left in France. The mother rarely appears except for lunch and then does not sit with her husband and family. A young Greek American now stationed in Germany with the US Army, is visiting Attica for the first time.

"My father has been a US citizen for a long time now but he will retire home to Greece," his matter-of-fact acquiescence to this circumstance suggests that retirement in Greece is commonplace among first generation immigrants to the States. There are too humble people looking for employment. And there are the well-heeled business travellers circulating in the Mediterranean melting pot which acts as a global node for all the Old World and much of the New World: among them a troupe of variety artistes with members drawn from as far afield as Brazil. One, Linda the Lebanese belly dancer, shares Anne's cabin spending most of the voyage lying on her bunk playing a mouth organ. She is resting.

"I must lie down" she explains. "I do so want a baby and I have lost four premature stillborn children. You see, my overdeveloped stomach muscles are no good for carrying a child. My doctor tells me that I will never succeed in carrying long enough to get a live baby but I still hope."

Poor Linda. But when the time comes for the ship's dance, held between Genoa and Piraeus, the variety artistes are a treasure house of song and dance: Linda has sinuous grace, a fluidity of movement rippling down her body. At the finale, every tassel on her torso is circulating wildly and the audience erupts in spontaneous applause.

Piraeus, on arrival, slow and bureaucratic, affords a long delay while Hercules is put ashore in slings. There follows a nightmare journey into Athens in the dark in an overloaded small car on potholed roads. Sometimes Cathy and Anne get out and walk behind Hercules.

Maison Pakis, when they arrive, is unashamedly Anglophile and they sit down to bacon and eggs. Madame Pakis is an owl, round, serene and wise with deeply lidded eyes, a short prominent beak of a nose and a dark, knitted cap on her head enhancing her owlishness. M. Pakis is the Man in the Moon, beaming geniality on everyone and especially the children. In Maison Pakis are found some of the flotsam of academia. The Professor, his wife and a friend are planning their Easter schedule.

"And of course we simply must be in Athens for Easter Week."

"But don't you think it would be more interesting to see Easter in one of the small towns?"

"Definitely not. Everything in Easter Week happens in Athens." The Professor is adamant.

"Well, I have made arrangements with my friends to be in Delphi for Easter" interrupts the friend.

"You must put them off. It will be difficult but I am sure you can explain your change of plan." The Professor brooks no argument.

April the First is departure day from Athens on the road to Salonika.

"Quick, Anne. You must get up and go and help Bob. Someone has jacked up the car and whipped off the wheels" reports Cathy as she enters the bedroom and wakes a tardy Anne. But it is April Fool's Day and soon the car Hercules is climbing ridge after ridge, each successively higher and possessing a more spectacular view from the crest and all of them part of the Kytheron Pass. The scenery may be magnificent but it is hot and the roads are a failure; in places, landslides and earthquakes have made them all but impassable.

In wet weather, the roads are dangerous and on occasions they see how savage the country can be; like a starved animal with the same wanton disrespect for life. Hercules is often pushed onto the verge, if there is one, by large American limousines, one of them carrying a coffin in its open boot. On the tortuous mountain passes, it is safer to stop while other drivers negotiate the sharpest hairpin bends. Coming cautiously downhill one day from a high pass in cloud and rain, they come suddenly upon an accident which can have happened only minutes previously; a bus and a lorry have collided head on, the lorry being overturned down a steep slope and the front of the bus being stove in. Bob and Anne run to see what can be done but apart from giving shocked and bleeding passengers all available nappies, handkerchiefs and rags, there is no alternative but to turn round and go back to the nearest village for a doctor and help. They vow not to drive back at the end of the fieldwork but to put Hercules on the train.

On the road to Salonika their principal attribute is the children. Young Bobby, in striped shirt and khaki shorts looking like a cross between a star footballer and a *sahib* on safari, has all the curiosity and some of the detachment of a born traveller. Jennifer at five years, more inclined to be insular and raise the voice of Kelvindale, looks older than she is and may resent having her cheek pinched by admiring Greeks. Nevertheless, the two blonde children act as passports to friendship.

In the villages, people are more than kind, also curious about and appreciative of the foreigners in their midst. Language is rarely a problem since some local people, having worked a lifetime in the USA before returning rich to their roots, can be called out to translate. Hercules causes much amusement since the ideal choice of vehicle in Greece is something big, long and powerful. The car is so hemmed in by youngsters peering and exclaiming, that nascent difficulties arise until a passing policeman strides over, clips any fleeing onlookers he can catch, scans the car sourly and demands passports.

"Do you belong to Arsenal? Me, I play centre forward." Suddenly friendship flows as the policeman, discovering that the aliens are British and, ergo, must be Arsenal football fans, grins happily and introduces himself.

The weather gets wetter and colder as they drive north; the plain is rain-sodden, the last high passes rise above the snowline where surrounding peaks are diamond sparked in the sunlight, and an eagle displays its aerobatics before plunging into the cloud below. Down on the ultimate plain the weather is again hot, the occupants of the overfilled little car, cramped and irritable; it is the sixth day on the road and nearing Salonika the traffic is heavy, inconsiderate and threatening.

***

Holy Week and they are fasting; for adults no meat, eggs, butter, sugar, cake, cigarettes or anything tasty: only bread, beans, macaroni, yoghurt, olives and weak tea. It is hardly a voluntary act but in the circumstances they are content to submit themselves to the rigours of Holy Week alongside the devout families with whom they are staying. It is a challenge to eat less well but perhaps not the hardship it could have been since meat seems rare in rural Greece and milk all but unobtainable except in the form of yoghurt. On the other hand, an aching smell of baking fills the street as Easter Bread is prepared for the coming celebration along with myriad heaps of dainty cakes, pastries and confectionary. Lamb carcasses decked with coloured tinsel and silver foil medallions hang in butchers' windows awaiting the week's end. The principal church in the square is ornately decorated, mystical, each huge chandelier draped with black ribbon bows, and galaxies of candles burn before highly coloured icons. Much chanting emanates from the porch door on Good Friday as the population files round the icon of Christ Crucified, kissing it as they pass. The story of the Burial is chanted, each phrase by phrase, twelve times.

All Saturday tension mounts, the square is a fever of activity. Posses of people are hurrying here and there, aimlessly purposeful, they pace to and fro; knots of children stand before the windows of the confectionary goods, fingers jabbing the glass; harassed housewives bear huge cloth-draped baking trays to communal ovens.

It is now eleven o'clock at night and the population begins to converge upon the church where crosses on the twin towers floodlit with pretty pastel colours, lure enticingly. Talking in whispers, carrying painted candles and clutching handfuls of hard boiled eggs painted red, the people come. Halting behind the horseshoe of soldiers which occludes the church door and its adjacent draped dais which bears the small overflow altar, the crowd is spontaneously hushed with a palpable mystique of sanctity. Shortly before midnight, the priest emerges, majestic in billowing white robe over pale blue chasuble, accompanied by two assistants clad in red and gold, all three carrying lighted candles shining bravely in the silent tomb night. As the priest chants the story of the Tomb, the crowd light their candles and every window of the dark church suddenly scintillates with candle flame.

At midnight the priest shouts: "Christ is risen." Pistols crack. Bells peal out. Fireworks rocket up shattering in showers of gold and silver sparks. A rising chorus of sound explodes as everyone shouts and laughs, claps their neighbour on the back, shakes their hand, kissing them on the cheeks wishing them *Hronia Pola* (many years). Then out come the red eggs and everyone competes to crack their neighbour's egg while safeguarding their own. One egg may make several conquests before being vanquished, peeled and eaten. Meanwhile the soldiers break rank and, joining in the fun, are swallowed by the happy crowd. The priests bless the crowd before retiring into the church to continue singing; a church now joyously hung with enormous blue and white bows on the chandeliers and sporting strings of Greek national pale blue and white flags across the aisles. Finally, everyone walks home carrying their candle to light the home shrine.

The place is Verria on the scarp of the Vardar lowland some sixty miles west of Salonika. The geographical work that Anne is undertaking involves making a survey of land utilisation, building up a picture of the whole from detailed studies of sample areas, most of which will be delta and reclaimed lakeland but with two upland scarp areas being examined for comparison. The data she hopes to obtain includes size of holdings and type of tenure; cropping practice; distribution and ratio of cash crops as distinct from subsistence crops; degree of mechanisation; any changes in yield per acre; and the marketing of produce. It involves a very great degree of help from local officials, agricultural societies and the farmers themselves and this is freely given. (Later, political confrontation between Britain and Greece over the status of Cyprus will disturb the study.) Bob's work concerns the people of the Vardar plain, in particular identifying those whose families were settled as refugees in the 1920s and recording how they have fared a generation later. Not an easy task.

Fieldwork presents many problems. Language, for instance. While some rural Greeks speak English after many years in America, most do not. Anne learns a smattering of colloquial Greek like: "How many acres have you?" "How many metres down to the water in that well?" and "How many bushels/kilos do you get from one acre?" Rain-swollen rivers without bridges halt her on the track until a kindly, curious farmer offers a pillion ride on his mule. Calling at farms as a student, a foreigner, a woman and a bona fide traveller on foot in the rain or the heat and dust, raises sympathetic curiosity and traditional hospitality: convention demands that the guest consume a helping of candied peel or jam by the spoonful, and/or a homemade liqueur and a tiny cup of rich black coffee. Mercifully, a glass of water accompanies these delicacies but several farms later, the strain begins to tell; Anne's embryonic Greek language is the first to suffer. Later in the season as weather heats up, field work starts earlier; they rise at five in the morning, get on the track at half past six, finish at noon and plod back to Hercules for return to base. Days, weeks, months pass in a semi-coma of exhaustion.

The visit to Verria is made early in the course of the fieldwork. Their arrival causes consternation. Around Hercules parked in the square, a densely threatening throng of people parts like the Red Sea for the Israelites and – oh joy – English is spoken.

"Can I help? What do you want?" A young man, dark-haired, slender and smiling peers in at the window. "My name is John."

"Yes, please help us. We are looking for accommodation and would like to stay as paying guests with a Greek family for a week."

"Wait. I will go and ask my father if you can stay with us. First, though, let us go to the Police Station to register. Follow me."

The Chief of Police makes them very welcome.

"Yes, I am a personal friend of Professor Gomme of the Geography Department in Salonika University. And of course I know that Greece has special relations with Britain. Why, didn't your Lord Byron die fighting for our freedom? I will phone the District Agricultural Office for you." He beams genial hospitality.

Thus it is arranged that Bob, Cathy and the children will stay with John's family and Anne will lodge with the family Petropoulou nearby whose daughter Athy (Anthoussa), is delighted to share her bedroom. John's family have a patisserie and confectionary shop with two large rooms above, one of which is assigned to the Common family. This means the three sons of the family will have to sleep on the loft floor while Papa, Mama and the two daughters occupy the other bedroom. Their generosity is overwhelming; with nothing to give away, they manage to bestow all. The room consigned to the Commons contains a double and a single bed, central table, a low cupboard and some beautiful embroidered rugs, coverlets, cushions, runners and tapestries made by the womenfolk.

Papa is a big man, though not tall, with a thatch of thick, dark, curly hair, grave in manner but with a twinkle for the children. Mama is plump with two long, shining plaits. She has a lovely skin, smooth and young-looking, but she is not well, often in pain and remains seated while her daughters manage the household chores. Only her hands are mobile and they have a life of their own, two attendant gulls which swoop down to scoop in Bobby for kisses and cuddles or to pluck Jennifer to her and pop a sweet in her mouth. Eleanor is reserved and serene; being the eldest daughter she never went to school, instead helped her mother at home, in her spare time stitching many of the beautiful embroideries around the house. Tasoula at thirteen years is a pet, a plump schoolgirl still who will be attractive in a few years' time. Of the sons, they see little of the eldest who manages the shop below with some help from Jimmy (Takhi) who is awaiting call-up for army national service. John (Yannis), sensitive, emotional and egocentric, has done his military service. He is at a loose end despite being a talented linguist, speaking Greek, Romanian, French and fluent English. Moody and depressed, he is desperate to emigrate.

For Anne the conveniences of modern living no longer matter: the standards and norms of daily life such as privacy, quiet, regular meals, cigarettes, radio, cease to apply. Television, of course, does not exist. From a wood-burning stove in the lobby on the first floor comes some heat for the whole building, and mama has a small charcoal burner near her if the day is cold. From daybreak until near midnight, there is a coming and going, movement and commotion, loud colloquy and shrill dialogue. But on the credit side is this wonderful family, with their photograph albums of weddings, name days, Christmases and traditions, their overwhelming hospitality and their obvious pleasure in sharing their home, their food, their recipes and their opinions.

Anne experiences a spontaneous revelation: she admires the simple life which, despite lack of labour-saving gadgets, affords enough leisure time to embroider, entertain and visit relatives and friends. Nevertheless, she recognises that it is a hard life; with no National Health Service, little spare money for serious illnesses, these people must be tenacious in endurance. Their religion helps with its visible and tangible comforts; the highly-coloured icons, the candles and the kissing of the priest's hand which may bring relief in hardship, which can impart the gift to bear pain with serenity. Theirs is a transcendent, sacred view of life that Anne finds profoundly uplifting, almost alluring.

When departure time comes, as it must, plans are public property to be discussed by the family, criticised and roundly condemned when a Tuesday departure is suggested.

"No. No. You should not leave on a Tuesday. Never do anything significant on a Tuesday. It is a most unlucky day."

"Why? What is so bad about Tuesdays?"

"It is because the Greeks lost Constantinople on a Tuesday."

And, since the Greeks, or Byzantines lost Constantinople to the Ottoman Turks on a Tuesday in 1453, the Commons and Anne in 1955, comply with their hosts' Greek tradition and arrange departure for Wednesday.

Leave-taking is emotional and exhausting, the visitors torn between regret at leaving the kindly cocoon of intimate Greek family life and, a longing to get back to the creature comforts of the mid-twentieth century. On the journey, there is a surreal quality of being in limbo, in no man's land; the road is a tightrope between two worlds only sixty miles apart.

Chapter 3

A Byzantine Joke

In Salonika, the American Consul's apartment is a dream; huge airy living rooms with a long balcony facing the sea, a fully fitted kitchen with every conceivable gadget, a marble bathroom, plenty of cupboard space and parquet floors. There is a domestic staff of two maids who rarely come to work, having a string of well-thought-out excuses. More co-operative are the two big black poodles, the larger for being unclipped, who delight in walks along the seafront in the cool of the evening.

One by one, the Verria families Anne and the Common family have stayed with come to visit. Mama comes, when in Salonika to see a specialist, accompanied by Eleanor and John. Jimmy calls in on his way to do military service: Athy comes for the weekend. Is there envy when they explore the apartment exclaiming volubly at everything in it? No, not really; the womenfolk at heart prefer the security of their own homes in the bosom of their extended families. Only John comes time and time again on matters pertaining to his longed-for emigration to the USA.

On a later sortie from Salonika, the Commons and Anne spend a weekend with the Verria friends. It is a different Verria; no longer rain-sodden mud-running streets, a grey town amidst grey hills, but a warm, rosy terracotta tiled town against a mountain backdrop of blue, green and gold. Eleanor cooks an 'English' meal for them on Saturday but Sunday lunch is a Greek masterpiece with stuffed pumpkin, salad, yoghurt, pastries and wine. Sunday evening is family night out and all the families and friends go together to an open-air *taverna* with live music and dancing, with *retsina*, the local resin-flavoured white wine and a plethora of tasty titbits; *souvlaki,* pieces of lamb on a skewer; *susyakaki,* small spicy sausages; *koulouri,* circular bread glazed with sesame seed and *kolkithia,* pieces of grilled pumpkin.

As the weather warms up, fieldwork shakes down into a regular routine. Bob and Anne drive Hercules into a village at the far end of a dust track and adjourn to the coffee house which serves as information bureau, telephone exchange, bus office, moneylender and moot house (council chamber). After Bob and Anne have been to the same village for a day or two, the bush telegraph kicks in, reporting back to the geographers which farms they visited the day before yesterday. Over a tiny cup of sweet, strong coffee, their plans are heard by the village dignitaries, discussed, debated, changed, argued, amended and approved. If there is an English speaker, he will be delighted to accompany them describing, explaining, translating. If not, Anne must ask: *"Possu stremata?"* - how many acres - pointing to cotton, wheat, vines, tobacco or whatever. Or *"Possu metres?"* pointing down a well in order to get the depth of the water table. It is slow work. The farmers and village dignitaries, the schoolmaster, the policeman, the priest and the coffee house owner are embarrassingly well- meaning, desperate in their efforts to help. But if there is no English speaker, the language barrier is as high as Mount Olympus. When there is an English speaker however, tongues loosen, explanations fall over themselves in haste to be heard, anecdotes erupt, reminiscences roll out like barrels from a brewer's dray into a pub cellar.

It transpires that the village is not a hayseed settlement at the back of beyond, forever off the map. Joined to The USA by spider lines of family and friends as it is, the village, for dramatic action, is as a Hollywood blockbuster film.

In the coffee house, a bead curtain parts to admit a piercing shaft of light and the policeman.

Dimitri!" he shouts for the owner.

"Greetings, Plato my friend. I am delighted to see you because I am feeling melancholy. Can you spare time for a coffee?" Dimitri invites his friend.

"Thank you, I have a few minutes to spare." Plato unbuttons his grey tunic and seats himself.

"You, Dimitri, are the last person to feel sad today of all days when your brother arrives from Boston. How many years is it since he went to America?"

Dimitri has withdrawn to the back of the café to open up his wood-burning stove and grind fine oriental coffee. He takes two small copper jugs with long handles, measures coffee into each and adds sugar, a generous helping to one jug since Plato has a sweet tooth, and a speck to the other since he likes his coffee bitter. Dimitri's reputation rests on the fact that he makes it his business to know each client's tastes as well as a general practitioner knows his patients. Pouring hot water into each jug, he sets them on the stove to simmer.

"It is thirty-five years since Pascal left this village." Dimitri lifts the jugs from the stove just before the liquid boils, a delicious aroma arising as incense from an altar. "I'm afraid, Plato. My brother is a rich man now, you understand, and he is coming to see whether he will adopt my son Nikko. There is no other way for Nikko to get to The States. Perhaps my brother will not like Nikko, refuse to adopt the lad? It would break Nikko's heart." Dimitri rises to return the jugs of coffee to the stove for a second simmering.

"You must not despair, my dear friend. As for Nikko, I will read his fortune at the bottom of my coffee cup" Plato promises.

Plato, his coffee finished, turns his cup upside down on the saucer, allowing time for the viscous sludge to settle before righting the cup and gazing at the runnels, rosettes and eddies in the dark drying dregs. Intense as a medium, he announces: "I see waves. Nikko will make a journey by ship."

"But my brother is flying back to America."

Undismayed, Plato reverts to his cup. "Your brother must be *very* rich; I see many piles of money here." His face radiates reverence.

"You are right. He has a chain of patisseries all over Boston."

"Now I notice a girl. I think there are signs of trouble here." Plato regards Dimitri earnestly. "Perhaps Nikko has a girl in Greece and won't want to leave when the time comes."

"No. No. No." Dimitri flails the air with his fist. "Nikko has no girl. His only passion is America."

"Then it must be your brother's wife I see. But wait. There are many little ripples of laughter. I foresee a happy ending."

Soon Nikko bursts in to announce a taxi approaching the village. Dimitri stands outside his coffee house with Nikko flanked by Plato and the schoolmaster Costas, watching the bauble-bright limousine slow to a standstill. Pascal gets out of the taxi - stout, smart, smiling. Everyone embraces, talks, kisses, talks louder, shakes hands and laughs before repairing to the coffee house where Nikko prepares coffee. At last he brings the coffee accompanied by tumblers of water.

"I've not had coffee like this for years!" sighs Pascal. "There are many, many Greek people in Boston now. Nikko shall come back with me and make them coffee like this."

Next evening, Dimitri is holding a party for his brother. It happens to be Widow Rhodakes's Name Day and she and her friends are bound to come to the coffee house for the evening. Moreover, the local football team is to play an adjacent village in the District's Cup Final on the morrow and Dimitri knows it is the custom of the young people to wish their team well on the eve of a big match. Pascal sits in the cool of the coffee house watching Dimitri's preparations for the festival evening. Poor Pascal, he is feeling the heat, is not looking too well.

Later, as the brief opal twilight merges into night, Dimitri switches on the coloured lights round the coffee house and in the lime tree in the square. People arrive and Nikko is busy carrying out trays of drinks and coffee.

"Bring three coffees and three brandies," calls a lady. Nikko is astonished; sitting there like three sooty rooks are Widow Rhodakes, Madam Saliaris still in mourning for her son killed long ago, and Miss Evangalides who has never forgiven her fiancé for stopping a Communist bullet in 1949. They, who rarely come to the coffee house and never drink spirits, now sit tapping feet and fingers in time with the thrumming music. With an acrobat's agility, Nikko swings their order over the heads of the whirling dancers. Among them run children in pyjamas bouncing like Christmas tree balls. What a success the evening is!

Next morning however brings a shrill ring of the telephone and Dimitri receives a telegram from Boston where Pascal's wife has suffered a heart attack and is in intensive care in the hospital. Pascal must return immediately, without Nikko whose adoption procedure is barely started.

Some weeks later the daily bus lumbers into the square and the driver enters the coffee house carrying the mail. "Dimitri, I have a special letter for you, from B...OS...T...ON." He deciphers the foreign alphabet with difficulty.

"It's sad, his wife is still in hospital," Dimitri reports as he slowly studies the script. "Nikko! He says he is sending you some books to study. A neighbour of his, a widow, in Boston and her daughter will soon be visiting Greece and will carry the books for Nikko."

At this moment a shaft of scorching sun sweeps into the coffee house with Plato. "What daughter is this? Is she American? Is she coming to stay in the village? Is she rich?" Plato fires his questions like a revolver.

Dimitri recoils, losing his place in the letter. "Yes... Yes... I don't know" he stammers. Using his finger as pointer Dimitri pursues Pascal's handwriting. She is to be visiting Greece, it says, and will bring the books for Nikko."

"Books!" snorts Plato, "What books?" How long will she stay is more important. Quickly, Dimitri, discover if she's rich" he beseeches his friend.

Dimitri mops his brow. "Her parents came originally from Greece and have brought up their daughter well. She is their only child."

"Ah, an heiress!" Plato sighs with relief. The coffee house is filling rapidly now as news about the foreign letter flows like floodwater from street to street. Costas, the teacher, several farmers, a shepherd or two and the village priest; even the women and children are trying to squeeze into the small premises. Fragments of conversation drift round like dust in the sunlight: "Yes, yes, an American girl." … "Coming here, when?" ... "Of course! All American girls are beautiful." ... "Naturally, she's blonde!"

In the centre of the hubbub sits Plato, tweaking his collar straight and smoothing down his hair. At thirty-three it is time he thought about getting married. What better wife than a beautiful, young American millionairess!

Some weeks later arrives Fredriki and her widowed mother 'bearing the books'; she goes about her business with quiet efficiency. She is nineteen years old, wears her dark hair pinned in a plait against the back of her head, and has a child's pleasure in everything. She has led a sheltered life in a well-furnished home, not a thing missing in the kitchen where she is fully competent. Fredriki has never been to a cinema or dance and may not do so until she is twenty, this being the wish of the priest to whom she goes for Sunday school in Boston. She has, nevertheless, been away from home, summer camping with girlfriends from school. Having no brother or father, she will doubtless find it difficult to get to know young men. But she knows what she wants and soon Nikko is in love. Three months later, Nikko and Fredriki are married in the village church, a traditional Greek wedding with the exchange of crowns and the knotting together of bride's and bridegroom's hands. And in due course, the young couple sail for America where Nikko, in the fullness of time, presumably inherits Pascal's flourishing business in Boston. A marriage made in heaven? Perhaps!

One of the most interesting people whom Bob and Anne meet is Peter, a village grocer on the plain near Salonika. His English is good. "I learned it while serving two years alongside an Indian Regiment of the British Army," the Greek Army having served with the British in Crete and in North Africa in 1941-43. "My parents came from Turkey but I and my two sisters were born in Greece."

His father has a smallholding and Peter, now married, works long hours in his shop. "I never shut in the middle of the day because that is the time when farmers come home from their fields and need me. Nor do I shut on Sundays and holidays; I cannot afford to. You see, I am saving to go to Australia, to emigrate. But my wife does not want to go, does not want to leave her mother and the village she knows. She is afraid of trying to learn English. And of course, she will inherit some property here, fruit trees and such."

This young man, well-made and good looking, exhibits confidence and ability, both in his speech and his body language. He will go far. Fully aware of Greece's political history and current state in a framework of world affairs, he is distressed, hurt, to think that not so many years ago, Greece sweated blood to overcome Communism.

"And now" he sighs "There is again much Communist-caused trouble, this business of *Enosis* for example." By now *Enosis*, unity of Cyprus with Greece, has escalated into violence and terrorism, become a rotten canker. A well-planned, synchronised series of bombs has erupted in Cyprus on April the first, the day the Commons and Anne had left Athens to drive to Salonika.

"I have no time for Greeks who are ignorant about their own country, who shout: "Give us Cyprus" without having a clue of the implications. Their only opinions are what they read in the local papers and overhear discussed in the coffee houses" concludes Peter.

In 1955 EOKA, acronym for the militant arm of *Enosis*, reveals itself by violence; and will be blessed by the charismatic Cypriot Archbishop Makarios. *Enosis* will come to be regarded as more than a popular preference for Greek Cypriot joining with Greece: Archbishop Makarios will be identified as backing EOKA and for authorising Orthodox Church funds to finance its terrorist activities, which are aimed at injuring and killing British armed forces and civilians in Cyprus. He will be exiled, by the British Colonial Government, to the Seychelles. But in 1960, Britain will give up its millstone colony, its small hapless limb of Empire, and launch Independence, upon which Makarios will be elected President of the Island by an overwhelming majority. By 1963, there will be serious rioting between the Greek and Turkish communities in Cyprus. Indeed, with the British out of the way, there will begin the real struggle for Cyprus, the principal protagonists being the Byzantium-oriented Eastern Orthodox Church versus a Europe-looking Athens Government.[3] It will be a match between two champions, with Turkey, an audience with heavily vested interests,

---

[3] Clark, Victoria: *Why Angels Fall,* Macmillan 2000

breathless at the ringside. It is soon clear that the Turkish Government is not content to see Greece take over Cyprus, an island only fifty miles offshore from Turkey and some two hundred and fifty miles from Rhodes, Greece's nearest point.

Meanwhile, in 1955, there is more fieldwork to be done by Bob Common and Anne in their efforts to bring up to date studies made by the late Professor Alan Ogilvie in 1915. Rural Greece is delightfully appealing. While the geographers are moved by the villagers' heart-warming hospitality and sincerity, they nevertheless begin to recognise that farming is a poor man's business. Despite a measure of reform and the introduction of some machinery and chemical fertilisers, farming still relies on traditional methods. Much of the groundbreaking and all the inter-row tilling is still done by hand hoe or animal-drawn ploughs on smallholdings.

Tobacco, the oriental variety which demands labour-intensive work, is still the main cash crop. Finding a farmer drawing water from a well into old petrol drums on a bullock-drawn cart, Anne, with help from a kindly interpreter, is able to talk to him. He explains that he is now transplanting seedlings from seedbeds to fields and he needs plenty of water.

"And do you use any fertiliser?" queries Anne.

"Ah no, chemicals put on the soil would harm the aroma of the tobacco. You understand that we must keep the special flavour of our tobacco because there is a danger that people will begin to prefer the poor quality American Virginian tobacco which came to this country during the war (1939-45 World War).

"Do you only grow tobacco on your land? Have you tried rice, or cotton?" Anne persists, recalling that rice, only introduced into north Greece after 1945, is a good initial crop to flush out salts in delta soil and prepare the ground for cotton. Cotton, named 'white gold', has made encouraging progress for enterprising farmers.

"No, no, I grow only tobacco. Greeks are not rice eaters, you know. And I have not enough land for cotton growing."

This is a disappointing response since the Hellenic Cotton Institute, founded in 1931, has done much to encourage northern Greek smallholders. Among other crops which could be developed are sunflower and sesame. Vegetables and temperate fruits can be raised in sheltered and well-watered localities but at present inadequate marketing arrangements limit the value of these goods.[4] Anne moves off, followed by her kindly interpreter who now reveals that he is from the local police and she is in fact under arrest. With sudden shock, Anne notices his handgun in holster. Instructions have come from Athens, he says.

It was bound to happen sooner or later, as Cypriot violence against Britain becomes more ugly. Local officialdom is now disturbed by two Britons, tramping around the countryside in the heat, on foot, with maps, cameras and sketch pads, looking, asking questions about farms and crops. Permits! They must have permits. No fieldwork without permits.

The British Consul in Salonika has had to answer a range of questions from the Minister of the Interior. Reports are coming in that the Verria families have been contacted by the local police and questioned. The British Consul further divulges that two Britons, both engaged in social and welfare work for many years, are in trouble with the Aliens' Department, one of them being given nine days in which to leave the country.

One has to remember that Greece has undergone centuries of occupation, insecurity and fighting. Leadership has too often failed the country; legions of bureaucrats score off each other in competition for power plus all the status symbols and perquisites of high office. The true

---

[4] Prentice, Anne: *The Commercial Crops of North Greece,* World Crops Vol 9, No 4, pp 163-5, April 1957

villain is ignorance, well jostled by the media and massaged by unscrupulous newsmen. Suddenly Greece has an axe to grind with Britain over the status of Cyprus, as yet still a British possession. In the Greek press, accusations are lobbed daily at Britain and the British. The miracle is that so much kindness, hospitality and help have been accorded to Bob and Anne despite the politicians' antics in connection with Cyprus.

Barred from fieldwork, the daily preoccupation is Salonika market. Divided into sections, the narrow alleys teem with alternative markets; small boys with trays of combs and razor blades, farmers with baskets of garden produce, vendors of ice from the ice factory, pushcarts of snacks and confectionary. Vegetable alley leads into fruit lane; hardware crescent opens into furniture row, into meat court, into fish passage and so on. In the maze of narrow ways, merchants vie to attract attention, persistent but polite. "Come into my shop, lady. What will you have, this lovely piece of turbot or some tuna steaks? The sardines are fresh and I have swordfish in the fridge."

'Fridge'!

His English is impeccable, his wares well displayed and aromatic only of fresh herbs. "I have been a fish merchant for generations." He beams. "My family came from the Turkish Black Sea." Other fishmongers buy daily ingots of ice from handcarts and some of their fish is odoriferous, the gills dark and stained looking.

Some shops and kiosks are the proud possessor of a telephone, status symbol of prosperity and entrepreneurship: nearly always, such merchants speak good English and want to practise their linguistic skills, they demand to exchange names and addresses and hail from Turkey originally. As friends these marketers are a delightful group but as research data, they provide little substance.

Or do they? Quantitative and statistical proof is undoubtedly lacking but there is a gut feeling that some of the refugee families from Turkey have done rather better, are more able, than their native contemporaries. If fridges and phones are counted a measure of success, then it suggests that the trauma of displacement, the challenge of circumstances and competitive edge of an incomer, have combined to spur on refugee families to greater achievement. There is, of course, no mention of those that failed to make it, died or dropped out; nor of the deprivations, disasters and despairs suffered *en route*. The tragedies of history, which eventually prove to be ephemeral, demand dedicated anniversaries as generation follows generation. Success stories on the other hand are likely to be forgotten: or perhaps good fortune becomes the icon of youth, the stuff of romantic novel and cinema.

Eventually the permits are issued but it is too late; plans for departure are well in hand. Anne is joined by Ann Powell, the Fine Arts graduate and leader of the previous year's expedition to Salonika, who arrives from Italy where she has been doing her postgraduate study. By train to Athens and back on board *SS Corinthia,* the two "Anns" sail via Alexandria and Port Said to Beirut, thence by bus to Damascus for a week's stay to explore the city and its treasures.

The Damascus *Souk* is a triumph. Friends made on *SS Corinthia* escort them round. Wahlid, a textile designer who draws patterns freehand, explains the different designs for woven silk and cotton fabrics; this one is called 'Abdul Rahman Ali Kurdy'; that one is the oldest design, ninety years old, called 'Batteh'. Then there is the 'Princess Elizabeth' and the 'Shahin Shah of Persia', both of silk. They visit a workshop, watch weaving, reflect that setting up a loom takes forty days and record that real silk brocade requires some four hundred and fifty 'cartoons', that is pieces of paper the size of each repeat, and that two skilled weavers at one loom can make two metres of brocade a day.

Alas, they fail to reach one of their most desired destinations. A Damascus tourist office is offering one-day excursions to Palmyra by small, expensive private plane. Whilst the high price of the excursion would consume a large share of their precious financial funds, they deem it money well spent to see the fabled Palmyra, the ruined desert city where Queen Zenobia attempted to defy the might of Rome's armies in the third century AD. It is not to be. The tourist agency cancels the flight at the last moment giving no reason but returning their fare. Going back to their hotel, they discover that fire has broken out and a swift evacuation is being demanded. Sitting on their rescued luggage by the Barada River among the fire engines and police, the two "Anns" console themselves that missing Palmyra might be fortuitous.

They proceed by bus to Jerusalem for several days, visiting the British School of Archaeology. They judge the mosque of The Dome of The Rock to be more beautiful and more spiritually serene than any of the Christian sites. The latter are overfilled with assorted priests and myriads of guided tour groups.

In Amman, they stay at the YWCA (Young Woman's Christian Association) and at supper announce their intention of taking a taxi to Jerash on the morrow. "If anyone wants to come with us, they are more than welcome." Early next morning the Warden greets them: "Martha the cook tells me you have invited her to go to Jerash with you. Is this true?" They confirm it is and Martha is given the morning off. Flushed with excitement, she goes to put on her national costume, that of Ramullah district in Palestine. She wears a black dress magnificently embroidered in red, with a turquoise shawl and an eye-catching scarf hung with a solid row of coins round her brow. These are marvellous details of interest for photographers!

Difficulties abound in getting to Petra: it is now August and the tourist camp there is closed in the off-season. Only mad dogs and the English would try to go in the red hot months. Never mind, the two girls will go by train to Ma'an and hope that their letter of introduction to the Governor of Ma'an from the British School of Archaeology in Jerusalem, will somehow be able to move them further along the way to Petra. Travelling south through the thirsty land of Jordan, there are only rare signs of occupation, some herds of sheep and goats and a few huddles of black tents.

Arriving in Ma'an in mid afternoon, they find little more than an isolated police post, well asleep at this hour. Lady Luck is with them for the Governor alights from the same train and arranges a shared taxi with a family bound for Wadi Musa, some twenty-seven miles distant, the way, a stony track under a savage sun. At sunset, Wadi Musa fortress and police post is reached.

Hold on! Parked at the guesthouse, is a British Army lorry and a score of personnel.

"We are on desert warfare training with the Jordanian Army. This is our weekend leave and we are riding down to Petra at dawn tomorrow" explains a British soldier. "Do you want to join us? You can borrow trousers from us if you like; easier to ride in than those skirts. You'll get less chafed," grins another soldier. At the mid-century, women travellers in Arab countries wear calf-length skirts and long-sleeved blouses, always carrying a headscarf, essential for visiting mosques and public institutions, or for filtering drinking water.

The Jordanian police meanwhile allocate the two girls a room for the night and bespeak their two horses for the final five miles to Petra. A telephone call to the Governor in Ma'an excuses them the Petra entrance fee and orders them a police escort: perhaps the police don't trust the British Army.

At five thirty in the morning, goes a long cavalcade, mounted on skinny ponies each led by a lad. These boys combine in singing endless songs in thin high trebles. And so down the steep course of the Wadi Musa and along its stony bed, passing mysterious caves and rock cut facades. Suddenly the valley narrows; this is the *Bab es Siq*, door of the defile, rising in places to seventy-five metres high with room only for single file; a winding, water-cut gorge in bedded sandstone of brilliant reds, rusts, magentas, golds, baby blues and whites. The cavalcade skirts around another towering rock abutment and there, magnificently, is *el Kazneh*, the Treasury. Now the terrain spreads out into a broad bowl with vistas of colossal facades, of columns and capitals, architraves and pediments, all cut in the colourful living rock. Many of the tombs and temples, occupied by Bedouin using open fires in winter, have smoke-blackened ceilings intricately marked like watered silk. Local families have not the habit of begging as is so general in tourist cities such as Jerusalem: rather, they invite visitors to partake of strong sweet tea in tiny cups. It is considered good etiquette to refuse twice and accept the third pressing offer.

At length, it is time to leave these wonderfully hospitable countries of Jordan and Syria. Back to Damascus by road, change money with Wahlid in the Souk, pounds sterling to Turkish lire: they get twenty Turkish lire to one pound sterling when the official rate is only seven or eight Turkish lire. After travelling from Damascus to Aleppo by road, they take the train, the Taurus Express, alias the Berlin-Baghdad Railway, bound for Istanbul. The final stage of the journey is by ferry steamer, at dawn, across the Bosphorus with the minarets and domes of this splendid city sparkling gold and green against the still dark west bank sky.

Tourists from Europe would normally expect to arrive in Istanbul by train from the west, crossing into Turkey from Greece or Bulgaria and traversing the Thracian plain into the famous city. The two "Anns", travelling from the south across the Anatolian plateau and by boat over the Bosphorus, congratulate themselves on their finesse to achieve first arrival in Istanbul, alias Constantinople in Byzantium, not by train to a sooty station but by ship, as did many medieval Europeans. The girls are able to conjure imaginary visions of the fabled city of Constantinople and the richly mysterious Byzantine Empire. In the mid-twentieth century, however, 'byzantine' is a derogatory adjective denoting devious dialogue, labyrinthine argument and Machiavellian intrigue. Plunging into a quayside hotel for a wash and some breakfast, the two "Anns" have the first of several Byzantine experiences. The dining room waiter taking their breakfast order adds, in an undertone, "And do you want to change money?" A spirited debate on rates of exchange is whispered across the crockery and cutlery ending with an irritated hiss, "Seventeen Turkish lire to the pound sterling is my final offer, take it or leave it." The girls leave it.

Istanbul, on first acquaintance, has no apparent nationality and little of the courtesy to which the girls have become accustomed. Moreover, it is hideously expensive, its hotels and pensions alarmingly full and the weather atrocious with wind like gunfire and bullets of rain. The only accommodation they can find is in a private house, a room with a strong pong of drains so that the first move is to locate a pharmacy, purchase disinfectant and, while the landlady is taking her siesta, apply it to every sink and waste hole they can find. Madame Fifi is the lady's appellation, Greek her language and twenty Turkish lire to the pound sterling is her rate of exchange. Hurrah! They can now afford to stay in Istanbul and begin work on Ann's project.

Ann is in Istanbul to make a tracing and thereby a copy of an early fifth century mosaic from the Byzantine Palace of the Emperors. Professor Talbot Rice has commissioned this work for a Byzantine Exhibition he will be mounting in Edinburgh. Such is Talbot Rice's standing as a Byzantologist, that the Turkish Ministry of Culture is delighted to give them every possible assistance in their work for this prestigious exhibition. Ann has a grant from the Fine Art Department of Edinburgh University to cover her expenses; with judicious money changing and abstemious care, they can make it do for two during the fortnight before Anne must return to Europe. Thereafter, Ann's sister, Peggy, will join her.

Ann and Peggy will shortly be caught up in serious rioting in Istanbul, obliged to hurry to the Hilton Hotel and, after spending a whole day there, gratefully accept the offer of a Turkish Army tank escort trundling behind their taxi back to their digs. Madame Fifi is one of the *Romei*, or Romans as the Greek-speaking population has been termed since Byzantine times. Mercifully, her house is still intact and the girls are hauled hurriedly through the front door and entrance passage by Madame's *dragoman*. The violence, having exploded after reports of Greek Cypriot callousness to the Turkish minority in Cyprus, causes massive damage to Greek property and to Orthodox churches in the city. In its aftermath, almost all the Greek-speaking people will flee Istanbul leaving behind their homes, cemeteries, valuables and businesses.

The designated mosaic, now in a museum near the Blue Mosque, is known as the Kicking Mule.

"This particular mosaic is the only known joke in Byzantine art!" Ann explains. "It represents not a man kicking his mule but a manifestly delighted mule, kicking a man head over heels into the air."

The chosen method for copying a mosaic is to take a rubbing. In places, however, the surface is so worn and smooth that tracing becomes necessary. Lying full length on the museum's stone floor for hours tracing the outlines of hundreds of thousands of tiny tesserae is tedious; the more so of an area three metres by one-and-a-half metres in size. Later Ann will transfer the tracings and rubbings onto canvas and paint them. The following year the finished product will be on display in the Edinburgh exhibition looking so like the real thing that viewers cannot credit it to be a copy. By the end of a day's tracing, eyes are tessera-weary, fatigued by incessant fan patterns. Walk out from the museum and the street is cobbled; bold stones in fan patterns. To add insult to injury, the delicious boiled or charcoal-roasted maize cobs they buy from pushcarts along the way, have tessera-shaped seeds all over them. Eventually the girls settle for half a day's tracing and indulge an appetite for sightseeing in the afternoons.

When the time comes to leave on the Orient Express back to Europe, exhilaration sustains Anne on the journey. Looking back down the line of familiar Oriental heroines; Mary Wortley Montagu, Gertrude Bell, Freya Stark and even Agatha Christie Mallowan (not for her whodunits, but for her delightful archaeological memoir of Syria, *Come, Tell Me How You Live*), Anne is filled with gratitude that she has been privileged to visit so many of the places described by her heroines. The travel bug is vanquished, her wanderlust satisfied. For now, that is. She has no idea that, forty years later, her husband will be posted to Byzantium for a period of three years.

Chapter 4

Island in the Sun

T/S Irpinia, Linee Maritime Siosa, 9 September 1957

"Thank you so much for your letters to Vigo and Madeira." Anne writes to her parents. "Now we are more than half way to Venezuela but have run into terrible weather and the whole ship is battened down, which makes it very hot inside. Many passengers are sick; either 'Roman tummy' or seasickness, but luckily I have so far escaped both." This wind is part of Hurricane Carrie, which sank the sail training schooner *Pamir* with the loss of eighty-eight lives.

Their departure from Southampton has been confused, the ship delayed by gales. There is trouble with Anne's cabin. At first, the tourist class purser insists on putting her in a six-berth lower deck inner cabin, but brother Colin who is seeing her off, deals firmly and successfully with the attendants so that Anne is eventually assigned a two-berth upper deck cabin with porthole, as specified on her ticket. Her cabin companion is a delightful, vivacious Danish lady called Ebba going to visit her grown up daughter in Jamaica. Large by comparison with other cabins, it has a metal floor and walls, wash basin, two cupboards, an aluminium stool and a wastepaper basket. Two minimal tea cloths do duty as towels and there is no soap. Sometimes one tap runs a little warm water but the waste pipe is badly blocked up.

By the time Vigo in Spain is cleared, the ship is overfull and the purser has, alas, put a great many dormitory passengers into cabins. Spanish immigrants make up the bulk of the passengers; families going to the mines of Venezuela, travelling through the auspices of agencies which handle their tickets and deduct from earnings during the two-year contract. Other passengers are West Indian families going home on holiday. The vessel is old, stuffy, noisy and often malodorous.

Anne and the motherly Ebba connect with some other kindred spirits in tourist class. Vic is a Czechoslovakian Jew bound for Venezuela where he has relations; Stephan is a Venezuelan, originally from Hungary, returning, after eight jolly years travelling and studying, to take over his father's cattle ranch. Margit, an ex-Swiss Venezuelan, has been on holiday in Europe. Then there is Sam, a slow-speaking languorous Devon man.

"I went to Jamaica three years ago after my marriage failed," relates Sam. "I admit I lived wild for a year but then I settled to the island. I have my teaching job, a bit of rugby football, my interest in astronomy. I have been home to get a divorce and now I shall marry a coloured girl and become Jamaican."

And there is Cecile. At first the group, except Sam, heartily dislikes Cecile. The first night at sea she appears in a skin-tight brocade dress, every curve shouting and within the evening has changed twice. A White Jamaican with caramel-coloured skin, huge eyes surging restlessly round the bar and wide, moist mouth painted with palest lipstick, she is gorgeous, forever surrounded by men. Recently divorced from a rich husband, she is about to marry another monied man and has, as she tells everyone, 'a fan-tastic amount of luggage'.

"She is a typical Jamaican girl," observes the connoisseur Sam, "Well above the average in intelligence,

I'd say." She can talk well on a variety of subjects, is a trained secretary and about to start new employment in Jamaica with the international conglomerate, ICI. Cecile becomes a favourite with the children, telling them endless stories about the adventures of a spider called Anancy who is gifted with a talent for achieving the impossible.

The long monotonous crossing of the Atlantic is nearly over. Despite poor menus, "Good enough for the Spaniards," says the Italian tourist class purser, the small group of friends manage to enjoy themselves, joining with Jamaicans in dormitory class who organise excellent calypso dancing parties on deck. The Jamaicans' quarters are less crowded than tourist class because the Italian shipping company will not mix European immigrants with coloured people, yet the group finds cleaner conditions among the Jamaicans than among the Spaniards.

Arriving at Caracas in Venezuela where eight hundred Spaniards disembark, some of the group of friends venture into the city. It possesses a city centre obviously new rich, flaunting plazas on three or more levels connected by flyovers and subways. It sports enormous skyscrapers built, apparently, entirely of glass. Miles of wall are decorated with frescoes, mosaic designs, ceramic tile patterns, anything the city architects can think of. But around the central business district, hang shanty town slums seething with the rural population now flocking into the cities. Not a city Anne would wish to live in, it is a delightful respite from the ship where, everyone including first class passengers agrees, the accommodation and facilities, for their price, are unsatisfactory.

The Island of Curacao, the next port of call, is all oil; the sickly sweet smell of oil, smoke from cracking plants, oil opulence manifested in enormous limousines and nothing but luxury goods in the shops, where even water is imported because the island is a desert as barren as the moon. Willemstad is, however, a flourishing town and port with a distinctively Dutch style of architecture and an Old World appearance.

"There's Jamaica!" exclaims Sam at the sight of a long cloud on the horizon. "I'm glad to be back."

Anne is uncertain about her own response to the Island. Leaving home in Edinburgh and the security of a loving family is not the sole reason for her reticence. After a year's postgraduate study on the Greek fieldwork at Glasgow University, she has had to admit that an academic career is not for her. Having had the results of the Greek study accepted for publication in various academic journals, she quit academia and took a job in John Bartholomew and Sons Ltd, the Edinburgh cartographic firm. In brief, a living has to be earned; Father has generously supplemented University grants from time to time and living at home is economic financially, but the wanderlust is on her again. Moreover, a turgid affair of the heart has run its course. About this time, Father receives a letter from his sister Bobbie who is married to a Sapper Officer now posted in Kingston, Jamaica. "Philip and I are leaving at Christmas" writes Bobbie, "And I dread the sorting and packing that must be done. I am so very lame and sore with rheumatism out here in the damp climate. Alas, Patricia (her stepdaughter) does not really want to come out; too busy getting engaged and planning her wedding. I don't suppose Anne would like three months in Jamaica to help me out."

"There you are" says Father. "I will pay your passage and you can do Aunt Bobbie a favour."

But Jamaica is not on Anne's horizon. London is what she thinks she wants.

"Right, you go to Jamaica first and to London afterwards," reasons her father, who has explored the travel agencies and come up with this Italian shipping line plying between Southampton and Kingston, Jamaica.

Anne recognises father's wisdom. She knows little about Jamaica. While at Glasgow University the previous year, a Jamaican, Betty Ogle, had become a good friend but Betty has now gone to Australia and is about to marry there. At Edinburgh University she recalls a Jamaican in the final year called Hester Field. But final year students do not speak with first years and Hester is but a name.

Bobbie and Philip's house in the military establishment known as Up Park Camp is very pleasant; built on stilts to protect against termite ants, it has a verandah round half the building and ceiling fans for cool. Anne, in a bedroom with attached bathroom, feels luxurious. Poor Philip is obliged to sit in a court of enquiry into a railway disaster which killed one hundred and eighty and injured seven hundred people. Never mind; there is a drinks party this evening, it is polo tournament week and Saturday sees the Polo Club Ball. From now on it is all go. Subalterns are summoned to partner Anne, picnics to beach beauty spots include her, the Saddle Club invites her to participate. Bobbie has a second cousin (also father's cousin) in the Army and stationed at Up Park Camp; Steven Anderson and his wife Shirley being much involved in the social whirl. Life is as it is in Britain, cocooned in family, comfortably Establishment but, and it is a big 'but', it is a *dolce vita* in a tropical climate; wealth, pleasure and self-indulgence for days and nights on end.

"We're riding the polo ponies up to Newcastle for some rest and recuperation after polo week," says Steven. "I've suggested to Bobbie that you come along. Should be fun. There will be a bit of a party up at the army hill station."

Starting at dawn, Anne, mounted and one of a string of riders most of whom are *syces* (grooms), passes cheerful local folk carrying produce to market, one bright lass having put her city slippers on her head to save them from getting muddied. There are scattered shacks built of interlaced stalks with a tiny yard containing a vegetable plot, orange trees and banana plants. Some have chickens, a pig or two, or a cow. First impressions are of a sparsely populated country but the hills are criss-crossed with tracks weaving through thick vegetation with every shrub and tree hiding a homestead, intimate secret settlements. There are signs of a savage climate; fearful erosion and landslide scars disfigure the slopes, all unstable and unforgiving. Cotton trees with long grey beards hanging from branches, high bracken-like fronds with stems thick as a man's arm, furry bamboo, long trailing lianas like wire hemming round the jungle and the heavy scent of wild ginger lilies, unveil a garden of Eden.

With Philip's permission, Anne attends at the House of Representatives for the court hearing on the rail disaster to a crowded excursion train some weeks previously. The court is cool from overhead fans, the walls dark panelled and hung with imposing portraits of King George V and Queen Mary flanked by photographs of Queen Elizabeth and Prince Philip. On the floor, stand a couple of stout lawyers, a reporter or two and a Chinese-looking clerk, while behind a fence sit half a dozen members of the public. "They are retired railway workers," comments Philip. The Commission consists of Brigadier Langley who looks like a schoolboy trainspotter, and Philip. "We are concerned with the technical issues," explains Philip. "The other two, Colin MacGregor, the Attorney General and 'Whiskey' Gordon, are dealing with personnel and legal matters." After evidence about braking points on the track and number of brakemen per train, there is reference to a forged brake test certificate. Principal witness is Mr Magnus, a stout, dark brown figure with a tonsure of frizzy grey hair who is sitting in a heap of despair during the evidence. He seems to consider his defence but as time goes on, he is led to admit that he is lazy, inefficient and uninterested in railway management. His suffering is palpable.

In the meantime, there are short walks with Aunt Bobbie and their dog, visits to the Garrison Club, regimental matches to watch, tennis parties, cocktail parties for visiting ships, never a dull moment in the peacetime army. The regiment, hosting a barbecue on Lime Cays, an island all of a quarter of a square mile in size, sends out the working party by launch to set up braziers for roast chicken and to lay out the bar, construct a dance floor and hang hurricane lamps. Guests' launches leave Kingston at eight thirty in the evening with a calypso band aboard, a full moon just rising and flashes of summer lightning behind Jamaica's mountains. Swim, dance, eat, dance, swim, eat again and back into Kingston at three in the morning. It is all great fun, this lotus-eating life; delightful but quite meaningless, merely sounding brass and tinkling cymbal.

A slow-growing decision to remain in Jamaica after Aunt Bobbie's and Philip's departure, has been working its way through the turf of Up Park Camp into Anne's mind: stay on in Jamaica, get a job, see more of the country beyond army establishment society. Having contacted Mr and Mrs Ogle, Betty's parents, Anne is invited to tea at their attractive home in the suburb of Constant Spring where a stunning view of the harbour and the Palisadoes may be seen through the feathery branches of a fir tree in their deeply sloping garden. Mrs Ogle is artistic, paints and teaches art; Anne is impressed by the form, movement and colour of some of her pupils' work. They chat about Betty in Australia.

"If only she had married in Canada!" exclaims Mrs Ogle, "So much easier to visit than Australia." Her dark eyes blink, a hand brushes a strand of disappointment from her face. When Anne had met her previously in Glasgow, she had appeared as Mediterranean, Spanish perhaps, but now in the Jamaican setting, Anne can recognise the monied White Jamaican

"Come. We are taking you to meet my sister. She wants to see Betty's friend." Mrs Ogle leads towards the car. Mrs Crooks is a much larger edition of the family with crinkly grey hair, a comfortable, happy-go-lucky manner and a milk coffee-coloured skin. Both Mr Crooks and Mr

Ogle are pinko-grey Anglo-Saxons married into Jamaica, and both work in the Education Department. They beseech Anne to apply for a job in the beleaguered education service.

"No. I really don't think you should take a job. Just enjoy yourself until Christmas and give me a hand." Aunt Bobbie is adamant about Anne's inclination to remain in Jamaica.

"Teaching in Kingston would be too ghastly. Take a secretarial post if you must but believe me you won't enjoy teaching here." Aunt Bobbie's sense of familial responsibility threatens to intrude upon Anne's plans.

"I have just received a Bank Statement," Anne writes to her parents "And find I am £4 overdrawn. I can live on £5 a month here but alas I cannot cover the overdraft. Would you please advance me £5 to be paid back as soon as I get a job, about which more shortly."

"I am going to buy a bicycle as I shall be immobilised when Aunt Bobbie goes home. Today I heard of a second-hand Raleigh for £10 and Aunt Bobbie is taking me to look at it. If it is suitable I had better get it while the going is good. Please could you advance me a further £10 to be paid back shortly."

The job is temporary, part-time work in the Overseas Exam Office and in the meantime, Anne has written to five schools with details of her CV, two of which have requested an interview. About the same time, she hears about a Colonial Office couple who would like a paying guest while their own two daughters are away at boarding school in Scotland, a Mr and Mrs Stewart. He is a Scot from Perthshire and she is a West Indian Barbadian born, with a caramel-coloured skin, dark flashing eyes and a hint of hot Indian spice in her blood.

"You should accept their kind offer," advises Aunt Bobbie. "They are a very pleasant couple; far more suitable than trying to find digs in town."

"Umm!" says an acquaintance at the Garrison Club, "Gilda Stewart is not everyone's cup of tea. She's very managing, you know. But John is a dear, very sensible."

At last, Philip is on a week's leave and he and Aunt Bobbie plan a series of day trips beginning with Port Royal at the end of the Palisadoes, a lengthy bar protecting Kingston's huge natural harbour. In the good old days of the seventeenth century, Port Royal was acclaimed the greatest and wickedest city of the New World. In 1692, a terrible earthquake destroyed it and rendered an astonishing miracle. In the churchyard is the tombstone of a resident who was swallowed by the earthquake and disgorged into the sea at the next tremble: rescued, he lived to be eighty years old. Near Port Royal is Fort Charles whence Nelson as a young man commanded the Caribbean. The fort is damaged by recurring earthquakes, as is its church, wherein are numerous plaques to HM servicemen who died of plague and yellow fever; the ruins being full of sad little ghosts aged thirteen and fifteen years who died in the service of their country. In Fort Nelson is the two-quart silver tankard which belonged to Captain Henry Morgan, an entrepreneur who managed to persuade the Crown that his pirating was to its advantage and who was knighted for his efforts. Morgan's Harbour, now an elegant beach club, serves an excellent lunch.

Another day trip takes them to Dunn's River near Ocho Rios on the north coast of the Island. The four hour journey passes through flat reclaimed marshland now growing sugar cane, to Spanish Town, once known as Saint Iago. This was formerly the seat of government and boasts the Governor's house, a lovely regency style building now earthquake damaged and no more than an ornamental façade in a shabby little town. Then up a narrow deep-sided limestone gorge, known as Bog Walk after a settlement at the head of the gorge, to a plain with its market town famed in the calypso 'Linstead Market' where the soil is rich red in colour and full of extractable alumina. From the Linstead

Plain, the road climbs steeply to the watershed at Mount Diablo and twists down and down to the north coast.

Dunn's River beach is the blueprint for travel agency posters; hard white sand, palm trees bending to the shore and transparent tropical water. The river rushes down onto the sand from a long, stepped waterfall coated with travertine deposits, so that its bed is smooth and milky white, delightful to clamber upon.

"I have definitely got a job for January" writes Anne to her parents, "Teaching at St. Hugh's High School for Girls at Cross Roads which is a suburb near Up Park Camp." Anne's future begins to take shape. She will be teaching English rather than Geography but that does not present a problem. The girls all wear uniform, the headmistress, Mrs Landale, is a pleasant White Jamaican and Anne's salary will be about £680 per year.

"It's a good school by Jamaican standards I suppose," says Aunt Bobbie disparagingly.

Anne starts a temporary post in the Overseas Examination Office invigilating London GCE. It is an irksome job. She must patrol continuously a hot hall closely packed with a hundred boys, or rather young men, their aroma of anxious effort deepening as the day wears on. The girls' centre, less noisy, is even entertaining as a fashion show, for the girls have dressed as for a party, high-heeled court shoes being slipped off under the desks and toes clenched in concentration.

Anne emerges from the halls of toil and moil and returns to the *dolce vita* life of Up Park Camp. She is invited to ride well-trained polo ponies and observe Major James teaching children at the riding club. 'Jimmy' James is leaving shortly and cousin Steven, who organises polo and riding, expects Anne to assist with the children. Parties, parades, picnics, polo, receptions, balls, lunches, naval visits, swimming parties, barbeques and night clubs chase each other though the days and nights as Aunt Bobbie's and Philip's departure looms and Christmas approaches.

At one of these parties a large lady with cast iron curls bears down. Mrs Leach is something of a *bête noir* in Anne's mind.

"I can't stand the woman," says Aunt Bobbie, "She's so nosy, so snobbish." Anne, first meeting the dragon at Newcastle when she rode the polo ponies up the mountain after Polo Week, had mistaken her for the brigadier's wife and had spent half an hour being as charming as she could. "And where did you go to school?" enquired Mrs Leach, and "What pack do you hunt with?" and "Did you know so-and-so in India?" and "This is a photo of my daughter, married at twenty-two," and "Here is a photo of my son. He has travelled so widely and gained such experience that we don't consider it necessary for him to go to Cambridge!"

Now Mrs Leach introduces her nephew from the Argentine and invites Anne to drinks at her posh house in the foothills above Kingston, where she entertains Lady This and Lady That. "I have told one of the subalterns to drive you up. It's all arranged." Mr Leach, Argentine born and schooled in England's public schools, a banana boffin engaged on research into prevailing banana blights, is easy to talk to and interesting. Nephew Richard is also an agronomist, working on a sugar estate. 'Drinks' extends to include supper and it is late when Anne is delivered home. She wonders if she is being looked over.

Aunt Bobbie's and Philip's departure is imminent when Mr and Mrs Stewart announce that their new house is not ready and they will not be moving until early January. However, Major and Mrs Bowen offer to have Anne in the interval. Major Bowen is away on duty in British Honduras and his wife, Anne, would be glad of company during his absence. Indeed, Anne finds plenty to occupy her when Anne Bowen entertains their company's wives and children to a Christmas party, after which the two Annes hurry to the Police cocktail party. On Sunday, Anne accompanies her hostess to the Garrison Service of Nine Lessons and

Carols, after which they lose their heads and invite dozens of people back for drinks and supper.

Anne Bowen is a doctor and does some voluntary work at a local pre-natal clinic, work she finds harrowing. "I ask the patients if this is their first child and one young girl told me it was, but added she had had ten miscarriages. She has raging anaemia and will probably abort or deliver a premature stillborn. I can prescribe iron pills but she may not be able to get them, afford them. It's hopeless." Anne Bowen's response to her patients' plight is the only manifestation of emotion she allows to show in public. Normally she is efficient, tender to her children and casually jolly in company, but phlegmatic to the point of indifference in daily life.

Mrs Leach has invited Anne to spend Christmas with them at Harold Hill. She phones to say "I shall collect you on Christmas Eve before lunch. We are having friends in that evening including your cousins." Presumably she means Steven and Shirley Anderson: they are a popular couple and being their cousin is an advantage. Anne goes to Up Park Camp NAAFI to buy a Christmas present of a large tin of Crawfords shortbread for Mrs Leach and family and visitors, which means she does not have to buy something for the entire household.

The afternoon of Christmas Eve is spent with nephew Richard putting up cards, blowing balloons and preparing for the drinks party before the other houseguests arrive. Richard is twenty-six, tall and disastrously good-looking with blonde hair, blue eyes, dark brows and eyelashes. Mrs Leach says he spends all his time running away from women; also that if she wants him to do something she has to suggest the opposite.

Christmas Day is traditional; eight o'clock Holy Communion followed by ceremonial opening of presents. Then a swim at the Liguanea Club before lunch and a siesta followed by a walk with the dogs, two black Labradors of the Leaches and one of Richard's, before changing into evening dress for traditional dinner with candles, crackers, nuts and raisins, wine and port. Boxing Day sees a picnic to a long beach on the eastern end of the island where the dogs are well exercised.

"I wonder, Mummy" Anne writes to her parents "If you could write to Mrs Leach and tell her how much I enjoyed Christmas. I have become fond of her and she treats me like a daughter. She even murmured something about having me as a paying guest if I don't get on well with the Stewarts. She may be hoping I shall fall out with Gilda Stewart. I am very grateful to her and her family."

New Year is seen in with the Bowens, Bill having managed to get back from British Honduras on Christmas Eve. They invite the company subalterns and everyone goes to the officers' mess for a dance and party. Anne is given a free hand to do the flower arrangements for the event and enjoys all the preparations as well as the party. What a great way to finish the year.

Chapter 5

Small Island

It is 1958, the year of Federation for the British Commonwealth West Indian Islands.

When the year opens, Anne is still a paying guest at the Bowens in Up Park Camp. Her first commitment is an appointment with Mrs Landale at St Hugh's School where she discovers her salary will be a princely £710 per year. Then at a staff meeting to discuss timetables, she is introduced to other staff members. Head of Geography is none other than Hester Field who does recall Anne from Edinburgh University days. More significant is the senior English mistress. Miss Priestman, recently retired from many years teaching at the Froebel teacher training college in Britain, is the Head of English studies. Friendly, indeed motherly, she is the gift Anne needs. Her Quaker tranquillity eases the nervous tension generated by starting a new job in a foreign country and soothes beginning-of-term frenzy. Not only is it the start of a term, but it is the beginning of the academic year. Miss Priestman volunteers to pick Anne up every morning once she has moved to the Stewarts' house since she has a car and lives in the same direction, some distance from the suburb of Cross Roads where the school is situated.

The following week passes in a flurry of activity. Anne is invited to a twelfth night fancy dress ball by a Captain in

Bill Bowen's Company. School begins on a Tuesday. On Wednesday after school, Anne moves up to the Stewarts' new house which is still being finished and furnished in Gilda's absence, she having started a full time job as doctors' receptionist. On Thursday, as on all school days, Anne teaches from eight o'clock until one fifteen in the afternoon, then she has lunch in the school kitchen. She occupies the next two hours on lesson preparation before walking to Gilda's work place whence John Stewart picks them both up at four-thirty to drive home. At the Stewarts' house chaos reigns; furniture is still arriving and being unpacked and Gilda is a ball of dynamite throwing together a fork supper for seven guests before all go on to the pantomime. On Friday, Anne is invited to a private dance given by one of the Up Park Camp families.

What a week! To pursue a full time teaching job and continue as one of the few available, single British girls in Kingston is stressful. Anne hopes she has stamina enough to enjoy the forthcoming exhaustive Federation ceremonies plus an imminent change of Governor General, which will spark a further round of flag-waving, pomp and circumstance and partying. The British Navy's Home Fleet is visiting in style with bands playing and gold braid galore. Add a tropical setting and scented balmy nights. Put all into a small island and mix in a limited social circle. Continue this process for a month and the result is stultifying; gossip rages, scandals soar, boredom prevails.

The Stewarts' house, built by a Jamaican called Mr Mesquita whom Gilda loathes, calling him Mr Mosquito and the house 'Anopheles Pen' (*pen* being a local word for a smallholding), is well out into the country at an altitude of nearly 200 metres above the sea with marvellous views over the harbour. It is a good ten minutes' walk to the nearest bus stop and takes one hour to reach Cross Roads where St. Hugh's School is. Never mind: the Stewarts treat Anne as a daughter taking her everywhere with them, also sweeping her into household chores and making her work hard, but Anne can hardly take offence because Gilda herself works harder. One Sunday there is an invitation to drinks on board the frigate *HMS Ulysses* after which John, Gilda and Anne repair to the Garrison Club for some lunch followed by the weekly Scottish country dancing. Somehow Gilda manages to collect five young naval officers to bring home for a fork supper and urges Anne into a frenzy of activity as she prepares a gourmet supper table. It is exciting to be at the hub of official entertaining, though wearing for a beginner in the skills of a hostess. John's post of Colonial Undersecretary in the Chief Secretary's Office demands communication with all British comings and goings: Gilda sparkles when entertaining, her face glowing with delight.

The following week is fairly quiet, only two dinner parties at the Stewarts' home and an invitation to a fancy dress party at the weekend. Next week, however, there is a big reception at King's House for the visiting Navy, five or six ships in all and an admiral or two.

"Pick out a suitable sailor at the Reception," commands Gilda, "And we'll take him on to the Yacht Club Ball and invite him home for the weekend."

This is not as easy as it sounds when there are over fifty to choose from and many are married. Anne finds a suitable sailor and asks him if he is going to the Ball. When he says yes he is, Anne assumes he is already invited in a private party and rushes back to the source of supply for another. Meanwhile Gilda cannot resist a sailor she likes and invites him, at which point John comes across with the sailor Anne had first thought of, having issued an invitation to him early in the evening. They manage to farm out one of the three to local friends and bring only two back to supper before going on to the Ball. Bed at four o'clock in the morning and into school by eight o'clock.

On Sunday afternoon, Anne is obliged to go to Vale Royal, home of Mr Stow the Chief Secretary, to help entertain sailors, ratings rather than officers; it turns out to be an interesting and stimulating event. Then in the evening, the Stewarts and Anne are invited on board *HMS Maidstone* by the two sailors they have adopted, for a delicious cold buffet supper and film show on the quarterdeck. Highlight of the evening is watching the submarine *HMS Tiptoe* arrive and ease alongside the mothership *HMS Maidstone*; the other submarine *HMS Turpin* having had some engine trouble will not be in for a day or two. And Wednesday sees everyone back on *HMS Maidstone* for a reception; at the end of which the gangplank stairs down to the quay are many and steep. Press on regardless to a barbeque and dance at the Liguanea Club. Bed at one in the morning and at school for eight o'clock. Thursday evening the Stewarts go to dinner at King's House and Anne goes gratefully to bed at nine o'clock.

Anne is, after the first week of term devoted as it were to administrative matters such as form lists and mark sheets, beginning to enjoy the school work: the structure is not unlike the school she attended. Most of the classes she teaches are the two lowest forms of ten to twelve year olds: Miss Priestman recommends plenty of stories from the literature set books, play writing and acting, some choral speaking and poetry writing and, a minimum of tests and formal work, with just a bit of spelling.

"Why don't you get them to make a class magazine?" she suggests. "That way you find they do their own correcting and editing, which is more effective than a teacher's correction. Pick up any obvious weaknesses such as punctuation and sentence construction for the language classes and then let them get on with it." Anne is grateful for on-site training such as Miss Priestman can offer.

Geography for the little ones is also Anne's remit; not difficult to bone up on bananas and sugar cane for the youngest group and the Americas for year two. Current Affairs for the sixth form is more of a challenge: many of the girls now in their mid-teens are fully-formed women interested in boyfriends rather than school work. They walk with slow dignity and enviable grace, swinging their hips provocatively, regarding Anne with serious, aloof curiosity. There are, too, a number of Indian and Chinese girls who flaunt their greatest blessing, 'tall' hair, which is masterfully caught in a swinging ponytail or contained in a heavy net.

The staff is mostly White Jamaican varying in skin colour from café-au-lait to creamy white, and while the older teachers are friendly enough, some of the young ones are detached, withdrawn and difficult to know. Anne recognises Hester Field's shyness, and acknowledges the need to go more than half way to draw her out.

The lower school children are charming, all colours from ebony through caramel to gorgeous cream. Many have short, spiral hair parted in sections and dressed in four or five tiny plaits, pegged down with a kirby grip to their neat heads. Enormous eyes roll mischievously whenever there is a language problem. After reading from the set work, Longfellow's poem *Hiawatha*, Anne asks them to illustrate the piece. Walking round the classroom, she can recognise the wigwam - well, she had drawn one on the blackboard – and can distinguish the big lake and shining sun.

"But what are all these little crosses for? They look like kisses."

"Please Miss, that is the pine forest."

"But pines are great big trees, taller than me, taller than this classroom."

Gales of giggles. "Don't you know what a pine looks like, Miss? Pines are spiky bushes with a pineapple growing in the middle."

Anne struggles to recall the right name of a child and explosions of mirth follow if she gets a wrong name. It is all harmless fun. Not so on Friday afternoons when Anne has to take tennis from four to six o'clock. The good players go to a professional for coaching, so Anne gets the rabbits who are uninterested in sport, and noisy.

With the departure of several naval vessels, a more peaceful week promises.

"It's good to have a week of recovery" Anne writes to her parents. "John and Gilda have a visitor staying, Lady Noble, who says she knew you when you were in Singapore. Also claims to be General Montgomery's mother-in-law. She is an easy guest because she never stops talking. I don't know how long she is staying though, possibly until she is turned out by the arrival of 'Jimmy' James who is booked to come and stay with the Stewarts soon."

Lady Noble, now seventy-nine, must have been a great beauty in her youth. She has a delightful Edwardian grace and dignity; one would think she is royalty by the way she speaks. The Stewarts invite some elderly friends to supper to meet Lady Noble, including the Leaches. Mrs Leach tells Anne that she has a nephew on a ship called *HMS Narvik* about to visit Kingston; not part of the Home Fleet but just passing on its way to Christmas Island in the Pacific.

"You must meet Christopher. We shall invite you to go on board with us. And please don't accept other invitations at that time." Mrs Leach wags an emphatic finger.

Lady Noble cannot refrain from remarks about Gilda. "She is such a charming person, you know. One would never imagine that she is coloured. Quite astonishing don't you think?"

Anne has not given any thought to Gilda's colour. She is just Gilda, and marvellous. Born a Henriques, an old renowned West Indian family, she married early and has a son now aged twenty-four training at Ampleforth to be a monk. Her Indian subcontinent heritage is clearly acknowledged by her wide mouth with narrow lips, obsidian black eyes and shining jet hair; her skin a delicious cinnamon colour. Her brother, Cyril Henriques, who is much darker and more Indian looking, is nicknamed the 'Coolie Judge' amongst his legal colleagues. Gilda's second marriage to John Stewart has given her two daughters, Helen twelve years and Robina ten years, now at boarding school in Scotland. Anne, a proxy daughter in their absence, is grateful to Gilda for providing a tower of moral strength.

"You are in an impossible situation here," says Gilda. "Jamaica is no place for you. The women here are either the uninhibited daughters of local families or bored, married women with too much money and time heavy on their hands. They are posted from Britain by the Army or an international company, are given a big house, servants and a car. What can you expect? They have no idea how to behave. There's nothing here to buy, nowhere to go and nothing to do." Gilda picks up a stick, examines it closely as if it were a piece of Jamaica, then hurls it for the dog to chase.

Now comes a frenetic week. On Sunday, Anne goes with the Stewarts for pre-lunch drinks on the submarine *HMS Turpin,* which has limped into Kingston and is awaiting a tow home to Britain, after which she joins the Leaches and goes with them in the evening to a cocktail party on *HMS Narvik*. She is there to partner the nephew Christopher Tisdall, but alas Mrs Leach talks so much and so long, that neither Christopher nor Anne can get a word in edgeways. In desperation, Anne makes conversation with another officer who is handing round a platter of canapés. His name is John Sears and he spends time telling Anne about his girlfriend, Mary, in Britain whom he misses and whom he hopes he will find waiting for him when he returns in a year's time. "And what present do you think I should buy for her? What would you recommend?" More to the point, he suggests a night club after the party on deck. Christopher is Duty Officer that evening so he cannot come but John and Anne have a jolly time at the Glass Bucket. John presents Anne with a *Narvik* crest which, she is told, is a signal honour. "And what about coming to dinner in the ward room tomorrow evening?" Anne, not sure how to handle this invitation, suggests that he invite John and

Gilda Stewart too. They are delighted to accept a refreshingly informal invitation and enjoy the evening. *HMS Narvik,* under close inspection of a conducted tour, is an old rust bucket on its way to Christmas Island in the Pacific Ocean to land supplies for atom bomb tests there.

On Thursday, the aircraft carrier *HMS Bulwark,* arriving with a daunting one hundred and eighty officers on board, gives a monumental cocktail party. It is exciting going out in the launch at sunset to the skyscraper of a vessel anchored out in the stream, and proceeding through a trap door into a giant lift used for bringing up aircraft from the hanger to the flight deck. Anne again finds herself a suitable sailor, a New Zealander who invites her out to a night club after the reception. Thereafter King's House hosts a reception for the Navy, which is followed by a dance at the Liguanea Club. Then the Stewarts host a high-powered dinner party for senior officers from various ships which goes well but Anne finds exhausting: the thought of school next day alarms her. But it is not finished yet. *HMS Bulwark* throws another big party for everyone; a jaded Anne being reanimated by her friendly New Zealand sailor. At last it is over. Everyone is tired, satiated with the Navy. That evening Anne goes to a private party with friends. It should be fun, informal and refreshing, but no: gossip rages, scandals sparkle with a score of nuances: the zip of Scilla's sheath dress is hanging open, Audrey is flirting with a married man. There is a fragrant aroma of barbeque smoke and a balmy, scented tropical night with myriad lights scintillating on the still harbour. Everyone is busy living intensely and there is dancing, embracing, heavy petting. Someone she barely knows is asking too much of Anne. Is it imagination or is there a competition to see which lady-killer can make the greatest conquest? Is it an ego boosting exercise for damaged personalities induced by married women bored with their lot?

Anne's appetite for parties, balls, receptions and picnics ebbs, her antennae desensitised by the sexual opportunism all around her. She is too traditional, takes herself too seriously to treat lust lightly. Kissing is all very well but heavy petting, clothes fumbled loose to play upon the erotogenic zones is too much. She recognises that once her bra is off it may not be physically possible to stop going further. She sees herself as wife to the right man but never as a bauble in the crown of some philanderer. The fact that the contraceptive pill has yet to be invented is beside the point: Anne has no intention of bestowing herself on any Tom, Dick or Harry. Life in Jamaica is just a bowl of jello, all froth.

"What do you expect?" says Gilda, who holds strong opinions on Kingston's society. "These bored young women get into mischief, run amok. And the men aren't going to say no. It's a tropical night, drink is free or ridiculously cheap. Then in comes the Fleet with band playing, full of white uniforms with lashings of gold braid and buttons all over the place." Scorn scorches Gilda's speech.

Although Gilda can help Anne by rationalising the social circumstances of Kingston, she can also be very scathing, flinging squibs of satire at her friends.

"Jimmy James is a fool. He's taken a job out here with Rerries' Haulage Company. When Jimmy was in the Army, Rerries was his best buddy. Now the boot is on the other foot and Rerries has taken a rotten house for him. Jimmy should have known better." Gilda smiles craftily. "Perhaps Zena (his wife) pushed him. She would not want to have to run a home in Britain."

John airs a Solomon quip, simultaneously hiding a chuckle and Gilda with charming compassion puts herself out to assist Jimmy and Zena in settling back into Jamaica.

Anne, observing Gilda's jousting, is wary even as she admires and loves both Stewarts: better to tread with discretion and avoid the barbs even if it means foregoing the delicious charm offensive that follows. Or is it? Anne notes that John revels in the verbal arrows aimed at him;

positively purrs with pleasure at his wife's delectable winsomeness which invariably follows. Theirs is a coloratura marriage: nothing chiaroscuro about it.

There are two Gildas. One is caring, caressing, controlling; the typical British *memsahib*. The other is stormy, sensual, sultry and sexual; an Indian aristocrat, a vibrating instrument. John is a Celtic patrician from a Scottish landed family, cool, calm and calculating; more than a match for his lady's exuberant outbursts.

Anne is again unsure about her future plans. At the weekend, she goes down town to a travel agent to find out about passages in July to Britain or possibly Canada where a Canadian Edinburgh University friend, Mary Beacock now married to Geoff Fryer, lives in Toronto. Mary writes to say that she is expecting a baby in July, resigning her post as Librarian in the University's Geography Department and would Anne be interested in applying for it? The alternative is to go to Canada for an eight-week summer as an *au pair* and then seek a job in London thereafter: or return to St. Hugh's for another year. She will have to make up her mind soon if she is to give in her notice by the end of the Easter vacation.

In the meantime, the Stewarts' children will be out in Jamaica for their Easter holiday and Anne arranges to attend a geographical excursion from St. Hugh's School to Knox College at Spaldings in the mountains during that period. Anne travels up to Spaldings with Hester Field in her car while the others, thirty-five students and six staff, go up by train and bus.

Founded recently as an experiment in boarding schools by the Scottish Presbyterian Church, Knox College is the brainchild of its headmaster, Mr Davidson, who wanted something more modern than the old, traditional exam-oriented foundations of Jamaica. Run on a financial shoestring and co-educational, it offers vocational training as well as progressive intellectual education and is making a name for itself by holding Summer Schools with an international intake. It is situated at about 700 metres on a ridge, with views over a multitude of ridges to the north coast. In these rugged hills, water is always scarce and often absent: a patina of red dust coats the entire place inside and out. Anne is obliged to sleep in a dormitory with the girls and eat local food. This consists of boiled yams, plantains and corncobs, or maize porridge and roasted breadfruit. There is an infrequent beef or pork casserole or a rather unpalatable saltfish and *ackee*. This is followed by oranges, avocados or sweet bananas. In sum, the excursion to Knox College provides a stark contrast to the lavish life Anne has been accustomed to living in Kingston. It is a challenge she needs to meet if she is to understand the essential nature of Jamaica.

The central mountains of Jamaica are a far cry from the cocktail parties of Up Park Camp and the Liguanea Club; not in distance, for a mere fifty miles separates them, but in circumstance. This is the other side of the coin. Structurally, central Jamaica is an anticline with cretaceous and tertiary limestones on the outer flanks to the north and south, and older metamorphic rocks and conglomerates exposed down the spine of the anticline. It is a tortuous topography, a helter skelter of hillsides where valleys interlock and double-lock so that there is no exit but up and over the top. Precipitous slopes slashed with great red wounds of erosion offend the eye; a broken terrain, a jumble of crests, ridges and spurs, offers no horizon, unhinging one's cognition of locality. This, the Cockpit country, is a disturbing landscape; no place to be lost.

The district was settled in the 1830s as emancipated or runaway slaves took to the hills determined to distance themselves from their erstwhile masters. Not for nothing it is known as the Land of Look Behind. To the slaves these mountains were not claustrophobic but concealing, camouflaging, where they could build homes, clear vegetation, plant yams, maize, bananas and breadfruit for the family and cultivate coffee, pimento and ginger to sell.

Early settlers having prospered, the population began to multiply far beyond the capacity of the land. For many years, bananas in particular flourished and the womenfolk could carry spare produce to local markets and *higgle* (sell) them.

Then came the 1930s. Alas, the Great Depression occurred in conjunction with Panama Disease irresistibly blighting the banana crops and caused severe hardship in this remote, inaccessible mountain fastness. Desperate peasant farmers stripped further the vegetation, burned further to improve the soil fertility and planted other crops, cocoa, coconuts and sugar cane. The 1940s saw a brief boom in ginger for overseas export since Jamaica's ginger enjoys a reputation for good quality and excellent aroma, but by 1952, Jamaican ginger crashed as African and Chinese produce of poorer quality came cheaply onto the world market. In 1954, the Government of Jamaica established the Christiana Area Land Authority (CALA) to ameliorate the peasants' lot by land reform and social improvement.

One of the days' fieldwork is spent going round the district with CALA staff. Anne sees children with balloon bellies and stick limbs, a sure sign of malnutrition, even of starvation. A one-room shack is full of small children all belonging to a woman who is hoeing a row of maize. Anne enquires how many children she has.

"I got ten children now. But I been and buried another eight, or ten maybe."

"And your husband, what does he do?"

"He go to Kingston, look after work. I look after the *pen* (local word for smallholding)."

"How many acres have you got?" Anne asks.

"I don't know no acres. I got this *pen* and another two miles over the mountain. And my man he got a *pen* three miles down this hill here," she waves her arm towards a distant gully. "But it is far, and they steal my plantains."

It is a hopeless situation with plots divided infinitesimally among descendants, in tiny parcels miles apart. There is little incentive for improvement, theft is rife, investment useless.

The area of CALA corresponds approximately to the ginger growing region whose history is tantamount to the sorry state of the island's peasant agriculture.

"The climate up here in the mountains is good for ginger and it is a crop which can have a high value, give the farmers good money," explains a staff member of CALA. "The problem is soil erosion on these steep slopes. We tell them to plant contour strips of grass for animal fodder between the rows of ginger. But the farmers don't want to do that. They say it takes too much land away from their ginger."

Since 1952, the selling price of dry ginger has bounced between five shillings and one shilling per pound. It is a boom and bust story. Peasants invest in the heavy cost of ginger when prices are high, so that the market is flooded and the price drops to the point where smallholders cannot afford to retain enough green ginger for planting. In consequence supply drops and prices soar.

"If the market price is low the crop can be left undug in the ground," the CALA staff member explains. "But this means that farmers have nothing to sell and the women who wash, peel and dry the crop have no work, no income."

The Jamaican Government is trying to help the very small farmer by buying their ginger at a fixed price. This step is first taken in 1957 when the Government could offer a good price. But in 1958, the Government is more sparing with its offer and farmers face an outright loss. Undoubtedly they are not acquainted with a statement made in 1956 by Mr Norman Manley, the Chief Minister, in respect of banana production. He told his people that the world does not owe Jamaicans a market and, if the country is to survive, export competition production must be more efficient.[5]

What can CALA do to alleviate the misery of the smallholders?

"We are trying to persuade the farmers to plant other crops such as coffee and new disease-resistant bananas so that they can have something to sell," reports the CALA staff member. "But they can't afford fertilisers and the soil is exhausted." Scrambling up steep little tracks almost occluded by exuberant tree and creeper growth, Anne finds plots no bigger than a double bed of yam, vines and ginger. There is no one to be seen but she is conscious of hidden watchers in the wilderness.

CALA have tried to count the families in their district. "The survey results are always different," laments a staffer. "We have no idea how many homesteads there are on these hillsides. We are trying to register land holdings so that farmers have a more permanent claim to land tenure, but it is an impossible task."

Anne returns to Kingston dejected and despondent. Never having been hungry or in need, she frets over the disheartening existence of the peasants she has seen struggling for survival among Jamaica's unforgiving hills. Meanwhile, the *dolce vita* continues. Having decided to leave Jamaica in July and return to Britain, Anne hands in her notice with regret since she is enjoying the teaching. The summer term involves the chilling task of exam setting and correcting and of report writing. Miss Priestman, having cast a practised eye over Anne's efforts, is enthusiastic about a future in teaching, in London perhaps. As a farewell gift for Gilda, Anne buys an antique brooch; five oval corals in a chased silver setting. For John she chooses a set of eight Czechoslovakian sherry glasses, plain but elegant on tall stems. Her affection for the Stewarts having deepened with time, she suffers feelings of bereavement at her departure. Someone born under a

---

[5] Macmillan, Mona, *The Land of Look Behind,* Faber and Faber, 1957

wandering star has inevitable appointments with departure, its disadvantages as well as its inducements.

Chapter 6

The Die is Cast

Having heard through Consular friends in Kingston about a Canadian family called Todd living in Toronto who would like a summer holiday *au pair*, Anne has contacted them with an offer to help look after their children for six weeks, leaving herself some time to visit Mary Beacock Fryer's family in Toronto and in Brockville on the St Lawrence Seaway.

Canada is a delightful interlude. Anne does not know much about the country or, indeed, about the USA. Canadians are those North Americans who spend their time convincing Americans that they are not British and enlightening the British that in no way are they American.

"Anne, would you please put the baby buggy out on the sidewalk for me," calls Mrs Todd, her North American accent clearly marked. (Put the pram on the pavement is what she means.)

Jocelyn Todd, known always as Jolly, is in fact an American, daughter of a Pittsburgh steel magnate. Tall, slim, auburn-haired, for the time being anyway, she is an organised woman always doing four things simultaneously. On this particular evening of Anne's arrival, she is supervising supper for Debbie aged seven and Julie who is three-and-a-half. She is cooking the adults' dinner for Don Todd, herself, Anne and Aline the French Canadian *au pair* staying to learn English. She is also is directing Aline, who is to look after the infant Jamie aged four months, as well as downing an old-fashioned cocktail.

"Toddy and I are leaving tomorrow with Jamie and all the luggage to drive to the cottage on Lake Joseph" Jolly announces. "You two, Aline and Anne, can clear up the house, put everything away, then you and the girls will catch the train and we'll meet you at Foots Bay station. It is about three hours on the train so you will have plenty of time for dinner. Here is the money for your taxi to the station, train tickets and dinner."

Anne, having not been in the country longer than a couple of hours, hardly knows a dollar from a dime so Aline takes charge of the money. Neither of the little girls appear to worry when their parents drive off. Maybe the train journey is treat enough for them?

The train, 'The Canadian', is a transcontinental stainless steel cylinder with bullet-shaped locomotives, soundproof windows and an observation lounge at the rear. Dinner is excellent; a salmon steak almost as big as its platter with vegetables, followed by blueberry pie and ice cream, served with limitless coffee and rounded off with digestive tablets. This is no train to compare with British Rail's steam puffers hauling 'The Flying Scot' between London and Edinburgh. Rather it is something out of an American movie, spectacular while it lasts, an experience to remember.

The Todds' cottage proves to be not the two-up-two-down wooden building with privy by the wood stack, but a colossal timber-built palace elegantly fitted with parquet flooring, a log fire burning throughout the day, and underfloor air conditioning, that heats, humidifies and cools. It has every convenience including washing machines for clothes and for dishes, electric waste disposal units in principal rooms, six bedrooms and an unknown number of bath or shower rooms. Next door is their fine boathouse containing a speedboat used in lieu of car, a rowing boat and a couple of canoes.

Lastly, the jetty.

Their private dock is used by everyone for sunbathing, for picnic lunches, for pre-prandial drinks starting at 10 o'clock in the morning, for cocktails from 4 o'clock in the afternoon onwards, and as a landing for Don Todd who, having been back to Toronto for a week's work, flies in by private seaplane for a long weekend. Some cottage! Anne, whose parents boast a small caravan as their holiday cottage, is amazed and awed by the American life style.

The lake, a limitless labyrinth of water, islands, channels, inlets, bays, and the surrounding promontories and peninsulas among pine and fir forest is most attractive, as are the myriads of modern mouth-watering summer villas. A pleasure steamer, Mississippi River Boat model, carries holidaymakers. Other vacationers delight in driving powerful micro-launches, with the noise of a fortissimo mechanical mosquito, crazily through the turbulent wake of any available vessel including their own. Clearly these North Americans are deeply serious people when it comes to vacationing.

One weekend, the Todds invite some neighbours to dinner. All day Jolly, Aline and Anne clean, polish and prepare; chop, grate and shred; cook and taste a dinner for twelve. Vegetable hors d'oeuvres, roast turkey with all the trimmings, blueberry pie with ice cream of course, coffee and petit fours. The table looks lovely set with candles, handsome with white paper napery and elegant cut glass goblets.

At last, Anne runs to change into a colourful cotton skirt and jersey blouse with pretty pumps instead of her daytime sneakers while guests arrive and wander down to the dock now hung with lanterns. Soon the bourbon, the rye and the scotch are flowing. Glancing round the crowd, she observes that all the women are in trousers or bermudas and shaggy pullovers with moccasins or clumsy casuals on their inelegant feet. This must be the North American fashion: it is a far cry from British Colonial as worn in Jamaica for a private dinner party. Men, Anne notes, conform, being gaily dressed in coloured shirts and well-tailored slacks with shoes and socks on. More bourbon, rye and scotch. Decibels rise as the discussion heats up: it is civil measures of defence for an atom bomb attack on Toronto which exercises the gathering, manifestly a matter of urgency and gravity.

Several bourbons, ryes and scotches later, guests file into the dining room carrying their drinks with them. Anne wonders what the cut glass goblets are for: can it be cider? Or iced tea? No wine has been seen or opened or chilled. In come the hors d'oeuvres: out go the empty plates. The turkey, crisply roasted and fragrant, is borne in for Toddy to carve. Jolly looks proudly round her dinner table.

"Oh! You've got nothing to drink" she exclaims with concern. "Now, there is pasteurised, homogenised and skimmed. Let me ask around each of you."

Milk in cut glass goblets is a novel accompaniment to a proud dinner. And why not, after all the spirits that have been consumed? All the same, Anne settles for water. Her neighbouring guest remarks that the British are 'quaint'. By that he may mean 'tedious': there is no doubt that these Canadians work and play immensely hard compared with the British back home. Nevertheless, Anne is grateful to the Todds for the wonderful opportunity they have given her.

Back in Toronto, Mary Beacock Fryer is adamant that Canadians are definitely not Americans. "We escaped from America nearly two hundred years ago," she cries indignantly. "At huge risk to our lives and livelihoods we outwitted the Yanks and found our way northward and across the St. Lawrence River to liberty."

Mary will, in 1976, be published in a book called *'Escape'* in which she fictionalises her Empire Loyalist ancestors' persecution at the hands of American Revolutionaries after the War of Independence, and their departure at dead of night from their home town of Schenectady in New York State. The family of Caleb and Martha Seamen and their eight children, ranging in age from sixteen years to eighteen months, made a perilous journey up the Mohawk River and down the Kahuago (now Black River) and Indian Rivers to Fort Oswegatchie (now Ogdensburg) where they were grateful to get a bateau ride across the St. Lawrence to Johnstown and safety. It is a gripping tale aimed at Canada's High School children and it will become a bestseller. Mary will follow '*Escape*' with '*Beginning Again*' in which she recounts the Seamen family's struggle with Canada's severe and extreme climate, with isolation and with pioneer survival. No wonder Canadians resent being lumped together with Americans.

***

Home again to Edinburgh after one year away. It is 1958 and Festival time. Among the marvellous cultural treats is a Byzantine Exhibition, including a 5th century mosaic of the kicking mule from the Palace of the Emperors in Istanbul.

"Oh yes, it is real stone" one of the attendants on duty assures Anne. It looks it too.

London. At last. A flat in Pimlico: romantic area of London. Anne recalls a film called 'Passport to Pimlico' wherein the residents of that quarter regard it as a place apart, drawing up in Dickensian manner, a unilateral declaration of independence. Warwick Street market, featuring largely in the film, still flourishes. Gone are the colourful vendors of sweet lavender or fresh strawberries but street cries persist as costermongers wheel round their barrows. "Paraffin, pink paraffin," they cry. London is a huge, sprawling, amorphous city in which it is easy to flounder amid a surfeit of social openings. There are hobby clubs, cultural, leisure and sports interests, club nights, pub nights in which to sink quietly among numerous acquaintances but few friends, until life consists of nothing but the job, the flat and a cat.

There are four people living in the flat, single sex of course in those days; Ann, Alison, Aileen and Anne. They decide to take a leaf out of Gilda Stewart's book and entertain. To all friends and acquaintances they announce: "Open House on Sunday evenings; bring your own beer," and start cooking delicious hot-pot, goulash or not-very-genuine curry with mountains of rice. Luckily brother Colin, having finished his medical training at the adjacent Westminster Hospital and now a houseman there, has colleagues and friends all over town.

Some of Anne's Jamaica friends turn up: Tom Riddell, the nice New Zealander from *HMS Bulwark*, Tony Shaw from Up Park Camp and John Sears of *HMS Narvik* now back from blasting atom bombs on Christmas Island in the Pacific. Anne is astonished to greet the latter when he knocks on the door of the London School of Economics Geography Department where Anne is employed as secretary. This is one she did not expect to see a year later. And what has happened to the girlfriend for whom she was asked to advise on the buying of a present?

"Oh, she got married to a Spaniard. Couldn't wait, I guess" John chuckles. "And you, Anne? What are you doing in the LSE? I know it well and always thought one half was mad and the other half Communist. Would you like to come and have some lunch or a cup of coffee or something?" he adds.

"I can't leave the office just at this moment. It's vacation time I know, but there are students about and post-grads. Why don't you sit down and pretend to be a student until I can get away at lunch time for an hour?"

It is a warm April day and they wander down to the Embankment, buying a few sandwiches as they go.

"I'm out of the Navy now. Rather regretfully perhaps: I so enjoyed the free travel and foreign parts. Now I belong to the ranks of the great unemployed while I look for a job. I've got a number of letters of application out but nothing's fixed yet. I'm enjoying life meanwhile."

They pass Wyndham's Theatre on the way back to LSE where 'At the Drop of a Hat' is playing. "Why don't we see if we can pick up a couple of tickets for this evening?" he suggests.

They are lucky and, after work, meet for a meal. John sketches in his Civil Engineering background; a degree from Imperial College in London and a burning desire to work 'on the job' rather than 'in an office'. "I shall have to do some time in an office. Part of my training for the 'Civils', Institute of Chartered Civil Engineers, must include design work. Let's hope I can do it in London."

That is in April. By May, he has joined a large Engineering Contractor, George Wimpy and Co Ltd, and is drafted to a site of multi-storey flats in Birmingham. So begins a summer of wonderful weekends either in London or in Birmingham. An outstandingly hot summer occurs in 1959 albeit punctuated by short snaps of intense summer storms and cold winds. John buys a second-hand car, a 1950 MG TC and becomes mobile.

"My life is now rather absorbed with cars, or should I say one car," he writes. Starter motor, electrics, gear box, brakes, engine tuning, carburettor... all give cause for concern but are patiently examined, cleaned and eventually methodically fixed. While it is fun to cut a figure around London in an open MG, the envy of one's flatmates, Anne is not amused when it stalls in Eaton Square, in The Mall and other enviable environs and she has to push it. Nevertheless, they pack picnics to the South Coast and to Wales, to Stratford-on-Avon, Warwick and all over The Midlands.

Is this a wooing?

Fortnightly weekend jaunts and increasingly frequent letters begin to spell love. The letters, three a fortnight then five a fortnight, pounding up and down the Royal Mail lines between London and Birmingham, are hardly love letters but they speak of personal things that matter; budgets and bank balances, hopes and expectations, anxieties and misgivings, yearnings and tenderness.

17 Gravelly Hill North, Erdington, Birmingham 23
8 July
"Dearest Anne,
To some people I find letter writing irksome but not to you because I know I shall receive a more than worthwhile reply... In some ways, Anne, I have been surprised at the great pace with which our relationship has developed, but we are both old enough to view it sensibly and logically." And, "All my love, John."

Physical love is much more difficult to manage sensibly. The MG gives them freedom and privacy denied to many carless young people. With the beach in this heatwave summer demanding minimal swimwear, how does one handle the fire of desire? The joking relationship is a standby.

"You looked just like a bucket of concrete coming down the pulley as you sat down on the rug." Thus speaks the engineer to his love as she plumps down beside him. Ruderies about knickers, anatomical appreciations of suntan lines, all are dwelt upon with relish. But more significantly, the two protagonists hold fast to an unwritten code of non-interference with erotogenic zones.

17 Gravelly Hill North, Erdington, Birmingham 23
Wednesday 5th August
"My dearest Anne,
Wednesday already – how quickly the time flies. I must say it was a most enjoyable weekend, and I am already looking forward to the next one. I know you enjoyed it as well and that makes it even better.
. . . In some ways we have spoilt ourselves by going to the coast together, and our petting has certainly gone

further than it would otherwise have gone. But what fools we would have been if we hadn't taken advantage of the wonderful weather, and we have never gone further than our morals (and society's) allow."

And: "All my love, darling, John."

17 Gravelly Hill North, Erdington
Tuesday 12th August
"My dearest Anne

What a wonderful letter you wrote on Sunday! It was so different, so chatty instead of just a series of facts and happenings… it was so much warmer and represented you as I know you now."

And: "What sort of a girl? I still cannot answer that question and feel it would be easier if it were phrased: "What don't you like to see in a girl? …one thing I can't abide is looseness. A girl can, theoretically, always say 'No' and I always admire a girl when she says that early on. A girl makes love to an extent by retreating behind her physical attractions and a man enjoys nothing more than attacking these. Once he starts this he finds an urge to go on until he is stopped and if he isn't stopped, he goes on, waiting to be halted."

So! This then is serious; a relationship constructed upon respect, forged on personal freedom, trimmed by trust.

It is August 1958 and there is still much water to pass beneath the bridge but the die is cast.

John is posted to London in the summer of 1960 to Head Office for a stint in the drawing office and in September of that year, they are married. With no finesse happens their swift primitive coupling as is the way of a man with a maid. Thus a rite of passage licences them to a healthy, vigorous enjoyment of *lust*: Old English for appetite, pleasure, relish, longing, eagerness to possess, sensual desire and sexual desire (Chambers Concise 20th Century Dictionary).

Remaining a further year at Head Office in London on design work, John is then transferred to Kent as Site Engineer on four concrete bridges on the Medway Motorway (M2). Anne resigns her secretarial and tutoring jobs at the London School of Economics and becomes a lady of leisure living in a rented farm cottage in Grafty Green, Kent. The farmer is Joan Thompson, a substantial lady and pillar of the local Women's Institute: those hearty ladies singing with relish about William Blake's vision of Jerusalem in England's green and pleasant land. It is not certain how successful she is at farming her 60 acres, Jersey dairy herd and poultry enterprises but with the help of the cowman, Sam, who lives in a caravan in a tangled farmyard, Joan and her sister Lorna make a modest living. In the fertile, fruitful, fecund Kent of the ebullient Larkin family immortalised by H E Bates in *The Darling Buds of May*, it is not difficult to eat well. For Anne, it is another delightful interlude; soaking up rural life, learning basic farm skills, idling to Nature's rhythmical routine of seasonal change and marking time, waiting.

Waiting for what?

Waiting for the full term of a first pregnancy in the first instance. One evening in her seventh month, John comes home, full of suppressed excitement, waving a copy of one of the national broadsheets.

"Would you like to go to Pakistan? I see here that Binnie and Partners are advertising for engineers for the Mangla Dam Project."

Chapter 7

Biggest is Best

"We have created water as the basis of all life'; so goes a verse of the Holy Quran" writes Mir Bashar Khan.[6] Appointed by the West Pakistan Water and Power Development Authority (WAPDA), Mir Bashar Khan is chief engineer of the biggest single construction contract ever awarded on a competitive bid, Mangla Dam.

Now, Pakistan has a number of capable engineers especially in the field of irrigation. S K Balach[7] calls to mind with proud words, the genius of Ali Mardan Khan who contributed so much to Mughal waterworks. A Kurd by birth, Ali Mardan Khan came from Kandahar via Kashmir to Lahore where he met Shah Jehan in 1638. Professional soldier rather than engineer, Ali Mardan Khan made his name constructing a good road between Srinagar and Lahore through the Pirpanjal range of the Himalayan foothills. Later he arranged festival celebrations for Shah Jehan in the royal gardens with illuminated water cascades and multi-coloured fountain displays which so pleased the emperor that he granted funds for bringing canal irrigation into Lahore and for creating the lovely garden of Shalamar.

---

[6] *Indus*, Journal of the West Pakistan Water and Power Authority, Dec 1962, p5

[7] *Indus,* ibid, p 14 - 18

Shah Jehan, initially appointing Ali Mardan Khan Governor of Kashmir and subsequently of the Punjab too, showered money and gifts upon this giant among engineers including an elephant aptly named *Koh Shikan* (mountain breaker). Ali Mardan Khan later cemented his reputation by laying on canal water to Delhi and also to Agra where he is credited with assisting in the design of the Taj Mahal.

However, Mangla Dam is not the whole project, nor indeed the largest component within an even greater plan. Such is the magnitude of the total scheme that only the combined skills and funds of the globe can expect to achieve completion.

Since the Partition of the Indian subcontinent into two countries in 1947, ownership of the lifeblood waters of the Indus Basin has been disputed; contested to the brink of war. What was one before 1947 must now be shared between two. Alas, the new frontier bisects the Indus basin, the 'Punjab', literally translated as 'Land of Five Rivers', which are the five tributaries of the mighty Indus and all the many millions of acres of potentially fertile interfluvial flood plain.[8] How are the great rivers of the Indus system to be divided between two independent, suspicious, recriminatory neighbour nations?

Muslim League and Indian Congress, the two protagonists both overly anxious to be rid of the British Raj, sincerely thought that they could handle the power vacuum created by British departure; neither side considered that precautions against violence might be necessary. British civil servants commissioned to help Congress and League draw the new frontiers were told, repeatedly, that all points of difference could be handled amicably by the future India and future Pakistan governments. No one foresaw the bloodlust slaughter of millions of people. When the new frontier line was drawn to give India the headworks that controlled water from the

[8] Tayeb, A *Pakistan, A Political Geography,* Oxford University Press, 1966

Ravi and Sutlej rivers upon which Pakistan's eastern region depended for irrigation, the British Chairman was reprimanded by both sides for even suggesting that a precise plan for the supply of water to Pakistan was desirable.[9]

Thirteen years later in 1960, the constant and real threat of conflict subsides with the signing by India and Pakistan of the Indus Waters Treaty. This allocates to Pakistan the three western rivers, to India the waters of the three eastern rivers, and undertakes to replace water that will be lost to Pakistan from newly developed stored water on the three western rivers. The scale of this water transfer, due for completion by 1970, is the biggest in history.

The Indus Basin Settlement Plan (1960–70), an astounding international remodelling of one of the world's major river systems, calls for the initial creation of a colossal storage dam on the river Jhelum at Mangla to conserve melt and flood water for release through a series of new and improved link canals. Above all the new dam, on an aggressive and violent river, must be safe since its failure would devastate vast and populated areas downstream - a safety factor of double the maximum historic flood in 1929 being built into the design. On the credit side however, it is calculated that the new dam will provide cheap, hydroelectric power, regulate fearsome annual floods on the Jhelum and lastly create a scenic lake of great natural beauty, which will attract hordes of tourists. Later in the programme, a very much larger storage dam will be built on the Indus River at Tarbela. Not surprisingly, the Indus Basin Settlement Plan carries the biggest price tag in history for any engineering feat. Biggest may be best but, in the words of Robert Burns, 'the best-laid schemes o' mice an' men / Gang aft agley': Mangla reservoir is expected to silt up in about 100 years

---

[9] Rushbrook, Williams L F, *The State of Pakistan*, Faber and Faber Ltd, 1962

unless drastic measures to reduce its sediment load can be achieved.

The main contract, the civil engineering works of Mangla Dam, is won by a consortium of eight United States of America companies, led by Guy F Atkinson. The consortium styles itself Mangla Dam Contractors, known thereafter as MDC. Binnie and Partners of London are appointed Consulting Engineers.

So much for the theory; reality may be different.

In the final days of 1962, Anne sets out by plane for Mangla, clutching a well-packed carrycot with her ten-week-old daughter lying near the gunwales atop a miscellany of essential, and other weighty, dispensable, items of hand luggage. No longer is it a Peninsula and Orient (P & O) passage through Suez and the Pink Arabian Sea, but a Pakistan International Airways (PIA) flight via Moscow to Karachi. John, having already been in Mangla for two months, billeted in the batchelor quarters, is waiting at Karachi Airport.

"Wonderful to see you both. The downside is that our house is not yet ready. I have agreed to accept an invitation to stay with a couple we knew in London whose house is now just completed. Should be about six weeks, I think, before ours is ready."

The Americans are quickly putting together three camps. One, at Till, will house a labour force of 12,000 drawn in from the plains, from the hills, from the villages and cities, from near and far, bringing in their own languages, customs, clothes, cultures, songs and dances to the huge encampment complete with canteens and a community centre. Secondly, Mangla colony, on the left bank of the Jhelum River, is to house some 400 Pakistani engineering and administrative personnel plus their families, complete with a school, mosque and bazaar. The third, Baral colony, lies on the right bank of the river and houses nearly 500 expatriate contractor's staff and their families and, a further 84 expatriate staff and families of the

Consultant's team plus a few senior Pakistani executive officers and their families.

Baral has the movie-inspired look of a nineteenth century American frontier town, stockaded behind high brick walls and gated, erected at full gallop. Never mind appearances; get the essentials up and running. Needed immediately are homes for the floods of expatriates now arriving. MDC builds A Street, B Street, C Street... and, at right angles, 1st Street, 2nd Street, 3rd Street... Spine Road is the hub of the colony whereon are found MDC's Residents' Bureau presided over by MDC's representative sheriff, his principal duties to maintain equanimity among some 600 disparate households. The Bureau must also administer one international school for 400 pupils, one community room, one club with restaurant, one gymnasium, three swimming pools, two squash courts, one Golf and Country Club, one air-conditioned cinema, three churches for a multitude of sectarian religious persuasions, one bowling alley – results to USA league tables, and one supermarket known as 'the Commissariat'. There are, in addition, dozens of small service entrepreneurs entreating permission to establish a coiffeur, a beauty salon, a boutique, a travel agency, a photographic studio... Baral's recreation, energetically organised by the recreation officer, holder of a college degree in recreation, is all-embracing. Courses for everything from aerobics and astronomy to yoga and Zoroastrianism; competitions, sweepstakes, duplicate bridge with scores remitted to the USA, swimming galas, sports ladders and leagues, an in-house weekly Bulletin. There is no time to pine for any of the two thousand persons contained in Baral colony.

A state-of-the-art, air-conditioned, 50-bed hospital staffed by eight doctors and two dentists serves the entire site of some 15,000 people. The first Mangla baby is delivered within minutes of the hospital's official opening ceremony.

The Commissariat, 'department charged with the furnishing of provisions, as for an army' (Chambers Concise 20th Century Dictionary), is open only to the expatriate population. Sealed wagonloads arriving on Mangla's newly built branch railway, deliver a myriad of imported goodies, which are sorted and labelled by Pakistani *koranis* (clerks). Among the more interesting terminology of the fresh meat counter is 'Sir Lion' attached to a hunk of bright red meat and, 'Bost on Butt' (transferring in the British mind to 'Bust an' Bott'), 'Boston Butt' being a recognised American cut of pork. "Send your cook to the bazaar to get some proper meat" writes father. And mother exhorts: "Do watch that your meat is thoroughly cooked, preferably in casserole; there is a risk of parasites from undercooked meat."

Anne's parents decline an invitation to visit Mangla and Pakistan. Little more than twenty years have passed since 1939 when they left Rawalpindi, only 76 miles distant. Mangla metamorphosis would irritate them. "Do visit the Officers Club when you are in 'Pindi," urges father.

With time, Anne and John, plus the infant Marion, do manage to get off the compound out of Baral's nanny housing estate to visit the real Pakistan. Down the Grand Trunk Road to Jhelum which is still a significant railway junction with a cantonment population of dedicated railwaymen anxious that, say, the No. 2 Down Mail is not running late. There they visit a British engineer friend and his wife. Malcolm, working for Halcrow and Partners, is a Resident Engineer on a new bridge over the Jhelum River.

"All this bund (bank) is being built by animal power," says Malcolm. Strings of donkeys bearing panniers of clay plod up the incline; at a signal from the foreman, the donkey-*wallah* tips out the clay and winds down again; and again; and again for months. "The amazing part is that compaction tests indicate that donkey hooves are adequate for compressing the fill"; Malcolm discusses technical details with John.

On down to Lahore 130 miles away where John, as Captain of the rugby football team the Mangla Muckshifters, leads them against the Lahore Locusts: alas the Locusts win 13 – 9.

Up the Grand Trunk Road to Rawalpindi where they locate the army quarter in Gwyn Thomas Road, occupied by Anne's parents in 1938-39. The house looks much smaller than Anne remembers but, yes, it is the same driveway where she first learned to ride a bike. The 'Pindi Club welcomes them; a stately old Bearer in enormous starched *pugri* (turban), white drill jacket and sneakers silently, languidly, insinuates himself into a position just behind John's elbow.

"Two Murree beers please" says John with a grin.

"Have you been here a long time?" asks Anne.

"Yes, memsahib, very many years."

"My Father enjoyed this Club when he was stationed here in 1939. It doesn't seem to have changed much since then."

"His name, memsahib?" And, "Ah yes. I do remember the Major. He played much polo I think. Please tell him my salaams when you see him." The Bearer's hand touches his *pugri*, a vestigial salute to a bygone era. Anne goes to the Ladies Room, 'The Powder Room'. Faded Sanderson chintz curtains and chair covers, the *London Illustrated News* of 1937-38 on a low table, all speak volumes: the lares and penates of yesteryear persist amongst the Pakistan Army personnel who perpetuate the club institution.

There is, too, a less auspicious excursion to a nearby ancient ruin, Rohtas Fort on the far side of a wide sand river or *nullah*. The sand is heavily criss-crossed with tyre tracks, which are followed confidently in the land rover until suddenly, the ground is slow, soft, sinking. Too late; the land rover is bogged down irrecoverably. Is it imagination or is it still sinking?

Within a heart-warmingly short interval, a group of farmers is heading towards the calamity. A string of lean villagers in *lungi* (loincloths) or *salwar kamis*, the traditional long-tailed shirt and baggy trousers, their heads wrapped in wisps of turban, is threading its way across the *nullah*, carrying, alarmingly, wooden planks which prove to be old railway sleepers, and spades.

"Salaam, sahib. You stuck?"

Grinning sheepishly, John shakes the headman by the hand and nods.

"Last week land rover stuck; it go down to windscreen."

"You, memsahib, and baba please to move other side. Land rover can be coming on top."

The gang is busy shovelling out a hole by the nearside front wheel and inserting a sleeper. Three men sit on the end of the plank and as, with a resounding plop, the sodden sand relinquishes its grip, another sleeper is thrust into the void. The process is repeated all round with breathtaking speed by this thoroughly professional posse of Pakistani peasants and the landrover is soon safely backed off the sleepers onto terra firma.

"Thank you, thank you, my friend" says John, digging in his pocket for a handful of rupees.

"Oh no, sahib. We no taking money. You to village coming now for *chai* (tea)."

The villagers during this exchange have stowed all their props and planks in the land rover, and set off single file for home, the vehicle following slowly, forming a mini motorcade behind a triumphant troupe. *Chai* is made Pakistani-style by boiling half a *datchki* (saucepan) of water on a wood fire, tipping in tea leaves from a twist of newsprint and adding a tin of sweetened condensed milk. Anne and John contribute a couple of packs of cigarettes, kept in the travel bag for just such circumstances, half a Dundee cake packed for their picnic, and a bag of oranges.

"You from London sahib? You know my brother there, Mohommed Hussan?"

John shakes his head. "London is a big place. Bigger than 'Pindi; bigger even than Lahore. But I will look out for your brother when I next go to London."

"You got only one child, sahib. You get more childs, sons, lots of sons, soon. How old you, sahib?"

"I'm 28 now. Plenty of time for sons." The villagers nod, satisfied.

Meanwhile, on the site, chaos rationalises into order. The huge civil engineering contract is separated into departments: main dam, spillway, five diversion tunnels, powerhouse and the three subsidiary dams to block holes in the reservoir rim. And the clock is divided into three shifts, namely day shift, evening shift and graveyard shift. Main dam, third biggest earth dam in the world, eventually to be almost two miles long, is a hive of activity as an armada of scrapers, dozers, tippers and rollers singly, in tandem or in triplicate, swarm down and up and round and up and down again. It is as an ant colony, that ceaseless community of insect order.

Teams of mobile maintenance men; the oilers and greasers, pressure hose people, hammer and spanner squads, the nuts and bolts brigades, the hydraulic jack pack and the outsize tyre troops shuttle here, there and everywhere amongst the hosts of heavy plant, the swarms of scrapers, droves of dozers and tippers and fleets of staff landrovers.

On a mighty and violent river, the spillway, needing to be immensely big, has two stilling basins each the size of two hockey pitches. It is calculated that in extreme flood, released spillwater could reach speeds of 90 mph creating 40 million horsepower of energy. The upper stilling basin will kill 30 million horses and the lower basin will consume the rest.

For the five diversion tunnels, the world's biggest mechanical Mole is created in Seattle USA and shipped to

Karachi. Thereafter, it is the largest load ever handled by Pakistan Western Railways and takes four weeks from Karachi to Mangla. Basically, it is a circular revolving shield 36 foot 8 inches [about 11 metres] in diameter, on which about 100 cutting wheels are mounted, spoil being collected in perimeter buckets and tipped onto a conveyor. The Mole is, however, not without its problems, particularly dust, and in summer, tunnel temperatures rise to an unbearable 50°C and more. The Mole has a cunning device at its rear for positioning interior tunnel ribs on which the steel tunnel linings will be hung. The latter, each 30 foot [10 metres] in diameter, are manufactured on site in the Chicago Bridge Company yard known as the 'Can Factory'. Its Chief Engineer is ironically a Mr McCann. Soon the riddle circulates: "How many cans can McCann can, if McCann can can cans?" He needs 56 in all.

The powerhouse will, of course, be one of the world's largest, ultimately capable of generating one million kilowatts of electricity. And the aggregate plant has the world's biggest stone crusher.

In Baral, colony houses are completed, roads tarred, gardens planted and social life is begun. Baral wives' luncheons, fashion shows, talks on cookery, flower arranging and facial make-up and of course the great standby, charity work, are no different from those in any other part of the world where there are ladies who lunch. The hot weather takes over from a delicious spring season. The magnificent Pirpanjal mountain range vanishes into a dusty heat haze, and two thousand air-conditioners are switched on ready to run continuously until November. Then, autumn having arrived, the Pirpanjal mountains re-emerge like endless waves of the sea, rising to a distant diamond sparkle of snow on the high peaks. The Peak of the mountain known as K2 may be identified on a clear day. Winter, following after Christmas, is short and sharp, with a chill wind whipping straight off the jewel-bright sunlit Pirpanjal. Crisp, dry, clear and cold outside, the interiors of the houses now offer expanses of glacial terrazzo: air-conditioners may be programmed to heat but are not as efficient at the job as they are at cooling in the hot weather. Some Binnie's staff have wood fires in their authentic fireplaces: unlike the contractors' accommodation, the consultants' houses, being built for eventual occupation by Pakistani maintenance staff, have *pukka* (proper) amenities. But in a country so acutely short of timber for burning, it seems too wasteful to indulge in log fires. Rather, Anne and John buy some *numdahs*, local embroidered felt rugs, treat themselves to buying a Baluchi rug and a small Afghani carpet, and turn the air-conditioners to 'heat'.

Investigations indicate that Mangla reservoir will receive annually an enormous load of sediment and will silt up in about 100 years.[10] Indeed, after 60 years, the reservoir will store only half its initial capacity of water. And this is an optimistic estimate, based upon the assumption that some measures will be taken to check the rate of soil erosion in the catchment area. It is a harsh alternative: less water versus proper management of the watershed.

What is the nature of the problem in the high hills? Firstly, farming on steep slopes is widespread. A rapidly increasing population and land hunger has pushed villagers ever upwards, cutting, burning, ploughing and hoeing so that the topsoil is lost and sheets of subsoil are swept away in the torrential downpours of rain. Secondly, the remaining forestland is largely in the gift of the villagers who use it freely for three essentials; fuel, timber and animal fodder. And when the peasants have exhausted the woodland available to them, they attack and deplete the government-managed forests. Swathes of bald hillside, scars of landslides, avalanches of mud across the roads and desolate looking trees cliffhanging as a slipping mantle of soil

---

[10] Ishaq Muhammad, *Role of Watershed Management in Water Development*, Indus, Dec 1962, pp 19-22

carries them down, down, down the slope, are a common and distressing sight.

WAPDA identifies a number of good-practice principles, emphasis being given to control of grazing habits, reforestation and fire control. Alas, given the truculent nature of the local peasant, these measures are easier said than done. Introducing crop rotation, contour cultivation, tree planting, mulching and cover crops to protect soil against heavy rain, are long-term solutions hardly attractive to villagers desperate for cash to pay for a marriage or a circumcision feast. Engineering works are however a popular innovation. Locals, instructed in building mini-dams and micro-blockades in gullies and ditches, happily devise ingenious barrages from such novel raw materials as a vehicle carcase. There is a latent engineering artist in many a Pakistani peasant: may they prevail in their running fight with soil erosion. In three years alone, twenty-five mini-dams and several thousand micro-dams have been completed by local people using boulders, earth, clay and gravel and, needless to say, without recourse to cement, machinery or access roads.

The main dam is to be 380 feet high in the first instance. Doomed, as it is by sedimentation, provision is being made to raise the dam in the future by a further 40 feet, which could, it is calculated, gain another 100 years if, and only if, watershed management can reduce the silt load. Thereafter, Rohtas Nullah could be adapted to receive Mangla storage water by means of a link canal between reservoir and *nullah*. Mangla dam may be an engineering colossus but its future outlook is daunting.

Chapter 8

Bradford, Bolton and Burnley

John's contract stipulates three weeks' local leave, plus, of course, the local public holidays. And home leave after two years. Using the shorter public holidays to explore the hill stations in the Himalayan foothills, to venture into *Azad* Kashmir (Free, i.e. Pakistani Kashmir) and to explore the North West Frontier as far as Kabul in Afghanistan, Anne and John pack picnics, travel bags and baby into their Ford Anglia car and slip out of Baral's strictures, as liberated as a snake having newly shed its skin. Bowling along the Grand Trunk Road towards Peshawar, keeping a wary eye on slow-moving bullock carts, wobbling cyclists, strings of donkeys or camels, pilgrims walking as if asleep, competitive drivers in ancient jalopies, mystifying buses travelling in a nimbus of diesel smoke, overloaded lorries with bald tyres and a list to starboard, all the nefarious traffic on this great artery of the subcontinent, they savour their opportunity to meet Pakistan eye to eye rather than from the superior confines of little America.

Beyond Peshawar and up the Khyber Pass they go. Rifle-toting tribesmen return their waved greetings. Hill forts spring into consciousness only after an interval for reflection. Is it a spur of onyx-coloured rock? No, it is a fort built of onyx-coloured stone. No, it is but a natural cliff. No, it is man-made, a fort. Other man-made features are the railway spiralling up to the railhead at the frontier village of Landi Kotal and a water pipe weaving out of and into the ground as it crosses narrow *nullahs.* Tribes people fill cans at a hole shot into the pipe. "No pay this water," they chortle. Bald hills, desiccated, ravaged by tearing wind, by unremitting sun and by occasional torrential rain, dun-coloured, dusty, landslip-scarred and threatening to road and railway, enfold the puny excrescences of civilisation. Visibility is but thin threads of tarmac and steel vanishing into the next hairpin bend, each corner swallowed by walls of rock which terminate the way ahead: it is good ambush country at every angle.

Suddenly, a straggle of mud huts borders the tarmac and, judging by the throngs of parked vehicles and tethered beasts, a bazaar in full commerce is surrounding the little car. Landi Kotal, the top of the pass, frontier between Pakistan and Afghanistan and a smugglers' paradise, has arrived. No man's land between Pakistan and Afghanistan is a lawless terrain where tidal waves of righteous Muslim fanatics have prevailed for centuries among the frontier peoples; a place where zealot *mullahs* incite war, where *jihads* are endemic. As the young Winston Churchill observed in 1897 in his 'Story of the Malakand Field Force', the combined allure of plunder and the promised pleasures of paradise is irresistible to these frontier tribesmen.[11]

After Landi Kotal, the journey is easy. Tarmac winds over a plateau surrounded by distant hills, a landscape painted in colours of golden topaz, amber, cornelian, agate and indigo. The distant hills metamorphose into a formidable mountain wall now penetrated by a new Russian-built road up the Tangi Gorge past a brand new hydroelectric power station; gift from the German Government to the people of Afghanistan. Then comes the summit, opening onto an even higher plateau all set about

[11]Churchill, Winston S, *Winston S Churchill Frontiers and Wars,* Eyre and Spottiswoode, 1962

with yet more lofty mountains, and soon Kabul lies before the travellers.

Kabul, en fête for the Eid feast celebrating the successful completion of Ramadhan's month of fasting, is full of bonhomie; its bazaar is humming with greetings and welcome gestures, sweets thrust upon little Marion, tiny glasses of scalding sweet mint tea offered with embarrassing frequency and many shakings of many hands. And carpets. Carpets galore pegged out on the roadsides flaunting rich ruby, crimson, indigo, oxblood red, mahogany, black and burnished copper colours, every one of them a handcrafted work of art, presenting a riot of colour to blazon forth warmth, luxury and beauty.

So back to Pakistan and, a stopover in Peshawar where Eid celebrations now mount to a crescendo point of the four-day holiday. On the *Maidan* (city park) is a funfair with roundabouts and swings, bumper cars, golden gallopers and a giant wheel. Equipment is powered by old recycled vehicle engines, whose not infrequent stoppages caused by a breakdown of the motor, are treated with the equanimity of old biddies on a country bus. Not so the giant wheel. That depends on people power. Lithe lads, members of a team of gymnasts, run up a ladder slung against the central column, tread lightly along the parallel bar of a radial strut and execute a marvellous somersault on the perimeter with body taut, legs straight at perfect right angles to the torso and toes pointed. Acrobatics or ballet? It is hard to tell. No uncalled stoppages occur on the giant wheel.

Another holiday takes them to Srinagar. They drive to Amritsar and fly Air India to Srinagar in Kashmir on the headwaters of the River Jhelum. Travel arrangements go as smoothly as water off a duck's back. Their host meets the flight and escorts them by taxi to the *shikara* (punt) rank on the Dal Lake, and by *shikara,* they are poled to a houseboat called the 'Good Faith'. Their host, owner of the 'Good Faith', is proud of his boat; Sandersons chintz curtains and cushion covers in the sitting room consort cosily with a wood-burning stove, black-leaded and with the unusual design of a chimney pipe which zigzags like a mountain road up the wall and out of the ceiling. A dining room, spacious double bedroom, small single room and bathroom extend to the rear of the vessel, while the sitting room opens on to a narrow verandah beautifully balustraded in walnut wood and fitted with steps leading onto the sunroof, likewise balustraded. The whole is gracious yet homely – in a 1930's style. Cooking, by his wife, is all done on the owner's own boat tied astern of the 'Good Faith'. Cut glass, silver plate and white linen napery grace the table and food is a mixture of British and Indian. Breakfast is fruit juice, porridge, a choice of eggs and *naan*, the flat Indian bread with tea. Lunch is *pakoras* and Cornish pasties with dressings of yoghurt chopped with cucumber and tomatoes. Dinner is often a curry with all the trimmings followed by plum duff or syrup tart and custard.

"Happy I am to have English visits. Only Indian tourists coming now and these *bandalog* (monkey people) bring all their own food, bring their stove, cook on the verandah." Sher Alam spits into the lake.

After breakfast, comes the ritual of visits from the pedlars poling punts laden with flowers: freesia, narcissus, lilac, hyacinths, roses and tulips, with pyramids of fruit, with Kashmiri and pashmina shawls, with papier-mâché dishes and vases, lamp stands and bookends all gorgeously gilded in gold and glowing colours with fine designs in Persian or Ottoman style.

"Sahib, you see this goods. This man, my cousin. He has fine woodcarving. English tables for the coffee. Cabinet for valuables. Jewelbox you like? Your wife has necklace? Bangles for Missy Sahib?" Sher Alam hails his wife Fatma in the cook boat to bespeak ceremonial tea in anticipation of protracted commerce culminating perhaps in a sale.

Anne and young Marion visit Fatma in her home, an interlude which stretches Anne's limited Urdu language.

Their boat is a scaled down version of the tourist houseboat; more like a narrow boat of the British canals, and divided between living space and sleeping quarters. Kitchen there is with wood-burning stove but no visible sign of a bathroom. Of the five children, three boys and a girl are at school and the sixth, a girl of Marion's age called Nadia, potters about on the houseboat.

"Aren't you afraid she will fall into the water?"

Fatma shrugs. "It is the will of Allah."

"When you go ashore to market, do you take Nadia with you?"

"I no go to market. My husband go."

"Well, if you go to visit your family or friends?"

"My family, friends come here. I no go anywhere. I come on this boat when I married. No go off again."

It transpires that Fatma has not set foot on land since the day she married; it would bring bad luck upon the family were she to go ashore. She did not get any schooling but is glad her children can become literate.

Sher Alam who, under his lambskin hat, has the face of a deerhound, lean, noble, patient and all-seeing, arranges *shikara* visits, with a cousin no doubt; another up a high valley, for some trout fishing; to the Shalimar gardens and to the city centre with its wonderful façade of buildings overhanging the River Jhelum. And, to the boat-building yards where new houseboats and *shikaras* are turned out by the score. Here is the local *quartier* in creeks of close-moored boats, presumably extended families on adjacent boats. Here live the artisans, craftsmen, merchants and farmers.

Dal Lake farming is an eye-opener. The lake, being only one to two metres deep over much of its area, contains a goldmine of nutritious silt for plants. Seeds germinated in tiny tumuli of soil, placed in rows upon a wattle raft, towed out into the shallows and anchored, yield outsize tomatoes, magnificent melons and marrows. Islands may be created by planting a rectangle of willow cuttings which root and sprout. Thereafter, the farmer will laboriously collect scoopsful of silt into his *shikara* then shovel it into the island arena between the willow saplings. Once the island breaks the surface of the water, grass grows, and a cow will be shipped onto the emerging enclosure: or a henhouse and half a dozen hens. And when the waters rise after storms in the high headwaters, the cow is up to its belly in water and the hens are sitting disconsolately upon the roof of their henhouse. Dal Lake farming is a worthy response to immoderate conditions demanding fine-tuned adjustment to weather and water conditions but it works, given the inherited skills, the patience and the perseverance of its farmers.

Another Eid, another end of Ramadhan approaches. Anne, John and Marion go to Kabul again: it is accessible enough for a four or five day public holiday. This time, they will drive to Peshawar, go by bus to Kabul and fly back PIA to Peshawar. Friends stationed in Peshawar offer to procure their bus tickets. Yes; they are assured that the Afghan Post Bus will be running. Eid or not, the mail must get through. No; there will be no problem about getting seats; everyone else will have already travelled in order to arrive in time for the vital first day of the Eid festival.

A predilection for bus travel is a characteristic that will surface again and elsewhere from time to time. With hindsight, one wonders why Anne and John should choose to forego their own private box on wheels, shipped from England to Pakistan at considerable expense expressly so that they may enjoy freedom of movement. Perhaps public transport holds more adventure, a taste of uncharted exploration, a tempting of fate, a defiance of established custom.

The first part of the journey goes according to plan. On the bus, besides the driver and the turn-boy, are two single middle-aged Afghani men and an Afghan couple who, speaking excellent English, introduce themselves. A former student in Germany where he met his wife, he is now Afghanistan's Minister of Education and Culture.

Landi Kotal, the border, is soon reached and once across the frontier, the driver pulls into the petrol station for fuel which is supplied via Russia and far cheaper than fuel in Pakistan. Having taken in about one hundred litres of diesel from a cheerful pump attendant, the driver, himself full of bonhomie on account perhaps of the Eid festival, steps on the accelerator across the wide plain. Suddenly the engine's smooth rhythm is interrupted: again and again the motor falters. Soon sporadically parked lorries on the verge, abandoned cars pulled off the tarmac become a sinister, sickening sight. The driver expresses his growing suspicion that the diesel he has just bought was adulterated.

"The boss is away for Eid so his minion puts water in the pumps and sells it at a profit to himself" explains the Minister of Education. "We will have to siphon off all the diesel and chuck out the water. It will take a long time with so much fuel in the tanks."

The bus has juddered to a halt. Much discussion ensues; much wagging of fingers, arms flying around like gulls behind a ploughing tractor. Body language and voices speak frustration, anger, resignation and aggressive action following each other in staccato succession.

"The driver wants to return to the Landi Kotal border post to do the diesel change. The weather is becoming stormy and he needs some shelter." The Minister of Education translates. Soon a corporate decision is achieved: the bus will return to Landi Kotal, siphon off the diesel into jerry cans known to be available at the border station, ditch the heavyweight water lying beneath the diesel and then refill the tanks with the pure diesel and proceed. It is an entirely achievable solution, albeit greedy on manual effort and time; two commodities which know no limits in the Asian outback.

Alas, the starved engine is unable to cope with all the backing and filling required to turn the bus on narrow tarmac. People power steps in, pushing rear then front, a thespian troop ably directed by the driver at his wheel. Once turned, everyone piles in and the bus hiccups along slowly, increasingly frequent bunny-jumps bringing the male stalwarts to their feet in willing expectation. The border post is reached just as the heavens drop ribbons of rain from a battleship-grey sky, a real gully-washer. For four hours, the driver and his turn-boy struggle heroically with heavy jerry cans, overwhelming diesel fumes and sodden slippery ground whilst the passengers, sitting in the waiting room, are regaled with tiny cups of scalding sweet mint tea and bowlfuls of sugared almonds, crystallised fruit and honey cakes, Eid offerings from hospitable, kindly customs officials. Young Marion comes in for special attention. Anne, worrying that the surfeit of sweets might cause tummy ache, thinks she looks a bit peaky. Nevertheless, there is a comfortable consciousness that the border officials, unhappily on duty over Eid, are enjoying the party. Outside it is still pouring with rain.

The diesel job completed at last, the driver relaxes with tea, Eid confectionery and cigarettes, relishing an animated discussion with local officials with all the Afghani passengers being riveted to the inner circle of the debate.

"Customs tell us that the Tangi Gorge road is closed for maintenance of the hydroelectric plant. They do the work at Eid when traffic is light. We have to use the old road, the Lataband Pass," explains the Minister of Education.

"The driver thinks it is unwise to go over this Pass at night in bad weather because the road is neglected and in poor condition. There may be landslides." As he translates, his hand comes down in a guillotine action.

"Driver says it would be better to stay the night in hotel at Jallalabad and go over the high pass in daylight tomorrow." This is an eminently sensible suggestion. Confidence in the driver grows ever stronger.

"But driver's contract says he must not stop the journey in any circumstances. He will lose his bonus if he halts on the route." Heads nod in sympathy with the driver's dilemma.

"He says he could stay in Jallalabad if all the passengers together write a letter to the company to say they demand the halt because they fear the Lataband Pass in heavy rain by night." The Minister of Education appeals for collaboration among the passengers. Unanimously agreed, and company paper and pen being supplied by the driver, a compensatory dispensation is written by the Minister of Education and all sign.

Eventually at dusk, the bus trundles off across the soggy plain, past all the stalled and abandoned vehicles, to pull up at a Government-run hotel in Jallalabad. And next morning in brilliant sun, the Lataband Pass is tackled.

The formidable mountain wall ahead presents hillsides of uniform donkey brown. In February, the heart of winter, there is no sign of the spring of the year. It is hard to know if this route was ever finished with tarmac - probably not. A surface of corrugated iron in the dry dissolves to a consistency of steeped cardboard in the wet; less damaging to vehicle springs but liable to beguile the unwary into a glissade. Rain-ribbed and rutted, the piste is but a ledge traversing spur after vertical spur where one side drops to violent depths several thousand feet below. Chiselled by hand, rough-hewn and boulder-strewn, the Lataband Pass will be, later in the year, one of the more testing stretches of the 1965 London to Sydney car rally. Meanwhile, the bus is grinding on, creeping up the hairpin bends, chugging noisily in the thin atmosphere, driven with consummate skill. The hillsides, streaked silver with streaming runnels of water splashing down the screes, sport a dozen mini-rainbows. A palette of ochre and umber, of slate, limed oak and polished pewter assembles in a harmony of colour, the whole composition highlighted by shrub-filled gullies which glisten with the patina of antique bronze.

At long last, the plateau is achieved. Villagers flag down and fill the bus thus converting the noble city-link coach into a rambling rural charabanc. The turn-boy has a hard time collecting fares. Passengers, reluctant as a student obliged to hand in an ill-prepared essay, hope to be overlooked. Expressive hands fly up and out in mock despair. There is much turning out of pockets, hunting in the hems of waistcoats, un-knotting of a shirt-tail or a turban end. An audience of fellow passengers happily watch these maestros of mime, knowing full well how the charade will end, if not when the fare will be forfeit.

So they reach Kabul. Anne and John again stroll around the carpet market and negotiate for two lovely rugs. They accept an invitation to visit the Minister of Education, Ahmed, and his German-born wife Uta in their home, where they enjoy delicious Afghani cuisine. All too soon it is time to go to the airport for their flight to Peshawar.

"The flight is cancelled due to bad weather," states the PIA ticket officer. "We are sending all passengers down by bus. Please be waiting over there."

Mercifully, the new road through the Tangi Gorge is again open and the journey passes without incident. To be back among Peshawar friends is a relief since Marion has measles. She sleeps on the back seat of the car all the way home to Baral colony and is soon recovering well.

At Mangla, much progress has been made. The eternal course of the Jhelum River has been diverted into the five tunnels and water is impounding in the reservoir. However, the Indus Basin Settlement Plan is a battle being waged on several fronts simultaneously, namely water availability and control, power supply, watershed management, soil care and, not least, the rehabilitation and improvement in quality of life for some 81,000 Pakistanis being displaced by the new reservoir.

As the Water and Power Development Authority (WAPDA) points out, the movement of displaced persons is a sentimental and delicate problem. Mir Bashar Khan calls for a considerable measure of sacrifice on the part of the people who are being forced to abandon home and hearth, their land and the graves of their ancestors. WAPDA promises landowners with half an acre or more land in lieu, most of which will be canal irrigated rather than dependent on rainwater or seasonal flooding. Those with less than half an acre and non-agricultural people, are promised cash compensation.

The heralded improvement in the peasant's lot is also expected to combat social and cultural evils in village life.[12] Dr A. Rauf writes of the villager that the mule or donkey he drives is more tractable than the Pakistani peasant. He is caught in a feudal time warp, undernourished, prey to all sorts of illness particularly water-borne diseases such as typhoid and cholera, or the insect-carried killers such as malaria, or to parasite-induced diseases caused by proximity to animals. Moreover, he has an oversized family, is liable to ferocious litigation, is slave to ancient notions of family honour and prestige, and is burdened by debt. He is prisoner to wastefully extravagant traditional customs, must empty his pockets to celebrate the birth of a son, or the circumcision of sons; is bankrupted by the marriages of his children, especially the daughters who carry his meagre wealth out of his family circle into the husband's hands.

The Government knows that education will do much for the rural population, especially the girls. On the other hand, as Dr Rauf who is Director of Education in Lahore points out, a little learning is a dangerous thing: it can empty villages as young men leave to pursue the perceived profits of city life. At the same time, the Government recognises a lack of guidance of a practical nature for the villages; no newspapers, radio, community centre or clinic. The population continues to soar at an alarming rate and the Government is desperately anxious to promote family planning, anathema to the Pakistani peasant. Rumour circulates that the Government will hand out free radios to

---

[12]Rauf, Dr A, *'Food Deficit and Social Evils'*, Indus, March 1962, pp 19-24

anyone willing to undergo sterilisation but since most villagers are beyond the reach of electricity, and batteries are an expense too much for the average household, this is a double-edged sword. The focus of the peasant's world is the village mosque but the *mimbar* (pulpit) is unable to lead or direct, the *maulvis* (clerics) being neither aware of nor able to discuss anything but the time-honoured matters of form and custom. In short, it is a Catch 22 situation.

Of the 81,000 people to be shifted as Mangla dam impounds the Jhelum waters, are a number from the town of Mirpur.[13] This habitation, which may be described as a 'poor little one-horse town' is a district headquarters in *Azad* Kashmir (Free Kashmir; that bit belonging to Pakistan as opposed to India). Founded 400 years ago, Mirpur some twelve miles from Mangla, is ill-connected to the civilized world, its only link being a thin thread of corrugated zigzag track along the bank of the Upper Jhelum Canal. This insalubrious town, a straggle of mud-brick dwellings, scattered as higgledy-piggledy as goat droppings on sun-baked earth, is devoid of any planning, devoid of electricity until the 1950s; is sans sanitation, treated drinking water or street lights. But it has a degree college, high schools for boys and for girls, a military hospital, a civil hospital and an officers' club. The town, razed in the 1947 battle for Kashmir and reborn, is 'home' to some 9,000 people. Now under sentence of extinction beneath the waters of the new lake, old Mirpur's evacuated premises are filled with some 60,000 squatters, traumatised Muslim refugees fleeing Indian-held Kashmir; disorientated families soon to be flushed out like rats by the rising waters of the reservoir.

The Government, however, paints a rosy picture of new Mirpur with an eventual population of 20,000. The planned town, about 3 ½ miles distant, will enjoy scenic lakeside views, soon becoming an international tourist resort and anglers' paradise. Houseboats and *shikaras* as on Dal Lake at Srinagar will grace the water; swimming, boating and

[13]Tahir M Aleram, *'Mirpur Old and New'*, Indus, Dec 1963 pp 30-32

water-skiing sports will be developed. Promised by the Government are many small-scale units for industries based on timber, fisheries and sericulture, including the planting of mulberry trees, raising of silkworms, spinning, weaving and dyeing the fabrics. Goodbye Old Mirpur, Hail New Mirpur, miniature Islamabad of *Azad* Kashmir.

Mirpur's citizens are assured by the Government that they are financially rich (some £750,000 a month flows in from overseas), and can afford to invest in their new town. Indeed WAPDA has already built expatriate Mirpur's money into the development equation. But Mirpur Man is busily choosing not a new industrial unit but instead, a ticket to Bolton, Bradford or Burnley. The narrow alleys of old Mirpur teem with ticket outlets; just a hole knocked through a mud wall between street and entrepreneur's parlour, barred, and emblazoned with a name such as 'Goquick Line' or 'Travelite Agency', serves very well for the flourishing business. No amount of promises about schools, colleges, technical institutes, industry, tourism or markets will hold New Mirpur Man.

On a weekend outing up the Upper Jhelum Canal road, Mirpur's circumstances are immaterial. Anne's brother Colin and his wife Jane are visiting, so a Sunday picnic up-country is a suitable escape from little America. Picnic, push-chair, baby, cameras, all are packed into the car. A run-around the dam site, a brief exposition on Mangla Dam as one item of the Indus Basin Settlement Plan, and then, out into the countryside for a picnic lunch. Peasant farmers are around but an innate courtesy forbids them to gather and stare. Nevertheless, the bush telegraph is at work and on the way home, a posse of young men stand on the route.

"Salaam, sahib. Please to stop and be talking." The invitation is heartfelt and irresistible.

"Please sahib, memsahib, you coming to village; take chai."

"Thank you friend. But it is late in the day and we must get home to feed baby."

"Where you from, sahib?"

"Well, one is from London, two are from Scotland and this memsahib is from Bradford."

"Bradford!" All attention focuses on Jane.

"You know my cousin Gulam Assiz? He live in Bradford. You know my uncle Azam Jamal? Bradford very good place. You come to tea please. Only two minutes to village. Tea ready now." One of the would-be hosts indicates a narrow footpath between fields of standing wheat. "Car stay here. You come."

"No, no, we must get home. We will come to tea next week."

"Please be waiting now. We like Bradford very much. Oh, very much and this memsahib born in Bradford. So happy we are to see you."

As this dialogue continues it become obvious that an early departure will offend. But how to exit gracefully? The village is just visible beyond a belt of shade trees, about half a mile distant. The prospect of a footslog there and back is daunting. No, really, they must be on their way. Wait. The vista to the village is quick with movement. A reel of people snakes between the standing wheat, a conga dancing energetically towards them. The first carries a table upside down on his head, the next a teapot, then a figure with a handful of cups, the man with a pile of saucers next, followed by the bearer of a sugar bowl, then a lad with a tin of condensed milk and another with a plate of biscuits. A white tablecloth carried aloft brings up the rear. In the middle of the road, theatre hands set the scene for a *pukka* tea party and the principals gather round. At this point the local bus arrives from Mirpur bound for Jhelum. Here is the audience; hanging from the roof, the windows and the doors they join in the chorus of: "Do you know my cousin, my brother, my uncle in Bradford?" Love, game and set to the men of Mirpur district.

If only this idyll could end here!

To understand something of Pakistan's troubled history, one must look at its beginnings. In 1947, at Partition, Pakistan was an act of faith, a divine miracle. It started with next to nothing in the way of a working government, India inheriting the bulk of the All-India Civil Service structure. Nevertheless, Pakistan did gain a number of highly qualified, efficient soldiers plus a quota of skilled engineers and professional academics, able administrators and educators all of them. At the same time, prominent in New Pakistan, was a religious element of Muslim clerics who offered the bulk of the population, that is the farmers and rural people, hope for a better life governed by Muslim social justice and free from oppression. While the doctrinal principles of Islam satisfied the masses, it was the social and economic element of Muslim justice that most appealed to them. Rushbrook Williams[14] lists some of the traditions adopted by Islam. There is the equality of all peoples in God's sight and the worldwide brotherhood of all Muslims. There is a duty to defend the weak against oppressors and to succour the needy. And, significantly, Muslims have an obligation to sacrifice even life itself in a religious cause. Mr Jinnah, founder and first president of Pakistan, recognised that some Muslim clerics could block, under the demand for orthodoxy, human development and progress: he was anxious to discourage what he himself labelled a '*Mullah* Raj'.

The shadow of disputed Kashmir falls over the Indus Basin Settlement Plan. In 1947, Muslim Kashmiris calling themselves the *Azad* (Free) Kashmir Force, invaded the three eastern districts of Poonch, Muzafarabad and Mirpur which they proudly styled *Azad* Kashmir. This Force was aided and abetted by a number of excited frontier tribesmen with an appetite for loot who declared a *jihad*, a holy war, in the cause of Islam. Had the invading Muslim force not paused for plunder; indulged in collecting the booty of

---

[14] Rushbrook Williams LF, *The State of Pakistan,* Faber and Faber Ltd 1962

weapons, cash, jewellery, women and boys, dividing it out and despatching it back across the frontier to Pakistan, it is possible that they might have captured the undefended capital city of Srinagar.[15]

As it was, the Maharaja of Jammu and Kashmir, hereditary ruler of a predominantly Muslim population but a Hindu by birth and culture, and encouraged by a coterie of wealthy Hindus in Srinagar, took fright and hurriedly acceded Kashmir to India. Bitter fighting continued and Lord Mountbatten, the retiring British Governor, only accepted Kashmir's accession to India on condition that a plebiscite be held when fighting ceased. Hostilities continued until 1949 when the UN effected a Cease Fire. The promised plebiscite has never been held and the *Azad* Kashmir government remains separate from the Government of Indian-held Jammu and Kashmir and, in theory, from the Government of Pakistan.

Thus Mangla dam sits near a line of major world dispute. The UN-drawn Cease Fire Line has witnessed cruel and savage outbreaks of hostility and incursion for half a century. Moreover, *Azad* Kashmir, in which area Mangla is situated, is an unsettled location. The population, swelled by Muslim refugees from Kashmir decades ago, is multiplying at an alarming rate. Confused and bitter about the absence of the promised referendum, frustrated and heartsick about exile from their Kashmir, these people offer ideal opportunities for extreme Islamic fundamentalists and terrorists. An article in *The Economist* in 2003 suggests that militant Islam is flourishing underground, the call for *jihad* issuing from many mosques.[16] Mr Jinnah's anxiety five decades ago about a '*Mullah Raj*' was not unjustified.

---

[15] Brown, William A, *The Gilgit Rebellion,* Ibex 1998. This account is based upon the diaries of Major William A Brown who was serving as a British officer seconded to the Gilgit Scouts of the Frontier Province at the time of the partition of India and Pakistan.

[16] *The Economist,* January 18th 2003, p. 60

Chapter 9

Families

Algeria! A paper mill near Algiers is the next contract.

"Can we fly, please, please" begs Marion, now in 1970 aged seven years.

"Oh no!" wails three-year old Robbie with earnest concern in his voice. "I can't fly." Presumably he imagines they would all leap from the bedroom window, as did Peter Pan, Wendy and her little brothers, and wing their way to North Africa.

"Maybe we will go by car and boat. We shall need a car out there," observes John.

John is now working for a civil engineering contractor called John Mowlem and Company Ltd, who has been awarded the contract to design and build a modern paper mill at El Harrach on the outskirts of Algiers.

First glances in the city reveal some women purdah veiled, enveloped from crown to ankle in huge white curtains, voile scarf tied round the face just below the eyes. A sprinkling of turbaned heads and long Arab robes stand out among the commuter crowds of stylishly dressed men and some young women. There are no driven donkeys, mule carts, bullock wagons or horse-drawn *tongas* among the vehicles swirling past in furious frenzy. It feels more like Greece than Pakistan. Moreover the Algerians speak French even when talking among themselves. Not infrequent views of the beautiful city with its pale sunlit buildings, often terracotta tiled, falling away to the harbour and cobalt sea below, are as a cream and coral carpet flung over the mountain slope.

Sunday brings a visit to a seaside resort managed by the Government Tourist Agency where the sand is clean and the littoral tidy. Weather beamed an azure sky and a sea of heraldic blue; creamy surf and creamy sand, sunbathers laid out like fish on a slab, no purdah veils but bikinis. Most of it might be taken from the pages of a glossy holiday brochure.

Another excursion organised by the State Tourist Agency takes in a visit to the *casbah* where 30,000 citizens live within the medieval fortified core of the city built during the Turkish occupation. From a steep, narrow alley, the guide leads the way through a low, dim doorway into a tiled courtyard, clean and cool with a gay central garden. First and second floor balconies are draped with bright blankets hung out to air. Women sit at doorways and there is a peaceful chatter of children. So up more stairs and out onto the flat roof suddenly hotly brilliant, like a dark stage when the footlights come on, but for one canopied corner of easeful shadow.

"The women come here after dinner," explains the guide.

All around are series of bright white squares, rectangles, triangles and cubes juxtaposed as a Mondrian painting, masterpiece of chiaroscuro, the roof patios of the *casbah* where women take the air. In the casbah, stronghold of tradition, most women are veiled, secluded in purdah, and their menfolk do the household shopping.

In the *Djeziratal Maghreb,* 'Isles of the Sunset' (ie West), from Morocco to Libya, there is a history of colonisation and invasion: the Greeks, Phoenicians, Romans, Vandals, Arabs, Normans, Portuguese, Jews, Spaniards, Turks, French and Italians have all come and gone leaving their mark. In Turkish times, administration and tax gathering spread through the land, meanwhile El Djezaïr grew on piracy and plotting, on conspiracy and commerce into the citadel of Algiers. The Turkish administration made a fortune from the land but it did not colonise. Not so France. The French entered Algeria in 1830 ostensibly to punish a corrupt and uncouth Turkish ruler. Soon, land was being accumulated into French hands despite Arab resistance. *Colons* arrived from France and from all over Europe while the military dealt with rebellious tribal opposition. Administrators imposed the law and order of the French Republic until such time as France annexed Algeria to become a part of France, an overseas Department.

In his introduction to Albert Camus's book 'The Outsider', Cyril Connolly in 1946 wrote: "What is an Algerian? He is not a French colonial, but a citizen of France domiciled in North Africa, a man of the Mediterranean, an *homme du midi* yet one who hardly partakes of the traditional Mediterranean culture... For him there is no eighteenth century, no baroque, no renaissance, no crusades or troubadours in the past of the Barbary Coast; nothing but the Roman Empire, decaying dynasties of Turk and Moor, the French Conquest and the imposition of the laws and commerce of the Third Republic on the ruins of Islam.' Since then the Algerians have fought for and, in 1962, gained their independence.

John Mowlem and Company have found a villa to rent in El Biar, a good residential suburb of Algiers, four miles from the city centre and some 250 metres above sea level. The house, brand new, stands at the end of a cul-de-sac lined on either side with hillocks of brick, rubble, sand, gravel and various building materials. A feeling of frontier settlement pervades, a pioneer persuasion that here is a feverish rash of prosperity and property investment. Not long ago, the valley was farmland and forest; indeed, beyond the villa is open ground, an inviting hillside of pasture blazing with wild flowers where children, as numerous as the dandelions, play from dawn to dusk. Three years later a school will have sprung up on this meadow alongside apartment blocks for six hundred families. Meanwhile, there are a few old French farmsteads dotted around. Beneath the villa is garage space for four cars but with an approach so steep and constricted that it takes skill to get one small Ford Anglia in, let alone out again. Three years later, the proprietor will have constructed another house in the 'garage' area and be about to move in below with his family of six children.

It is discovered that refuse collection takes place early every morning. "All the rubbish will be around the road by morning. The cats and dogs will see to that," Anne says as she places a large boulder on top of the bin. First thing next morning, it is not the cats and dogs, it is children carting off armfuls of empty bottles, tins, bits of plastic, some rubber sheeting. The boys are from the neighbours' families some of whom live in pricey property like this company villa yet they are scavenging, searching for something with which to make a game, to fill an hour or a day, to squabble over and crow about amongst themselves, for they have little else to do.

Whatever the neighbours, this villa is 'home'. Home is where the *lares* and *penates* are: Anne's sewing box and battered kitchen scales, John's toolbox and piles of files, Marion's drawing things and her dressing-up clothes, Robbie's striped cotton bed sheets and his collection of dinky cars. These are the family's household gods. The shape or location of the house is unimportant.

The house, having just been built, is filthy. There is no clothes washing machine nor automatic dishwasher. Moreover, the gas water heater is not working so warm water must be temporarily heated on the cooker.

Anne has a fit of depression. In Britain friends often asked: "How do you like moving about so much?" and "What do you do about schooling?" These are standard questions: the answer shifts with place and time but at its root lies the habit of the army life of Anne's childhood. Perhaps Marion will go to a French *lycée*: she has already adapted well to two primary schools in three years. In the end, she goes to the American School of Algiers since *lycées*, now closing for the summer, have filled their registration.

A *femme de ménage* is needed, urgently. Word is passed to the next-door neighbours and two days later, a white shape stands before the gate. Pulling aside her drape, or *haik*, she exposes a kindly face full of assurance. Yes, she has worked for French or Spanish families for fifteen years. On the debit side, her gums are toothless except for one small black stump and two steel fangs, her upper eyeteeth. Times and price are arranged but she never returns. Two days later another woman comes, young and in western dress without *haik* or *voile*. She has sad, tired eyes and a pale pinched face but there is little alternative but to let her come and try.

She says her name is Lena but her identification papers record the name Khadijah, name of the Prophet Mohammed's first wife. Taking off her dress and working in a black rayon slip, she proves efficient at washing, ironing and cleaning but nevertheless there is a disquieting, hungry look. She has a tiny box in her apron pocket, which she wishes to conceal. Perhaps it contains opium which poor people take to allay the pangs of hunger. More likely, it is snuff.

"No good at all," prophesies the Company's Accountant, Mike. "What you want is a widow, fat, forty and heavily veiled. Don't trust the unveiled ones. Now my *femme de ménage,* Byah, always goes out veiled.

Two weeks later, Lena looks more like a fashion model than a *femme de ménage* when she comes to work, hair rouged with henna and either folded up in a chignon or caught back in a dark auburn cascade; both styles accentuating her high cheekbones and narrow slanting eyes. She is a petite person, faintly Mongolian in appearance, a characteristic frequently seen among the Berber peoples of the Atlas Mountains. Her print dress is modish, her sandals stiletto-heeled, never mind the strap sores on her feet. Quick in her work and thorough with a professional pride, she brings considerable intelligence to planning the morning's work exactly as would her employer, Anne.

The Berbers were the original tribes of North Africa long before the invasions of the Greeks, Phoenicians, Romans, Arabs and others. It is generally agreed that the original Berbers were Hamitic in origin, not Semitic as were the Arabs. According to ancient Egyptian records, the Berbers were established in the Maghreb well before 4,000 BC. Referred to by Egyptian historians as 'Libyans' and by Roman writers as 'Barbari', overrun and colonized (but never conquered) by successive tides of invaders, they have mingled and adapted so that it is difficult to speak of pure Berber and pure Arab in Algeria. According to Ibn Khaldûn, a Maghrebi who finished writing 'The Muqaddimah' in 1377, the Byzantines took possession of Berber lands in the fifth and sixth centuries AD and Christianised them.[17] Certainly Saint Augustine of Hippo, a Prince of the RC Church and his formidable mother Saint Monica, were Berbers. Then in the eleventh century, the Arabs overpowered the Berbers stripping them of their land and converting them to Islam. However, history records that the Berbers rebelled and 'apostatized time after time'. The Berbers refused to be controlled, "remained disobedient and unmanageable,"[18] says Ibn Khaldûn.

The Berbers live mainly in the mountains of the Atlas and Rif of Morocco, the Aures and Kabylie massifs of Algeria and the Jebel Nafusa of Libya: they speak a Berber tongue though written Berber has now lapsed from use.

---

[17] Ibn Khaldûn, *The Muqaddimah; An Introduction to History,* translated from Arabic by Franz Rosenthal, edited and abridged by N T Dawood, published by Routledge and Keegan in association with Secker and Warburg, 1967, p 30.

[18] Ibid, p 131

Although the Berbers may have adopted the customs and beliefs of their colonizers, they have kept a degree of local custom, individual independence and a flavour of racial superiority. Although Moslem in religion, their womenfolk have more status and freedom than many Arab women: they go unveiled in their own villages though many would veil to visit the cities. The comparative licence enjoyed by the women is probably an inheritance of prehistoric and pre-Islamic times when many of these tribes were matrilineal in structure. Traditional Berber homes are very private places, windowless to the outside world. Ingress into a parlour, a public room, offers labyrinthine access to an inner sanctum, the wife's abode, a concealed core of the home, screened, cloaked in mystery where are kept all things pertaining to fertility. Here rituals, superstitions, ceremonials and magical observances to ensure the continuance of the family, are performed by the officiating matriarch and her daughters-in-law. In some households the married women never go out, not even to the health clinic; to cross the threshold would court disaster. Some women still cling to their ritual role within the home, from womb to tomb enclosed, believing that rites will protect.

Meanwhile, their menfolk fulfil all public duties exercising civic rights on behalf of the family. But where Rites are strong Rights are weak; such women risk being regarded as second-class citizens by the developing world. On the other hand, these women perceive that they have much to lose through modernisation and democracy. Urban Algerians speak scathingly of hillbilly families, which have migrated from the mountains to abandoned properties in the city. "They have no idea how to live: they put the goat in the shower, plant potatoes in the bath and parsley in the bidet."

Born in the Kabylie mountains, Lena talks of her childhood in the *montagne.* Her mother died when Lena was an infant.

"My father he was killed by a falling rock when I was seven. I lived with my grandmother until I came to the city. You know, my aunt she worked in Algiers and I came to the same *patron* to look after the children. I used to go everywhere with them: to the beach, to the restaurants and eat *bifstek,* on excursions to the oases, everywhere."

She had met and married a good-looking policeman from Biskra in the Aures district.

"I had no parents to find me a husband. I got married in Algiers but none of my family were at the marriage."

Lena has not complied with custom: she has cast off on her own and chosen a husband for herself. Now, in effect, she has no family. She and her husband live in an apartment of a council block. Photos of the family are produced. Lena, her husband and three children, Lena in her apartment reclining seductively on a bed, carpet on the floor, curtains, furniture, bed covers. She looks something of an Eve in the snap, but she has a kind heart and a sense of humour.

"My house is not like that now," she announces. "My husband he has no work, and he drinks: too much. He has sold everything."

"Why did he leave the police?"

"He was wicked," she says simply.

One hot afternoon, it is a surprise to see Lena coming through the gate carrying a baby. Behind walks a short crocodile of three other children. Dressed in their best, they stand hot, silent and overawed. Orange pop and biscuits are handed around in the kitchen, Lena talking all the time in an excited nervous manner and rising, as a champagne bubble, to wash up when the drinks are finished. As soon as the pop has been downed the children, full of curiosity, flow like a flood tide through the house. Robbie's dinky cars have magnetic effect and Anne gives the children one each quickly before any of his favourites vanish. They are chubby children, well washed and dressed for the occasion.

Lena is stealthily taking a pill each morning with her tea. "It's against a baby" she grins. A Moslem woman using birth control! It is surprising in a country such as Algeria not yet facing overpopulation. In Pakistan when family planning had become a national programme, advertised in the press and on the radio, some countrywomen had braved the clinic for advice and treatment. But Algeria has no such programme. The Pill must be extremely expensive in this country. It is not clear where Lena obtained her carton of pills but it is not long before they are finished, never to be replaced. It is said that the Pill is available if prescribed by a doctor but many women refuse to use it.

Setting up Anne's new home in a strange country having been achieved, the next essential is company for the family. In Pakistan, on an enormous site cantonment, English-speaking families were all around. Here, the trouble is that most English-speaking families, British or International, are by this time away on holiday, or busy getting ready to go off to Europe, or occupied with a sudden influx of school boarders. The English-speaking Protestant Church is closed until September, so too the schools and the British Council Library. As far as English-speaking company is concerned, Algiers is shut. Here, in a capital city, there is no one with whom to talk. Why not go out and meet the neighbours: forget Britain and British for a time? Why not? One must go more than half way to meet them but once the initial effort has been made, in French, there would be company in plenty for Anne and the children. Marion, anyway, would pick up French without tears in the street and perhaps Robbie, too, eventually.

Next door the girl aged 10, Laalia, is delighted to play with Marion, riding her bicycle and having fun with the dressing-up box. Marion goes to their garden and sits in the shade with Laalia and Fouzia from across the road, singing French songs and beating an upturned plastic pail, that serves as a tom-tom. Laalia's little brother Ben Yusef aged six comes over to play with Robbie's dinky cars but the younger children, having no French, can communicate but little. Soon Laalia and her elder brother, Mahommed, are coming to the beach on a Sunday.

Anne, sitting with Madam Chalfut through a long hot afternoon, acquiring useful hints and tidbits of gossip with the avidity of a young cuckoo, is being trained.

"You don't keep your gates locked," Madame chides. "You should. There are so many thieves here, the family opposite us had *all* their washing taken while they were inside at dinner. You will lose your washing off the line and children's bicycles." She helps Anne buy eggs from the vendor, choosing the largest from the basket, advises on and identifies spices when the spice cart comes round with its hundred and one assorted spices, herbs, oriental perfumes, household remedies and aids to beauty such as henna for dying hair, hands or feet. Madame is a good neighbour.

Her home is the first floor of a villa they have just built. She has a sizeable lounge with modern sitting room and dining furniture and a television set. One of the two bedrooms contains a double bed and matching dressing table, the other, the children's, has a stack of mattresses and covers piled against the wall. The kitchen is small but well fitted and the bathroom prettily tiled in pale blue: the toilet oriental.

Soon courtesy gifts are being exchanged: a huge platter of *couscous*; a crimson brocade cocktail dress from Marion's dressing-up box that Madame admires, inserts her plump self into and pirouettes round her courtyard. Normally Madame wears the traditional *pantalon* and blouse that Algerian women use every day. Their *pantalon* is a long loose skirt joined between the ankles so that sitting or squatting to work, they have no problems about exposing the leg. Outside her gate of course she uses the *haik* and *voile* triangle tied over her nose so that she is difficult to identify once dressed for the street. Her French is good and she has a small circle of French friends, whom she occasionally entertains and for whom she wears a western style of cotton frock. Monsieur Chalfut is a good deal older than his wife. He has been in the French Army for many years serving in Indo-China before he retired in 1960 just before matters between France and Algeria became too extreme and ended with Independence for Algeria in 1962. Now he works in an office in the city, returning home for lunch each day, as do most Algerians. Mahommed, the eldest child, is the son of his first wife and soon to go to spend the long summer vacation with his own mother. Laalia and her three younger brothers belong to the present Madame.

"Marion is so helpful to me now," Anne observes to Madame. "She sees Laalia doing all the work and must do the same. She argues with Lena for use of the broom. In England, girls of her age are sent out to play rather than being taught to help."

"Ah no!" exclaims Madame, scandalized, "A girl should learn to help for her marriage."

"When Laalia is grown up will you choose her husband?"

"Of course."

"Will she have any training after school, for a teacher or a nurse perhaps?"

"No, only marriage. And if I find a suitable husband for her before she has finished school, she will leave school and marry. As I did. I was fourteen when I left school to be married."

"It is very different in England," Anne remarks lamely.

Across the road from Madame, live a large family with ten children, ranging from young women of marriageable age who do all the housework, to a flock of unruly youngsters whose main sport seems to be catapulting pebbles at their neighbours. One bright morning, there is a sudden howl from the street. One of Madame Chalfut's small sons has received a direct hit. For half an hour, the two madames range up and down their properties hurling criticism at each other, children cower behind doors as cannonades of condemnation volley to and fro; fusillades of insults are flung with the force of javelins. Their reserves of energy for the fracas are amazing. Later, when Marion is hit on the leg with a stone, Anne attempts a verbal tirade in poor imitation of the neighbours but has to retire from the field after half a minute for lack of ammunition.

There is little contact with the madame from across the road, probably because she speaks no French, but the elder daughters chat readily and Fouzia is often in the garden playing with Marion. Monsieur is a nurse in the emergency ward of the big national Mustafa Hospital in the city.

About this time, Monsieur and Madame Chalfut are preparing to move house from the first floor to the ground floor of their home, having let their first floor apartment to Europeans. The difficulty is that the ground floor is not ready for occupation. The walls are there but that is about all. The slow rate of progress as plasterers, plumbers and joiners set about the place, is cause for concern. Monsieur helps when he is not at his office but during office hours, the family has difficulty in supervising the work. Mahommed is away for the summer and Madame cannot be seen downstairs in her own courtyard without putting on her *haik* and *voile*. There is only Laalia aged ten years to see that the workmen are getting on with their job.

Madame is becoming more and more agitated. There is no cement available: her husband has managed to procure two bags only at a price over ten times the standard rate. One day, she hastily flings a bath towel round her head and shoulders and comes over.

"Will you help me get cement, please. We must go to the cement factory today. I've heard there is some there now."

At the cement factory she is inside the office for half an hour. "There is no cement here but I have an address in the city." Driving to the city, parking before a huge warehouse on the edge of dockland, Madame draws her veil in closely and hurries through the shimmering heat haze white with the cement dust that hangs like a curtain across the mouth of a huge cavern. She is nearly two hours.

"I have some cement, I think. But I don't know how many bags. I have been lucky, it was not quite so expensive as I thought." A small truck, *camion,* hired and loaded with ten bags of cement follows the Anglia back to El Biar.

A few days later, Madame is round again. "Can your husband take me down town when he goes to work in the morning? I must get more cement; the other lot I got is no good, too old." Her manner is nervous.

"Yes, I will ask him. He leaves at half past seven you know." John agrees to give Madame a lift next morning and seeing Monsieur on his way home, hails him.

"Please give your wife the message that I will be able to take her to the city in the morning." Monsieur stops short, surprised, then agrees to relay the message.

Next morning Monsieur pauses to speak to John. "My wife will not be going to the city after all, it's not necessary now. Thank you all the same for offering to take her." After Monsieur is out of sight, Madame pulls her *haik* tight around her and slips over as John is starting his car.

"Please take me with you. I *must* get some cement. Instead of turning right, please turn left and pass the petrol station where my friend is waiting for us." John does as he is bid and sure enough as he pulls up at the petrol station, a white shape steps forward and gets in. This is Madame's friend, Ayisha.

Later in the morning, Madame returns with Ayisha in a taxi. She comes straight over to Anne's villa. "I think I have found some cement. I must go down to the docks again after dinner."

Later Anne puts her two children in the car and drives Madame and Ayisha to a warehouse. Madame, reckoning on a long wait, asks Anne to return after two hours. This she does to find Madame satisfied and happy.

"You and I can go home in your car. I have some cement and Ayisha will wait to accompany the *camion*," Madame says. She continues earnestly: "Please, I have not been out today, my husband has forbidden me to go to the city and docks for cement. I told him I would not go out."

"But the cement? How will you explain seven bags of cement in your courtyard this evening?"

"Ah! I shall say my neighbour went to get it for me."

"Does her husband not mind her going to docks and cement depots?"

"Yes he does mind, but he is away in the week and only comes home for Saturday and Sunday."

The rest is left unsaid. How wily are the ways of women and how determined: husbands chained to tradition oblige intelligent, capable women to descend to deception.

"Why do you wear the *haik* and *voile*? Do you like to follow the custom of Algerian women or is it your husband who insists?"

"My husband," Madame says simply.

"When Laalia marries will she wear it too? I see many young married women in the streets of Algiers without a *haik* and *voile*.

"It will depend on her husband."

Although she may not like wearing her *haik,* Madame can if she wishes, use it to advantage as a social weapon. One day, Anne is chatting with Madame at her gate when the lady starts suddenly and withdraws inside.

"Monsieur is coming," she mutters.

The monsieur was none other than the husband of her neighbour opposite, the nurse at the hospital.

"But you know him. You go into his house to visit his wife when he is at home." When their new baby, their eleventh, arrived recently, Madame has been over at all times to give a hand, carrying in food, taking out washing, veil ignored. Now Madame shrugs and closes the gate. It is clear that Madame has had a tiff with the lady opposite and wishes to imply that her neighbours are no better than the common herd. It is significant, furthermore, that women may put their veils to diabolical disposal: during Algeria's war of independence from French rule, women used the veil to ferry grenades and guns until, that is, the French authorities rumbled the astonishing truth that the Algerian woman, she of the lovely bedroom eyes above a lace-edged chiffon *voile,* is no acquiescent, douce doe but a virago of the first order.

One morning, Lena comes in as usual at eight o'clock with a tight-lipped pinched looking face. She begins washing up but soon breaks down in tears. Out pours a flood of fast, broken French and she is indicating her back, her neck and her wrists. The account is difficult to follow except it is clear that her husband had given her a thrashing. When she takes off her headscarf there is an injury about the size of an apple, purple with bruise tissue, white with scrapes of bone and black with clotted blood and matted hair. Anne applies some antibiotic cream, hands her two aspirin and makes tea.

"My husband, he brought a woman to the house. He made me fetch water and cook a meal for them. Then he beat me." Lena sips at her tea. There is an animal-like quality about her, an acceptance of pain and suffering, also an animal odour of a creature that has lain wounded in its lair, too sore to lick itself clean.

"Have you been injured by your husband before?"

"Oh yes, one time I was in hospital for two days, and one time I lost a baby." Her voice is flat but without self-pity. The tea finished, Lena goes on working as usual.

Later Anne goes next door to seek advice.

"You do nothing," says Madame firmly. "She comes to your house. She does the work. You pay her money. She goes, nothing else, you understand. Her husband, he is good looking, he goes with women, he drinks; afterwards he has a row with his wife. Today the couple are like this." She lays her two index fingers across each other. "Tomorrow they are like this." She places her fingers side by side. "If it

145

happened in my house I should turn the key on my husband." She turns an imaginary key with a flourish.

A week later Lena is herself again, working vigorously, gay at times with almost childish spontaneity. She talks of leaving her husband, renting a room for herself and the children, asks the local grocer if he knows of any place for her to rent, but that is as far as she goes. Clearly for her, pain is a normal experience of life. Her story is no different from a great many Algerian women.

Lena belongs to the underprivileged in the world, the 'have nots'. Life is not kind to a woman without a husband in Algeria and doubly malevolent for the woman who must survive and rear her family despite a husband. Their tenacity and courage in the fight for themselves and their children, must be admired.

One day, Madame Chalfut comes round, beaming. "You and Marion are invited to a marriage. You will watch Algerian dancing, eat plenty of cake and *couscous*, see the Algerian ladies beautiful in their long dresses with gold embroidery, collars, bracelets, earrings, all."

Anne's mind gropes frantically with the flow of French and at the same time examines the contents of her wardrobe. On Saturday afternoon, Madame, Laalia, Marion and Anne set off for the bridegroom's house, have trouble turning the Anglia in a lane as narrow as a knitting needle, acquire three more veiled passengers and join the motorcade. Moving off with a burst of speed horns honking, the passengers suddenly begin squealing with intermittent high-pitched cries, between snatches of nasal Arab singing.

Near the house of the bride the ladies disembark, walking the last quarter mile, a tangled skein of white shapes, an honourable company of matrons gathered to welcome another to the sorority, to escort a bride to her bridegroom. Seated in the closed courtyard of the bride's parents' house, the ladies take turns with the tom-tom tapping out with finger tips and the heel of the palm rhythms of compelling urgency. One guest begins a song and all take it up. Another rises and, tying a scarf tightly round her hips, wiggles shuffles and gyrates that part of her anatomy. The dancer is not concerned with the audience as a whole, selecting one member and performing for her alone. Sometimes two dancers take the floor together vying with each other as they swing their undulating hips: the movement is nothing less than enticing though there is not a male in the room above the age of four years. Are these homely ladies, some portly, some pregnant, performing a dance traditional of the harem, where highly competitive women occupied unending hours displaying their sexual skills? Clearly, this is an exercise in self-stimulation to be compared with reading a titillating paperback. Anne is interested to observe that Madame Chalfut gives birth to her fifth child nine months later.

Coffee in tiny cups and mounds of almond cakes are served. Ten minutes later the ladies, donning their *haiks* and *voiles*, reassemble in the motorcade which moves off to the sound of gun fire above the din of revving engines: from the car behind the bride's, her uncle is firing the traditional wedding volley. All around the busy city goes the motorcade, thirty strong, honking hard and passing rival shows. Anne finds the pace fast, loses her procession, but her passengers know the route. Soon, seated in rows on a terrace of the bridegroom's parents' house, the tom-tom, cakes and coffee appear again.

"The bride, she is coming now," whispers Madame. Heavily supported by her mother and a sister, gorgeously attired in gown of silver lamé, pearl-embroidered, silver gloves bag and shoes, tiered and sparkling with matched jewellery, she is like a society debutante. But for her face which is expressionless, as if the owner is absent. She moves like a plastic puppet, her momentum being that of her two supporters. She is as if sleepwalking, a drugged or hypnotised victim.

"It would not be seemly for her to look round or smile. She must display all her new clothes and jewels: the bridegroom's family has given the money for them and they want to see how it has been spent. At last, she will put on her marriage dress, white you understand, with a veil over the face. At midnight, the bridegroom will lead her to the new bedroom, he will turn the key and – *enfin!*" Madame slaps her well-covered thigh with a flourish. There are shouts of laughter and a rush of bedroom anecdotes.

So to the *couscous*. The ladies eat quickly and with relish, mixing mouthfuls of *couscous* with meat or grapes; they know that the bride's family has to feed many more guests in groups of eight.

An Algerian marriage is a civil affair, a financial contract between two families with a fête on three separate occasions; the betrothal, the contract and payment of money by the bridegroom's family, and lastly the marriage feast to display the goods. The expenses are heavy for all concerned and a great many parents of marriageable sons find themselves borrowing money round the family and, worse, falling into the clutch of moneylenders. Families are sometimes large enough to support the financial burden, the ties and obligations of kin are strong, and those that lend can expect a loan when it is their turn to play host for a circumcision or a marriage or a funeral feast.

After an *Eid*, a four-day Moslem holiday, Lena does not come to work. Two days later Anne goes to her apartment in a city council block nearby. Her husband appears, glassy-eyed and shaking.

"She is ill," he mutters.

"Can I come in and see her?"

"She's not here, she's in hospital."

"Which hospital?"

At the hospital there is no mention of Lena's name.

"Go round the women's wards and see if she is there," says a sympathetic clerk. A search among the tattooed and turbaned faces reveals no Lena: more likely she is in the flat, bruised and discoloured from a thrashing he has given her.

Two days later Anne is allowed to enter. The room is empty of furniture and fittings, and against one wall Lena lies on a mattress under a blanket, her face like a cadaver, the skin stretched, putty-coloured over the prominent cheek bones, lips bleached grey, the veins of her head standing out like cables.

"I fell down and miscarried a baby" she says, her voice a tremulous sing-song. "Much blood came."

"When did it happen?"

"I don't know," she wavers. "Before *Eid*."

That was over eight days ago: she has been bleeding unattended all that time.

"I must get a doctor or midwife immediately." Lena closes her eyes on a few falling tears and averts her head. Mercifully an acquaintance, a French midwife, lives locally.

"She must go into hospital straight away," declares the midwife.

"No," interrupts the husband. "She will recover here in the home." He is adamant.

The midwife hands over a prescription. "She's a hopeless case, anaemic, undernourished, weak, with a brutal husband who is a lunatic for drink, and now she has had a massive haemorrhage. Leave her. You have done enough for them. You can do nothing."

"But she will die."

"Certainly, she will die," agrees the midwife.

Next day, calling round with the medicine for Lena and some groceries for the family, Anne finds Lena marginally more aware.

"If you left your husband could you return to your family in the *montagne*?"

"Certainly. But the children would have no schooling. I wish my children to have an education."

She is a brave woman, a fighter overwhelmed by poverty, ill health, and a swallow-hole of a husband.

"Take my coat to your house, also this bag," Lena whispers.

Three days later, Lena, still like a rag doll on the pallet, says she could go into hospital.

"You're going into hospital!"

"As you wish," she mumbles. Lena means she can go into hospital if Anne makes all the arrangements, because her husband certainly will not. The midwife provides the certificate along with some sound advice on the wisdom of leaving such people as Lena alone. "She will never thank you."

Anne drives Lena, propped up in the Anglia car, to the city hospital. Then she manages to contact her neighbour from El Biar who is working there. This kindly man escorts them to the maternity department, carrying Lena up the stairs, moves another patient from a small single cubicle and puts Lena into it. He also does the necessary admissions paperwork.

Lena is in hospital for eight days and has seven transfusions of plasma. The midwife had said she would need a minor gynaecological operation to scrape the womb after a miscarriage but the Sister says this is not necessary.

"She never lost a baby," reports the Sister. "She has been abused with a broomstick."

It will be many weeks before Lena is fit enough to work. She has a little money saved, talks of leaving her husband and finding her own apartment and is jubilant when he finds a job in his hometown, in Biskra.

"He will be back from time to time," Anne says.

"Ah, *non*. It is two hundred kilometres away."

A week later, when Anne calls in with some groceries, Lena's husband is there. "Oh, he has just come to collect some papers; he's going tomorrow." Lena is vibrating as if electrically charged; she is a chained to him as Nancy to her Bill Sykes in '*Oliver Twist'*.

With the exit of Lena, a new era begins with Zayneb, the proverbial veiled widow. Her figure is generously curved; she has a friendly face and lovely amber skin lightly peppered with freckles, like a ripe apricot. Being widowed and with ten living children, Zayneb must concern herself with marriages for the elder children.

Zayneb arrives one morning twittering with excitement. "A monsieur arrived yesterday asking to marry Fatmasurah. He is divorced and has a daughter of seven years. He asked how much money he should give for her and I told him as much as he wanted. She is divorced, you see, and I cannot ask a price for her."

"And what does Fatmasurah think about it?" asks Anne. This eldest daughter is a thin, peaky woman plain as porridge.

"She says nothing: always she says nothing, just puts her mouth tight shut." Zayneb pulls her mouth into a pencil line.

It is a rush job. Zayneb hurries about the city buying new make-up, shoes, underwear, aprons and *haiks*; also ingredients for the wedding feast. But in the event, the man fails to return with the money and certificates. Zayneb waits two weeks until she hears that his first wife had decided to return to the home and his divorce has been abandoned.

About her daughters Zayneb may not take the initiative; she must wait to be approached by the envoys of a marriageable man. For her sons she must be proactive.

It is a hot, humid afternoon when Zayneb goes suddenly to Medea some 100 kilometres distant. The journey by crowded bus can be nothing but purgatory but her need is great. She has heard of a possible bride for her son.

"How do you look for a son's wife?"

"I visit the family, I regard the girl and the home. I look at the mother too," says Zayneb wisely. "Ah, this little one is beautiful with long blonde hair." Zayneb's hands flutter to her waist. "She has green eyes. Just eighteen years old and has done a course in sewing at school." Zayneb eulogises, her eyes becoming moist as she recalls this little peach. "But I was too late. She is already affianced and I must look elsewhere." Three weeks later, Zayneb has good news. "I have found a bride for my son at last."

"How did you find her?"

"She is the younger sister of my nephew's new wife. She is pretty, the little one, and sixteen years old now. Her family are tranquil and she is calm and gentle with children, never a dispute with neighbours."

"Can she sew?"

"No, this one has never been to school. I shall now send my brother and the husbands of my two aunts to visit the girl's parents with the customary gifts to discuss the contract."

So the bride is illiterate: how would this country girl fit into Zayneb's family? Apart from Fatmasurah, the other daughters are all educated and show talent. The seventeen-year-old is a persevering student who hopes to gain a teacher's diploma. The thirteen-year-old is doing well in sport and has been selected to visit Morocco with a team of young athletes. Yet the mother of the next generation is to be an uneducated girl. Her children would risk being at a disadvantage compared with their cousins and neighbours. It is a backward step for the family on the face of things and yet, who knows, perhaps the girl will remain more content with her lot than some of her clever sisters-in-law whose demands and hopes are set higher on the scale of social maturity.

Many Algerian families remain strongholds of habit and tradition, the women themselves perpetuating their own bonds, raising sons with self-effacing acquiescence to archaic memory, some of it nomadic and pre-Islamic, when the girls of the extended family had to be safeguarded for the boys of the clan. Women may be devout and uncomplaining but some resort to superstition.

"Do you know anyone with a pig?" A neighbour springs an astonishing question. A pig! Pigs are forbidden animals, unclean and taboo. "My friend has a son with a weak leg; he cannot walk. They have tried doctors, x-rays and injections but nothing has helped. Now an old woman says the leg must be rubbed with water from which a pig has drunk."

Zayneb confirms the practice of using medicaments made from the pig. "If your child has whooping cough you get a pork steak and squeeze the juice from the meat. Then you rub the juice on the throat of the patient and the cough will go." There is no doubt that Zayneb believes sincerely in the efficacy of this treatment. "*Malheureusement* it is difficult to get medicaments from the pig. When the French were here it was easy enough," she observes.

Whatever the therapeutic value of the parts of the pig, there is among the natural Mediterranean flora a wide range of plant products and extracts which are of use to Man. There are innumerable edible fruits and herbs, flax for linen, giant reed for the cane industry, trees to give tannin, turpentine and mastic gum, the olive to provide oil for cooking, lighting and for anointing the body. There are aphrodisiacs and medicaments believed to subdue the sexual appetite used equally by monks or by mothers-in-law who do not approve of their son's choice, and herbs for hysteria in horses. There is also an impressive list of medicines which can be obtained easily from Mediterranean plants: narcotics, diuretics, febrifuges, emetics, antiseptics, insecticides. For the would-be murderer or suicide there is, with a little working knowledge of poisons and of Mediterranean flora, an ample choice of method. The country folk, beyond easy reach of a doctor, are highly experienced in herbal remedies.

One day Zayneb arrives in high good humour; before long her news spills over. "Bayah is going to be married. She is my third daughter, seventeen years old. The marriage is in three weeks' time and this Saturday is the feast to affiance the couple."

"Why so sudden and in such haste?"

"He came last week, the young man, to ask for Bayah, bringing with him the proper presents, and the money. Bayah is very happy."

"Does Bayah know the young man, then?"

"Yes, his sister is Bayah's school friend, and every day he takes his sister and Bayah in his car to school."

"Did you know his family before Bayah became friendly with the sister?"

"No, not before two years ago when he began to take Bayah in the car with his sister."

Here is no traditional marriage in the Moslem manner, but a love match between two young people. Thus Zayneb has in the same family, in the same season, two marriages, one traditional, one modern.

"Why is there such haste for Bayah's marriage?"

"The young man's father has recently divorced and remarried. The new wife is young and jealous and she does not like to wash and cook for the grown-up family of her husband. So the grandmother has decided the young man should marry."

This is indeed a practical and realistic, if unromantic, attitude for a family suddenly faced with disharmony in their home.

"And Nadia? What about her?" Most families will not marry a daughter while an elder sister remains unwed.

"Ah, Nadia says she will not marry this year: perhaps next year. She says there is enough in our family for this year with my son's marriage and now Bayah's as well. She has received a request for marriage but she says no, she does not wish to marry yet," Zayneb finishes.

As a result of these two weddings in close proximity, Zayneb has suddenly more demands on her financial resources than she can easily manage. When some money is missing from a padlocked trunk, the clasp having been forced, and a wristwatch is suddenly 'lost', John and Anne decide to tell Zayneb she must look for another job. There is no recrimination nor demand for salary in lieu of notice. Why did she take the money? Perhaps her requirement for ready money was so pressing that she began to regard her need as greater than her employer's at that moment in time. Expediently regarding her employer as part of her extended family, she would mean to repay it at a future date.

Indeed, this is not the first time that a code of communal property has manifested itself. Some weeks previously, a neighbour's daughter has come to the door. "I need your red jacket: I have an interview tomorrow." And Laalia has borrowed Marion's swimsuit when she has gone on a school outing to the beach. Families pool resources of food, clothing, money, energy and time to the benefit of members who have the paramount requirement. Alas, to be accepted by and incorporated into Algerian families is an honour too far. The people of Algeria are undoubtedly the country's greatest resource, but in the meantime, the social structures of Algeria and those of northwest Europe are still poles apart.

Meanwhile, the old habits and customs continue in the daily life of many devoutly traditional families who represent a conservative core in Algeria that will be slow to change. About this time, an Algerian film called 'The Charcoal Burner' is released. It is set in the Kabylie Mountains where the hero has fallen on hard times since gas is replacing charcoal for cooking and heating. The domestic life of the Kabylie is poetically sketched; the wife prepares the food and serves her men folk, her husband and small son, eating separately with her daughter after she has attended to all the needs of the men. Time slowly passes, the couple work harder and harder but the larder becomes more bare. Finally the husband picks up his *burnous* and walks out. He has decided to go and seek an ex-freedom fighter friend in Algiers, and ask for employment. The friend turns out to be now a rich bourgeois in a slick office spending as much time drinking coffee and ogling his secretary as working. Nothing doing there for the charcoal-burner. The poor man wanders alone in the city, confused and uncomprehending, until finally, for want of a better idea, he takes the bus back to the Kabylie, only to find that his wife has got herself a job in a newly-opened textile factory. Then comes the dilemma. Should he accept his working wife and the material goodies she is bringing in and leave her veiled, or should he unveil her and face up to the mockery of his men friends? It is an academic question and the climax is related only as a reverie in which the charcoal-burner dreams that he strips off his wife's *haik* in the street to reveal her standing shamed and silent before his mates. In the final scene, he steps in beside her and the modern family departs, wife walking with her son and the husband accompanying his daughter, in complete opposition to tradition.

The film is a dignified and deliberate attempt to show how the Algerian rural family can move into modern life, but omitting all the complications and pitfalls that may occur on the way.

Of this film, an Algerian acquaintance, Mouloud, says: "Ah yes, I saw *The Charcoal Burner.* It was a poor film, I thought, very dull."

"We thought it was interesting and beautifully made," says Anne.

"Oh it's interesting for the foreigners but I was brought up like that in the Kabylie. I don't want to see that sort of thing at the cinema! Give me a Western cowboy film any time." How gradual must be the social revolution, razing with road roller strength the customs and habits that have lingered two or three thousand years and more in the Middle East and Maghreb!

By September, the English-speaking international community is resuming life in Algiers. It is time for Marion to enter the International School of Algiers and for Robbie to attend a kindergarten organised by a British Embassy wife. Later, at the International School ball held at the USA Ambassador's gracious residence, the Ambassador for the USSR has the last word. "Algeria has had its bourgeois revolution. Next it will have its proletariat revolution," he prophesies in tones of infinite gloom. How right he is! This will be proved in the 1990s when savage outbreaks of fighting occur between Islamist political party activists and the established Government and its army.

Chapter 10

Reflections in a Palmerie

One does not live in Algiers very long without becoming aware that the city is unrepresentative of the whole country. First impressions of Algeria, gathered in Algiers, are of a Mediterranean country with a dual nature; a French outside wrapped round an Arab inside. The capital city is difficult to classify: one cannot label it Arab or European, Moslem, Mediterranean or African. Algiers is a blend of all these identities and the mixture varies from person to person, from circumstance to circumstance.

The Mediterranean littoral is only a small part of Algeria though it holds, understandably, most of the people, the cities, the business and the money. The Sahara, which makes up 85% of the country's area, contains only 6% of the population. Between the Mediterranean watershed and the Sahara proper, lies the transitional area of high, dry plateaux with their sporadic wet and fallow lands and pasturages for immense flocks of sheep. Occasional towns and scattered villages thin out southward until the only habitations are the infrequent palmeries built round an oasis, and the nomadic tents of the desert dwellers.

Their first experience of the desert is a weekend spent in Bou Saada only 200 kilometres south of Algiers, but nevertheless a palmerie, oasis and market town of 35,000 citizens serving a nomadic district. Bou Saada is under development as a tourist centre and the hotel is new. Built in a Moorish style of architecture, it features attractive tile decoration, a French cuisine and a high class of comfort. A guide, dressed in loose, cotton robe, baggy trousers and turban, entirely in white as befits a well-dressed gentleman of the desert during summer, is engaged to extol the town's chief attractions. There are artisans at work casting silver bracelets or weaving blankets and burnouses, and the knife smith grinding cut-throats for the barber trade, the metal for the knives being obtained from old car springs. They saunter through the narrow lanes of square-topped mud buildings. The guide raps a door lintel with his stick. "This wooden frame has been here three hundred years. It is very hard wood this juniper, but there is no more to be found in the hills now."

The old homes built of mud and plastered with mud on their juniper frames, are more durable than any modern brick or cement job. Here is an antique house, which with the mere addition of a little more mud plaster, is still in excellent condition. In the excessively dry climate mud and wood both become very stable: desiccation holds decay to a minimum.

"Here is the donkey garage," says the guide, stopping before another antique, mud building whose heavy wooden door rests ajar. Behind is a straw-filled courtyard with five or six donkeys browsing lazily. "You can leave your donkey here all day for 40 centimes (about 4p)."

"How much would it cost to leave one daughter in the garage?" grins John, indicating Marion.

The guide never hesitates: "With or without hay?" he twinkles.

Walking round the extensive palmerie, the guide explains how the small gardens are worked and watered by a family, produce being divided among the members. There are vegetables down below, fruit trees such as apricots, figs, oranges and lemons growing above the vegetables:

and high overhead, frayed palm fronds hang, like dusty umbrellas, over their burdens of golden brown beads.

"Date picking begins on the first of October," explains the guide, pausing in a pool of shade. "But the flavour is best on the twenty-fifth and twenty-sixth day of the month. By the tenth of November, it is all over." What precision! How an orchard owner in the Vale of Evesham would laugh if asked to forecast the approximate dates of his apple harvest. But the dry desert climate is infinitely more constant and predictable than the erratic, changeable seasons of the Atlantic seaboard.

Several date palms are growing from out of the middle of a house. The tall trunks appearing through the roof are incorporated into the structural framework of the dwelling: not so surprising since date palms can live and bear fruit for up to a hundred years. Ambling through the palmerie, one becomes aware of a quality of indestructibility and immutability: nothing here has changed, generations come and go but the desert environment remains, preserved in the airtight container of its climate and its space.

And yet, on the edge of the palmerie, is a large modern construction site, the new college of hotel management not only for Algeria but for all Africa, soon to be opened. Modernisation, employment opportunities and new stimulus are rocking the palmerie people to their roots.

Anne and John go to Biskra and the Aures Mountains, stronghold of the Chaouia, an original Berber tribe. This is a strange world of red, white and orange plateaux, canyon-cut and scree-scarred: a lunar landscape quite nude of vegetation, awful in its remoteness: there seems to be no living thing in the badland. The route snakes downwards and suddenly there is the floor of the canyon, bristling green with a carpet of palm crowns. They pass a cluster of sun-baked, mud brick homes and come out of the glare into a cool, green cavern of palms. Below the high canopy grow fruit trees and beneath them vines, vegetable plots and tiny patches of ripe wheat. Not a square inch of soil lies untilled right up to the very boulders of the canyon bed. A mere trickle of water glistens in the stream but, in July and August, storms in the mountains bringing flash floods will inundate to many feet, the river banks, spreading fertile silt over the gardens.

Biskra is a dreary town, dusty as a pie dog, built of mud bricks, the same hue as the desert around. Three times the size of Bou Saada, its palmerie is nothing like as productive. "The water here is no good," explains a local man. "It's too salty." Biskra is, however, the market and service centre for villages embedded deep in the Aures Mountains.

The day is suffocatingly hot. Dust spirals race across the dun-coloured stony surfaces. Still hotter grows the day and the wind is rising. Like a flame comes the *sirocco* wind from the south, parching the skin and mouth, carrying dust and sand by the hundredweight. Everything is shrouded in an ochreous fog of fine silt, which settles in hair, clothing, luggage and in every garment inside the suitcases. The desert is alive with shredded paper and plastic rags. All night the wind roars with a plangent clattering of nerve-shattering volume; trees fall, doors bang throughout the hotel.

The hotel, sepia-coloured in a sepia-tinted alleyway, is old and due to be replaced by a new one now under construction. There is a ghost of former grandeur about the spacious rooms and the heavy, mud-constructed verandahs and balconies. The garden behind high, meter-thick mud walls is sheer delight, cool and green, with fountains playing rainbow colours. There are palms, fruit trees, scarlet and purple bougainvillea, flame hibiscus, hollyhocks, roses, geraniums. No wonder the Prophet Mohammed described Paradise as lofty gardens of darkest green planted with fruit trees, the palm and the pomegranate, watered by flowing springs and gushing fountains. For the righteous, as recited in the chapter entitled *'That Which is Coming'*, are 'gardens of delight' where the exalted shall be brought near their Lord. 'They shall recline on jewelled couches… and there shall wait on them immortal youths with bowls and ewers and a cup of purest wine (that will neither pain their heads nor take away their reason)… And theirs shall be the dark-eyed houris, chaste as hidden pearls.' But for the damned, the wretched who have lived in comfort and persisted in heinous sin, 'they shall dwell amidst scorching winds and seething water: in the shade of pitch-black smoke…'[19] As N J Dawood says in his Introduction to *The Koran*, that word means literally 'Recital'. This beautiful literary masterpiece of the seventh century is regarded by Moslems as the indubitable message of God, as recited to the Prophet Mohammed by the Archangel Gabriel. Even in translation, the exquisite imagery, the jewelled language and the eloquent expression of the ancient Arabic prose, is piercingly profound.

Ghardaia on the fringe of the desert is an unusually beautiful oasis. One sees it first from the top of a plateau, the road dropping suddenly into a canyon and there below, lies Ghardaia built on a hill in the middle of a broad bowl. The town has a classical quality, a mosaic-covered cupola rising from the floor of a concave courtyard, the tessera of the mosaic being the buildings which are brightly painted in white, blue, yellow and orange. Beyond the town lies the green needlepoint tapestry of the palmerie.

According to legend, Ghardaia takes its name from the wife of its founder, a sagacious and worthy lady by the name of Daia. In the unsettled centuries after the death of the Prophet Mohammed when rival Arab factions fought for supremacy, a group of religious refugees camped on a bluff overlooking this valley. They spotted far down below, a lazy trail of blue smoke and the leader sent a henchman down to investigate. The man returned with a beautiful young woman.

---

[19] Dawood, N J, *The Koran,* Penguin Classics 1968, pp. 108-109

"I was travelling with my family's caravan," she explained. "They moved on, forgetting about me. For two days I have lived in a cave by the *oued* down there."

The leader of the refugee band offered the stranger protection and security if she would marry him.

"I will consider the matter. Give me four days for reflection," replied the wise girl. Clearly she did not intend to exchange a lonely but speedy end for a lifetime of slow suffering should the marriage turnout unhappily: death in the desert would be preferable to marriage with a brute and a tyrant. But marry him she did and the small band settled down beside the *oued* to flourish and prosper. The marriage must have been happy since Daia's tomb and those of her sons stand beside her husband's mausoleum.

Ghardaia, together with a cluster of small towns and palmeries, which share the same *oued*, combine to form a prosperous desert district known as the M'zab. The men who founded it were a religious sect of Islam, more orthodox and austere than the contemporary Moslems of their day. They have a reputation for exclusiveness, also for business, habitually wear a skull cap and can often be identified by their conspicuously white skins, small black beards or, by their poor eyesight and need for thick-lensed spectacles. The Mozabites constitute a small but wealthy and fanatically orthodox facet in the composition of modern Algeria.

Being rich, the people of Ghardaia often have more than one house. A great many citizens have a home in the city and another in the palmerie, some three miles distant. When summer temperatures soar to 45° – 48° (110° – 115°), families move out to the town beneath the trees, to a cool shady community beneath the lofty green ceiling of a myriad date palms. There are schools and mosques and markets built among the trees. But the most striking feature of the town, is its regular street plan constructed on an intersecting basis, a remarkably rare feature in old Arab towns.

At the time of Ghardaia's foundation, there was adequate water to be had from wells 60 – 100 feet (20 – 35 metres) deep and the *oued* filled and flooded two or three times a year. The men of Ghardaia, eleventh century Arab engineers of great skill, designed underground conduits to the palmerie, which led from a barrage across the *oued*. When the *oued* filled after rain, water would be conducted via the tunnels into the main streets of the palmerie, which did duty as canals for a day or a day and a half. Not a windowsill along the streets stands lower than 3-4 feet (1 meter) above ground level. At intervals, angled stone slots in the mud walls either side of the roads serve as valves to lead off water into individual gardens. Nowadays, the *oued* rarely fills more than once a year. Well depths are greater than in the past and today, three or four gardens share a diesel pump. The Sahara is gradually becoming drier and water more valuable as rainfall diminishes. This would be disastrous for a desert city like Ghardaia were it not for one thing: Artesian water underlies the Sahara. Subterranean water first flowed in 1940 and today, large modern pumping stations lift water into hilltop reservoirs from 2,250 feet (750 metres) below the ground.

At dawn, the prayer call from many mosques rouses the sleeper. Wait! There is another sound: heavy drops of rain falling fast. Rain? In the desert? When the tourists peer from the window into the night, a sea of goats trotting along the tarmac is just visible: not rain but the pitter-patter of a thousand hooves going out to graze. At sunset, the shepherds bring the city's goats to the town gate, leaving them there. Running through the streets, grabbing any mouthful of greenery or a carrot as they pass the market, the goats return home. "Stop thief!" shriek irate vendors of fresh-cut grass who have brought the precious stuff from the palmerie for sale to goat owners who might wish to treat their pets to a *bon-bouche* on arrival. Each goat runs to its own front door, up the stairs and onto the roof in search of a tidbit.

Another excursion to the desert occurs in the spring of the year, when the desert is in bloom during a three to four week period of flowering which comes to the fringes of the Sahara following rain. The stony surfaces are spangled with mauve crocuses, miniature wild wallflower, diminutive marigolds (calendula), carpets of tiny blue scabious and dwarf irises. None of the flowering plants reach more than four inches (10 centimetres) high: well adapted to the climate, the vegetation wastes no time growing tall, it must complete its growing, flowering and seeding cycle in haste before the soil dries out. In fact, the water table is in parts of the Sahara, not very far below the surface: in places such as dry *oued* beds and in local areas of inland drainage, digging to depths of three feet (a metre) will show dampness or even water, probably brackish. In such places are found, later in the year, tiny melons growing wild, dependent on their massive root system for the moisture they need. The melon is truly the fruit of the desert, as the date is not: the date is more the meat of the desert, a staple item of the diet, supplying much of the protein and a large proportion of the vitamins consumed by the desert dwellers.

The destination is Messaad, an oasis situated on one of the principal nomad routes, passed twice annually by the nomads and their herds going north in May to pasture on the spacious stubble after the wheat has been harvested, and going south in October in time for the date harvest in the palmeries. These migrations are as regular as the ebb and flow of the sea. This is why Messaad was offered to the Save the Children Fund as a base for setting up a clinic. Not only would the clinic serve the children of Messaad, but it would have seasonal contact with a much larger population as the nomads come in for essential supplies during their migrations. Naturally much of their work is preventive medicine; immunisation against smallpox, tuberculosis, diphtheria, poliomyelitis and such endemic killers, but ante- and post-natal care is covered where possible. Messaad is destined to be a considerable desert medical centre with plans for a hospital approved by the Algerian Government; meanwhile, serious cases must go to hospital in Djelfa 50 miles (80 kilometres) distant.

Messaad is a typical oasis township, a mud brick-built town of small, angular, mud buildings ranged randomly around a principal square, the whole dominated by an imposing new mosque, set against a bleached background of grey-green palmerie and framed all around by the tawny tones of the desert. It is a harsh, indomitable landscape, yielding nothing, daily challenging human life to survive or surrender. Add an inclement climate. No wonder the desert folk are proud, intolerant and, as intractable as their environment.

Of the 'veiled Berbers and Arabs who roam the waste regions' whose nourishment consists of milk and meat, Ibn Khaldûn, the fourteenth century historian says, these people 'obtain no more than the bare necessity, and sometimes less, … In spite of this, the desert people are found healthier in body and better in character than the hill people who have plenty of everything. Their complexions are clearer, their bodies cleaner, their figures more perfect, their character less intemperate, and their minds keener as far as knowledge and perception are concerned'.[20] In contrast to these noble savages, Ibn Khaldûn records that urban peoples, having affluence and ease of living, are prone to obesity and slowness of mind, which may be followed by ill-health and early death.

At close quarters Messaad is uncompromising. The narrow lanes of the residential areas are high walled corridors with hardly a door and never a window. They are heat traps in summer, chill wind tunnels in winter, always dusty, alive with flies, muddy trenches after rain storms, a permanent threat to car springs and shock absorbers in all weathers. Messaad does not appear to western eyes anything but a dump. Yet the Save the Children Fund team are cheerful and happy there despite the isolation, the

---

[20] Ibn Khaldûn, op. cit., p. 65

grilling summer heat and the long unscheduled working hours of the staff.

Anne accompanies a nurse, Jenny, on a round of visits. With them are two Algerian health visitors, Messaad women who can converse both in French and the local dialect. The first home is a poor one but clean. Entry from the street is through a heavy wooden door into a small courtyard.

"I came here this morning," says Jenny. "But I could not get in. The husband had locked the women and children in and gone off with the key."

This is one of the big problems of medical or social aid in a place like Messaad. Many of the women never go out, not even swathed from crown to toe in a *haik*. It is quite common for wives to be refused permission to attend the clinic during their pregnancies or to take a sick baby to the doctor or nurse. Sometimes father brings a baby to the clinic, sometimes grandma comes with a child, but as often as not, sick infants are treated in the homes or not at all.

In the home, just one room with not an item of furniture but some cooking utensils and a pile of covers, mats and blankets to one end, is an old woman seated among the mats and beside her lies a bundle of clothes. Jenny glances quickly round the room and makes for the bundle of old clothes, beneath which lies the baby asleep. Jenny crouches down and lifts one of the baby's eyelids.

"Oh dear: it's worse. This baby has both pneumonia and a gastric infection. Look at it. It is so cold and its garment is wet through."

The mother comes over. She is a beautiful young woman with her hair neatly done in plaits round her head like a crown, a gauze scarf looped into the plaits and arranged about her head in a bridal way. Her dress is a brilliant turquoise colour falling to her ankles. She belongs to the Oulad Nial tribe whose women have practised the oldest profession in the world for many centuries. The mother's face is serene, she appears unmoved that her youngest is dying: Allah, the Lord, is recalling her baby. Besides, she already has eight living children and four more who have died in infancy.

Jenny gives the baby an injection and then undresses it. Casting around the room for a dry garment, finding a piece of towel, she wraps the infant. Then she feeds it a little boiled water with a teaspoon. Later, in the evening, Jenny will have to come back to see to the baby again.

Back in the car, a little '*deux chevaux*' Citroen that bounces gamely through the uneven alleys of Messaad, Jenny talks about some of their cases.

"Gastric infections are the worst to deal with and the most common illness among the babies. Pneumonia is easier if caught in time because most infants respond well to penicillin. Several children are being treated for tuberculosis and they are coming along nicely. Most of the little ones are now vaccinated against tuberculosis."

Jenny stops the car suddenly and speaks with a child in the street using her little bit of Arabic. Then she grins.

"Come and see our twins, one week old today. They are off to the Sahara tomorrow."

Inside the big, tidy courtyard is the one-room home full of ladies chattering and toddlers crawling about among their skirts. It is like an aviary of tropical birds so bright are the dresses: scarlet, emerald, lilac and maroon; chiffon fabrics embroidered with gold thread and hung around with gold and silver necklaces, collars, bracelets and brooches. Most of the women are young and their faces exquisitely beautiful: high cheek bones, huge eyes and aquiline noses give them a proud patrician appearance, the Oulad Nial women being renowned for their beauty and also for their skill in dancing. On this occasion they have gathered to say farewell to the young mother of the twins.

Jenny and Anne enter and greet each lady. In the far corner sits a young woman on a pile of blankets among which she rummages to produce a doll, the same shape and size as those gaily painted wooden Russian dolls which open to disclose a smaller but identical wooden doll inside, which in turn opens on a smaller replica and so on. Except this is not a doll but a baby tightly swaddled from head to heel so that its limbs should grow straight. The other doll is handed up; both have their eyes blacked with *kohl* from temple to temple so that they appear to be wearing outsize dark glasses, like screen stars incognito. *Kohl* is said to have medicinal qualities for the eyes.

The twins' mother has come in from the desert for her confinement, though many nomad women have their babies in a tent out on the hills. Twins had not been anticipated in this case, and the delivery was attended by a local midwife. There are plenty of midwives in Messaad and the Save the Children Fund has spent a great deal of time encouraging them, arranging demonstrations in hygiene and discussions about their work.

"Now we have four good reliable midwives and a number of others who are not so clean and thorough," reports Jenny.

They squeeze back into the little car and start searching for the next house to be visited among the labyrinth of corridors that pass as streets. Eventually, after many pauses to enquire which way from local children, Jenny finds the door. It is not such an orderly home as those visited previously and more crowded, with grubby children. Grandma sits on the floor with a phalanx of women beside the inevitable bundle of clothing, which proves to be the sick baby. The infant seems asleep. Jenny examines its eyelids and then demands boiled water.

"No," says the grandmother. "The baby does not need anything, it is peacefully sleeping."

The tiny mite is gathered up, at Jenny's command, by its mother and Jenny administers boiled water for some seconds.

"It's no good: it is too dehydrated." Jenny turns to her Algerian assistant. "Tell them we must take the baby to the clinic for treatment. We'll put it on a drip."

The old crone flares up. "You'll do no such thing," she as good as says. "The baby will lie or die here in this house." She is frightened that the infant might die outside the walls of the home, a very undesirable event: the traditional Algerian family embraces not only those living but also the dead and those yet to be born. Large sums of money may be spent returning the dead to their homeland, packed in salt on camelback in the old days and nowadays, preserved in ice by air. Indeed, the baby's family has been sitting patiently waiting for death, having composed the infant comfortably and gathered in a circle around it. Only the strongest can survive the rigours of Saharan infancy: no wonder the tribal people are so hardy.

Jenny turns to the young mother. "What do *you* want? Do you want to have your baby taken to the clinic for treatment?" The girl nods. Again Grandma protests vehemently.

"Be quiet, old woman," orders Jenny, exasperated. The crone subsides into silence but one wonders how she will spite the young mother later when she gets the chance. The girl looks browbeaten enough without adding further salt to the wound of altercation between her and her mother-in-law. However, the girl puts on her *haik* folding it round her so that one eye only remains, clamps the edge of the cloth between her teeth and picks up the baby. Later, it is reported that the infant recovered from that particular crisis.

The next visit is to give a baby a penicillin injection. He has had pneumonia but is recovering well. Anne shakes hands with the two parents and peers at the plump and well-grown baby.

"I don't know how they managed such a healthy family. Both parents are polio cripples," says Jenny. "They have five other children. This baby has done very well. She's breastfeeding him and gets Farex for him from the clinic. The mother has gone on the Pill now." Jenny turns to the Algerian health visitor. "Ask if she has taken her pill today." The reply is satisfactory.

Later in the day a man comes to the house where the team of nurses and the doctor live. His wife has just been delivered, he says. When a woman who has attended the clinic regularly for pre-natal care gives birth she always receives a post-natal visit from one of the nurses, just to check that all is well. More important, she receives a set of clothes and blanket for the newborn. At the home of the newly delivered woman, the baby is unwound from the swaddling cloth in which the local midwife has wrapped it, and dressed in a white knitted dress and matinee coat. Bonnet and bootees complete the outfit and then the baby is re-swaddled, wrapped in a gay new patchwork blanket and held up for the mother to see. But she averts her head, refuses to look. It is the custom for mothers to disregard new babies: one can never be sure at that stage whether they have come to stay or whether Allah the Lord will want them back. It is all a matter of destiny since the place, time and manner of death are determined at the moment of conception: all very comforting for families facing grief, bereavement, remorse or guilt.

For the believer, Islam, a way of life demanding total surrender to the Will of Allah, offers serenity and solace in a rigorous world and the tribal people are on friendly terms with destiny. There is a well-known Moslem fable about a king and his minister who were talking one day when the Angel of Death appeared before the minister. Extremely agitated, the minister beseeched the king to send him on an immediate mission to furthest India.

"Excellent," remarked the Angel. "I have just been commanded to fetch you from India and I was wondering, when I saw you sitting here, whether a mistake could have been made."

In Algiers time passes, summer moves again to autumn and the rains come. For two or three days at a time, waterfalls like the Deluge and city roads become running *oueds* of cinnamon brown and turmeric yellow as the soil washes off the steep slopes of Algiers. These are the waters that every year replenish the great underground artesian reservoirs of the Sahara, vital water for the south, but bringing disruption and distress to the littoral. Roads lying across the city's major fault settle 30 cms (12 inches) in a week. Water, gas and telephone services are disordered, in the streets, passing vehicles fling curtains of dirty water over pedestrians.

This is the time to go to the Sahara. That word, translated from Arabic to mean 'serenity', conjures up visions of sand, space and silence in one of the world's remaining wild places. Man has shaped the cities, fashioned the farmland and forged the machinery of technology to suit his purpose but climate designs the desert. Books on the Sahara are written by those who have been infected by space, exhilarated by silence, hypnotised by distance and inspired by challenge. Is it really thus?

Two weeks of leave are all that is available to see the Sahara and destination Tamanrasset is chosen because it seems the furthest achievable point for a fortnight's holiday. "Tam," as it is known by those who have been there, is as far south of Algiers as London is to the north, and is the frontier post for the Algeria-Niger border, (although the actual frontier lies a day's drive beyond), and is thus 'across' the Sahara. How to get there? Fly; daily scheduled flights take some five hours including several oasis stops en route but this is no way to experience the Sahara. Drive; but a round trip of 2,500 miles (4,000 kilometers) is not for the old Ford Anglia. Besides, the fact that the *piste* has a notorious death rate for saloon cars and that Tam and back would be too far in one fortnight, travel as 'carriage folk', insulated from the country by hopping in and out of a private world on wheels between tourist hotels where staff are conditioned to European whims, is not suitable for the present mood.

What is needed is a holiday of complete relaxation, with nothing planned, no schedules, time forgotten: moreover it should encompass the Sahara and the desert people as they really are. Alas, there are no camel caravans plodding slowly south: a holiday at camel's pace would have suited the mood. There are, however, local buses in lieu. Doubtless, there is even a bus to Tamanrasset. There were desert buses in Syria and Iraq, why not in Algeria? The idea of being obliged to live at the pace of the local people germinates and grows. If the bus does not go today perhaps it will go tomorrow or the day after. It is not important. One would be required to learn how to do nothing for an hour or two, or a day or two. Perhaps one would achieve complete disregard for time, 'desertability' for want of a better name. Why not spend two weeks getting to Tamanrasset and then fly back.

"You are mad," observe friends. "Just think of the dirt and think of the facilities you'll have to use." True, but it seems a minor sacrifice for the challenge and spirit of this now compelling adventure. Kind friends agree to look after the children.

It is decided, for variety's sake, to make the first stage of the journey by rail, as far as the railhead Djelfa. A little planning is necessary; a railway timetable, and a taxi to the station ordered the evening before since the train leaves early.

Arriving at Algiers station, loudspeakers announce that the express to Oran is ready for boarding. A porter approaches.

"You are going to Oran?"

"No, to Djelfa."

"The Djelfa train has gone."

This is a promising start to the journey. In fact, a slow train to Blida, which is the junction for the Djelfa narrow gauge line, has departed. But the Oran express is scheduled to arrive in Blida a few minutes before the Djelfa train leaves and it has given another hour in bed.

The Oran express fills up entirely before it leaves Algiers. The eighth and last seat is revealed reluctantly by the seven occupants of the compartment to a magnificent young woman, junoesque in stature, swathed entirely in a black *haik*, whose huge soft chestnut eyes above the *voile* over her face, gaze down soulfully at the miniscule portion of seat being allotted to her. The carriage immediately shuffles again and an ample share of cushion becomes hers.

The train wastes no time and Blida is reached just as the Djelfa connection arrives in the station. Swept in with the crowd, one is lucky to find a seat in spite of it being the second-class coach. However, a few minutes after starting, the guard comes along and turns most of the crowd out into the third class carriage. A man in a crimson fez opposite grins, slips off his shoes and tucks up his feet cross-legged on the seat. Behind, sits a tall young man in country tweeds of huge beige and ochre checks. He sports a vast floppy silk tie in black and white Op Art eye-shaped lozenges. Had this been a British train, he might have been an American Tycoon going to Perthshire for the twelfth of August.

The train attacks the magnificent Chiffa Gorge with energy. The landscape in October on this, the seaward side of the Atlas Mountains, is deliciously green with pine forest rising above the shallow river. Above the gorge, the terrain opens out into an upland basin of farmland rimmed by forested hills. The occasional ruined farmhouse or roofless barn tell of the wartime activities of the F.L.N. (Front de Libération National), the guerrilla fighters who engineered independence for Algeria only ten years ago. A small station: on pant the two diesel engines, one at either end of the two-coach train. Fifteen minutes later, the same station comes into view again 300 feet (100 meters) below. Another twenty minutes sees that station again, now 700 feet (250 meters) below. Then the train plunges into a tunnel carrying the line through a crest of the watershed and the drainage will be reversed, leading down to the distant inland depressions, or *chotts* on the fringes of the Sahara. The upward journey from Algiers to the top of the Atlas Mountains has taken about three hours; the downhill journey is to take ten days.

By now, the train has lost its bustle and resembles a county bus: it stops or dawdles for no good reason: it picks up a cardboard box from under a tree, a pouch of mail from a lad at a lane end. The passengers drowse, hypnotised by the heat and the persistent buzzing of a fly on the window pane.

The scenery is monotonously flat and rather saline. This belt of inland drainage which lies behind the Atlas watershed was, many centuries ago, a chain of *chotts*, inland lakes, filled with fresh water, fishing grounds with fertile fringes for farming. Now the *chotts* are saline flats, marshy after rain, at all times nearly useless to Man, depressing in their desiccation.

Will Djelfa never come?

This is not 'desertability'. The station, when it does come, is dead at three o'clock in the afternoon. Djelfa's claim to a name was originally as an assembly point for desert grass, which makes fine quality paper. Known as *alfa* grass, it is cut by the nomads and brought into Djelfa, the railway being built to haul out the grass. Also a garrison town, Djelfa once held a flourishing French community; fifteen years ago the central hotel would have been as lively as the fountain playing in the interior courtyard. Now there is damp on the ceilings, an aroma of mould, chipped plaster and peeled paint; the plumbing is at a standstill and the fountain supplies the kitchen with water. In the hotel's Sahara Bar, a camel, huge and mocking, marches out of a mural.

Their route continues onwards to Ghardaia by brand-new coach, built to carry fifty-six, in which some seventy people are now sorting themselves out. Burnous-wrapped tribesmen, their aquiline faces almost hidden by swathes of turban, hunker down in the corridor or settle on the lap of an acquaintance. An hour or so later, a remarkable thing happens. Those with seats stand up, and those in the passage move into the seats. It is a truly chivalrous gesture.

Now the landscape is stony and angular, almost nude of vegetation. Gradually the hills close in on the road in a sinister manner. Good ambush country this. How many pairs of eyes watch the progress of the bus from behind the encroaching cliffs? The road passes through a minor defile and suddenly the landscape is reassuringly open once more. Drop downhill through a small pass, over a wide, dry *oued* and into Laghouat, palmerie, oasis settlement and garrison town. Then out, across expansive open ground for miles and miles and miles. The road is straight as a taut tape, wide and well surfaced. Other traffic is sparse and the bus bowls along at a steady seventy kilometres an hour eating up the stony wastes. More sparse becomes the tufted coarse grass, more boulder-strewn and gully-scarred the surface. It is a landscape coloured in muted tones of yellow, rose, grey and indigo.

In the mid-afternoon, the road drops suddenly into canyon and there below spreads Ghardaia, its citadel ascending to the tall tapering minaret, giant needle piercing skyward, universal symbol of Islam and the Moslem faith. The Moslem religion, a way of life and, as revealed in the Koran, a manual for families, communities and politicians, may seem, by contemporary standards of the 1970s, demanding, especially on time and, rightly or wrongly, many professed Moslems do not follow rigidly all the prayer stipulations, as in the same way many busy, modern Christians cut church and forego religious obligations. On the other hand, a great many Moslems do still follow the rigid conditions of their faith, especially outside the cities where European influence is less strong. Pre-school Moslem children attend the mosques to learn by heart long passages from the Koran from the *iman* or leader of the religious community. One hears them chanting as one passes by mosques both in the city and elsewhere, and there is no doubt at all that this infant influence has a powerful and long-lasting effect on Moslem minds.

The bus from Djelfa pulls up at the bus station. Now for the burning question:

"Is there a bus to Tamanrasset?"

"Of course."

"When does it leave Ghardaia?"

The clerk consults a calendar. "The next bus will leave in four days' time. It goes twice a month, on the first and the fifteenth day."

At this moment, a man wearing bus company uniform enters the office, his Negro face smiling broadly.

"Here is the driver of the Tamanrasset bus," says the ticket clerk. "He will tell you about the route." John and Anne shake hands with the driver. He is a man of about forty with a disarming twinkle and a firm, assured manner as he introduces himself by the name of Midane.

"Is the bus old or new?"

"Old. It is not good with a new bus. The *piste*, you understand, is not smooth and sometimes there is much sand."

"Do you get some troubles on the route?"

"Yes, yes, we do. One bus is now broken down in En Salah. I have sent to Algiers for a new transmission box and shall take it with me when we go on Friday."

"And how long does the journey to Tamanrasset take?"

"Four days on the route: first night *au natural* along the *piste,* second night in En Saleh, third night *au natural* and fourth nigh in Tamanrasset, *Insh' Allah,"* the driver smiles. "Come and see the bus," he invites. In the yard behind the bus office there it stands, four square and plum red. The front end looks like a normal heavy Berliet cab, which indeed it is. The crate at the back, converted from a ten ton truck, resembles a container belonging to the cargo fleet that trundles off the Channel and North Sea ferries. As buses go, it is truly an unique model.

"You made this in your workshops?"

"Of course."

The bonnet of the cab is propped wide open, yawning hugely; the radiator lies on the ground and various little piles of nuts and bolts are arranged on the coachwork. The bus is being prepared for its desert crossing in much the same way that the camel caravans must have made ready in the past. Ghardaia is an ancient desert port, once handling cargoes of slaves, salt, spices, drugs, ebony and cloth. The camel caravans would come and go, hundreds strong, often taking three or six months on their voyage. They were the ships of the desert and cities such as Ghardaia, Damascus, Baghdad, Mecca, Medina, to choose a few at random, were the desert ports; caravaneers being like sailors with the same reputation. And in these desert ports, lived the rich merchants epitomized in 'A Thousand and One Tales of the Arabian Nights', Arabs who were rich, cultured, suave and chivalrous: cosmopolitan too, for some possessed businesses and commercial interests in many a Middle Eastern city. Mohammed the Prophet came from such a merchant family, and Mohammed himself travelled with his uncle's caravans in his early years. Mohammed was appalled by the corruption, avarice and hypocrisy that were standard practice among the traders and merchants with whom he came into contact. Their behaviour preyed upon his mind and subsequently he had a vision, which revealed the new faith and his own role as the messenger of Allah. Wisely, Mohammed absorbed some of the pre-Islamic pagan worship into his new creed, including the Kaaba or meteoritic black stone of Mecca[21] as similarly Christianity, absorbed pre-Christian practices. Mohammed borrowed religious background and doctrine from both the Jews and the Christians with whom he had many contacts, but later in his Ministry, he turned harshly against both Judaism and Christianity.

In the 1970s, in the Sahara, the *camion* is replacing the camel: one lorry can carry as much as a whole caravan of camels (a camel's load is 300 – 600 lbs and it can only

---

[21] Mahmud, S.F., *The Story of Islam,* Oxford University Press, 1959

work part of the year, will lose condition unless turned out to graze for six months). Camels have been crossing the Sahara for at least twenty centuries but suddenly their day is done.

Meanwhile in the bus yard, scrutiny of the crate reveals some windows, one of which has no glass. Inside there are seats for about twenty, some oil and water drums, a metal tool chest, and a carpet of sand covering the floor. However, three of the four tyres on the vehicle look brand new and there is one new, one not-so- new and one ancient tyre as spares. The engine standing naked and exposed with its radiator down looks clean and tidy with no sand about, no undue oil or grease. Perhaps the bus would reach Tamanrasset. Above all, the driver has such a responsible manner and quiet dignity. Full of confidence, tickets are purchased: £6.50 each, single to Tamanrasset.

The prosperity of Ghardaia has previously been remarked. Now is the time to enjoy the desert city. Boys cycle to school on smart new bicycles, the market stalls are left unlocked at night and very often, produce remains all night in the open. The only thief is a young camel who helps itself to some vegetables while its master gossips. They visit the museum of folk art and watch a football match. Sipping mint tea in a café on the pavement, they are interested to see dozens of travellers and tourists from a variety of nations, people who are about to, or have just, crossed the Sahara. Their vehicles range from Volkswagen 'Beetles' undergoing works endurance tests to Bedford trucks carrying overlanders to South Africa.

Nevertheless, the day before the bus's expected departure, they decide to take an offered lift to El Golea, the next oasis 120 miles (200 kilometers) southward and await the bus there. They must seek out Midane and tell him about the change of plan. He agrees to keep seats since the full fare from Ghardaia to Tamanrasset has been paid.

"El Golea!" the driver smiles. "That's my home town where my wife and family live. Be opposite the market in

El Golea tomorrow, Friday, at noon. I will look out for you there. The bus will leave Ghardaia early tomorrow morning and reach El Golea before midday. *Au revoir*."

In the Muree Hills, 1937

Antiquing carpets, Kabul, Afghanistan, 1965

Dal Lake, Srinagar, Kashmir, 1965

Algiers: women wedding guests being marshalled by their
menfolk, 1971

Dawn in the Sahara, stranded in the desert, 1972

This is how they lived, Mowlem site houses at Kitale, 1978

Smoking Nile Perch in the giants rock garden, Mwanza,
Tanzania, 1988

Learning water rescue at Mwanza Public Library, Tanzania,
1988

Lake flies hatching, Lake Victoria, Tanzania, 1988

A Georgian bridge eastern Turkey, 1998. Photo Ann Powell

Chapter 11

Sahara

Reaching El Golea without difficulty, it is tempting to calculate that Tamanrasset should be reached on Monday next, six travelling days after leaving the Mediterranean seaboard. There is really no challenge to crossing the Sahara by bus. At El Golea nearly half the journey is done: there may even be time in Tamanrasset to take a tourist camel trek around the Hoggar Mountains.

El Golea is a garrison headquarters with extensive barracks and spacious cantonment built around the small palmerie and mud citadel of an ancient caravanserai at a time when the lawless tribesmen of the Sahara were being brought under French control towards the end of the nineteenth century. France recognised the value of the Sahara particularly for minerals and attempted to construct a trans-Saharan railway. It was a disastrous undertaking: among other mishaps, a survey team under Colonel Paul Flatters was ambushed and massacred by tribesmen. Eventually, the line petered out a few miles beyond Béchar. The French army in the Sahara was strengthened and a series of garrison towns and forts established as bases. Wisely, the French founded a corps of irregular men recruited locally, well-mounted on fast riding camels, as mobile and desert-wise as their adversaries. This desert corps was the brainchild of General Laperrine, of whom more later at Fort Laperrine, now called Tamanrasset.

Next morning, it does not take long to walk round the market and buy supplies of bread, cheese, tins of sardines, tomatoes and melons; also some tins of concentrated grapefruit juice to flavour the water in the five-gallon plastic jerry can which they filled in the hotel and laced with water-sterilising tablets. The date season has recently begun and Anne regards a mound of dried dates and, below the counter, a crate of fresh dates at double the price. "May I try one of those?" she points to the dried variety. "*Bien sûr*. Those are for the people," says the merchant as Anne munches a sweet but flavourless morsel. "But these are for the capitalists." He flashes gold teeth with an identifying grin and points to the fresh dates. The sample is delicious, manna from heaven.

About mid-morning, with luggage placed on the roadside opposite the market, John and Anne notice a handsome young Algerian who approaches politely. "Are you waiting for the Tamanrasset bus? Does it come today?" They assure him that today is indeed the day for the bus. Now the market empties like a bathtub as all the men go to the mosque for Friday prayers. At one o'clock in the afternoon, a man in baggy desert trousers bicycles past, pausing to inform them that the Tamanrasset bus always comes at half past four in the afternoon. At three o'clock, when even the flies are asleep, a car pulls up about two hundred yards further down the road in the direction of Tamanrasset. Out gets a boy of about fourteen with some luggage, boxes and bedding rolls. This is a good omen. Suddenly attention is caught and riveted by two girls, both blonde, in brilliant long cotton dresses of clashing orange and crimson, approaching with rucksacks.

"Are you going to Tamanrasset?" they enquire in English. "We're Swiss, touring Africa. We just missed the last bus and have been waiting twelve days in El Golea."

The Swiss girls have it on good authority that the bus stops in El Golea not at the market place, but at the post office in the cantonment town some 400 yards distant. They prefer to wait at the post office; John and Anne choose to remain opposite the market place.

At four o'clock, there comes a tall Algerian in blue *djeliba* and black *chechi*, a length of cloth wound round the face and head, to join the lad on the luggage. This suggests that the bus is indeed expected about half past four. But at half past four, a local on a bicycle skids to a halt beside the man and boy, speaks with them and, shouldering the luggage, they all set off quickly on foot in the direction of Tamanrasset. Presumably they have found a lorry willing to transport them, illegally and expensively but much more quickly than the bus: lorries normally expect to make Tamanrasseet in two days, time being money. At five o'clock, an exciting brum-brum is heard in the distance. A motor scooter comes into sight, its two-stroke engine no longer resembling the counterpoint of distant diesel music. At half-past five, the two Swiss girls reappear accompanied by a young couple, who prove to be honeymooners from Cologne. They, having motored as far as El Golea but prudently chosen there to leave their new car and take the bus to Tamanrasset, have heard a rumour that the bus is broken down and still in Ghardaia. The market is now filling with Algerians out for their evening constitutional, the strolling crowd well-dressed in white: any old colour for morning, spotless white for evening. Night comes swiftly in the desert and at half-past six, John and Anne decide to pack it in for the evening and go to the hotel, taking a room and ordering supper. The Swiss girls prefer to remain at the market; having waited twelve days for their bus they are taking no chances.

At supper in the hotel, the waiter comes over with the soup.

"A car has just arrived from Ghardaia. They say the bus left at five this evening but there is much new sand on the road so it may take longer to reach El Golea."

In the desert, news travels with the travellers. The telephone is there, the line is distinct and reliable but the sort of news now needed could not easily be obtained from the telephone.

"Maybe the bus will arrive at midnight. The driver will stay the night in El Golea and go on at five next morning. You stay the night in the hotel, get up early and catch the bus." The waiter is anxious to help. Perhaps! But what if the bus driver, already late, decides to press on through the night and make up lost time? The dilemma is put to the waiter but he merely shrugs his shoulders and goes off to fetch the meat dish. In the course of events, the bus driver does exactly as the waiter said he would. Desert logic is much more straightforward and less demanding than European reasoning.

They finish supper, linger over coffee, cancel the hotel room and carry the luggage back to the roadside by the market. There the driver had said he would meet them and there they would be waiting. They join the Swiss girls and the German honeymoon couple. Sleeping bags are pulled out in which to lie on the ground, heads on canvas grips. It is not as uncomfortable as it sounds. At half-past ten, the German gives a shout. All leap up encased in sleeping bags and jump as in a school sack race to the tarmac. The bus looms overhead.

"*Bon soir*," shouts Midane. "I have been looking for you at the hotel to say we rest here tonight. They told me at the garage you were in the hotel." The desert network is amazingly, astonishingly efficient. "Never mind, be ready at four o'clock in the morning. *Bonne nuit*." His eye is arrested by the other four in the background. "There are six of you? I have seats only for two." With that he swings the bus away towards the old citadel where his family will be awaiting him.

They sleep a little under the stars, which are huge with a diamond glitter. About four a.m., stiff and chilly, it is good to get up. At five o'clock with the first thread of dawn comes the bus and canvas grips are handed up to the luggage rack on the roof. Midane has good seats for John and Anne, but the place where their feet should go is occupied by two lads sitting on the metal tool trunk. Every inch of the bus is occupied by bodies, silent and formless at daybreak. The Swiss girls and German couple are absorbed into the interior like drops of water in a bucket and the bus moves off. It is fiendishly cold once the vehicle is travelling and as the light strengthens, it becomes apparent that everyone else in the bus is huddled under blankets for comfort. Theirs are stowed in the luggage on the roof. There is yet much to learn about desert travel. Chilly and hungry, a knob of bread and some cheese suggests itself as a good occupational therapy. Yesterday's bread is like marble so they nibble the cheese alone. At seven a.m. the bus stops. Out get the driver and cleaner. They are letting air out of the tyres to reduce pressure because this is the end of the tarmac and beginning of the *piste*. Beside the bus, construction is in progress on the next stage of the macadam road that will soon bisect the Sahara from north to south, the Trans-Sahara Highway.

The bus gets under way again, now a shuddering, jolting ship straining every nut and bolt as successive potholes hit the bow like waves in a storm. The coach is filled with swirling silt, darkening like London in a November fog and they realise the need for a *chechi*, that long length of cloth, to swathe round the head and face but have to make do with anorak hoods, dark glasses and some head-squares; resembling Scott of the Antarctic rather than Saharians.

At eight o'clock, the bus rounds a bluff of rock, passes close in under the walls of a massive mud-brick fort, and pulls up at a well: Fort Miribel, a scheduled stop. Everyone clambers out of the bus and the Algerian men go off among

191

the dried shrubs and tall grass of the *oued* to gather firewood. Two or three ladies with babies clutched close under their *haiks,* make a camp behind the broken walls of a ruined sheepfold. The Algerians brew tea while John and Anne eat a tomato each and wander over to the well where stand six date palms and a tanker truck loading water for a desert mineral research station 50 miles (80 kilometres) distant. Close by the old fort, a British Bedford truck and landrover is being loaded: the men wear nothing but beards, shorts and sandals, the women being curiously clad in knee boots and bikinis. The Algerian men cannot take their eyes off this third sex, the European woman in the desert.

Half an hour later, the bus is again under way. By now the day is fully switched on, the metal coachwork of the bus scorches: blankets and burnouses are discarded, adding further chaos to the contents of the bus. They sit gazing across the spaces, hypnotised by distance, mesmerised by the glare and passing kilometre stones, when all of a sudden, there is an alarming noise from the engine and the bus jars to a quivering stop. The driver and cleaner jump down and raise the bonnet, releasing a plume of steam. Finally John gets out since he is nearest the door, and soon others follow him.

It becomes apparent that the nuts and bolts holding it having worked loose, the radiator has moved back on to the fan and been minced up. Stranded on a stony wasteland, as flat as a blackboard and about the same colour, extending from horizon to horizon in all directions, the sun has still two hours to go before its zenith and already it is blast furnace hot with the area of shade diminishing further every five minutes. Gazing around, it is clear that the Algerians, wise folk, have already occupied the last available strip of shade and are reclining comfortably against the edge of the *piste*, their legs stretched out beneath the bus.

A mushroom of dust is approaching now across the desert. It races in and sinks to reveal the British Bedford lorry and landrover with their load of Overlanders.

Stopping, the leader gets down to assess the situation. A few minutes later he turns to John and says briefly: "I can take ten, women and children first." John selects the Algerian ladies and babies plus their men folk to guard them. They go off towards the south and the rest remain in the middle of an unending featureless plain. During the next two or three hours, two *camions* going southward halt to confer and each one takes one or two of the bus passengers. A northbound landrover stops and the cleaner is dispatched to El Golea to try and locate a new radiator: there may be a spare in El Golea or it may have to be sent down from Algiers. Now they are truly stuck in the Sahara in the middle of the Tademait Plateau and it appears they may be there for some time.

A passing *camion* donates an empty wooden box to the shipwreck, this being pulled apart for firewood to brew mint tea. Midane beckons everyone over and all sit for hours drinking sweet mint tea in tiny glasses, smoking and talking.

"Once I was twelve days in the desert broken down while my mate was away getting some spare parts," reminisces Midane. That sparks off a round of desert incidents and anecdotes for several of the passengers are themselves long distance lorry drivers now coming or going on leave. One in particular has a very commanding manner; 'Lofty', they call him, on account of his height. He owns enormous hands, feet like shovels, and gazelle-skin Saharian sandals like snow shoes. Perhaps he has French blood, a father from France in the days when the French army permitted its desert garrisons to take local girls as wives. The girls were spoken for and married in accordance with their own custom, bride price being paid, the ladies taking prestige and privilege according to the husband's rank. Eventually when the soldiers returned to France, the wives and children remained, enjoying social status in retrospect: Madame le Colonel and Madame le Capitaine still guard their rank with jealous care.

Some of the Algerian lads on the bus have been out searching for firewood and they return with armfuls of dried roots and prickly herbs. Evening comes and all pull in around the fire, which smells delicious with fragrant smoke. The sun goes down with a glittering green flash. Lofty organises the lads to make dinner and soon a savoury stew of beans is brewed, the bus company's supply of dry groceries and spices being ample for an army stranded for a month. Everyone contributes what he can to the cooking pot; an onion here, some tomatoes there, and the result is delicious. No matter if the bread is like rock, it soaks up the sauce all the better. More mint tea, and a comfortable camaraderie exists. In spite of the national variety around the fire, Algerian, French, German, Swiss, English, Japanese, all are united by the situation, all stranded in the Sahara.

They get out sleeping bags and choose a spot in front of the bus out of the wind.

"It is forbidden to sleep on the *piste*," warns one of the Algerians. But the *piste* is here five miles wide, so what? The *piste* seems softer than the surrounds, which look like a tarmac tennis court. Midane, having glanced around once everyone is settled, seems satisfied. They sleep very well, occasionally conscious of lorries passing, like ships at sea, far out in the desert.

Dawn of the third day is again chilly and the Algerians sit around the fire, hands tucked into the loose sleeves of their *djelibas*, statues on a level landscape. Mint tea is being brewed but bread is in short supply. Soon a passing lorry stops to dole out six long loaves and refill the two goatskins of water, which hang on the outside of the bus. The water is refreshingly cool but has a slightly bitter flavour rather like quinine; probably it is the curing agent, or else the resin applied to skins to improve their water-tightness.

"Midane, what can we do to help?" Anne and John are anxious to furnish support.

"Go down to the *oued*, three kilometres in that direction, and bring back firewood" his eyes, all that can be seen among the draped swathes of his *chechi*, gleam with amusement. What *oued*? The desert here is as flat as a billiard table. John and Anne tramp across the plateau, a dead land of small black pebbles quite resonant when struck, which prove to be flints rounded to pebble form. Where heat waves ripple over the ground like summer wind over ripe barley, there is a break in the ground but it is no more than the workings of a chalk borrow pit from which the *piste* is resurfaced from time to time. Here are sharp arrowhead flints and several pieces of fossil bone but no *oued*. They trudge onwards and on over the stony emptiness; small black pebbles operate as ball bearings restraining not expediting the feet. What began as a morning constitutional, an occupational therapy of sightseeing to an *oued*, is now a protracted trek, an infliction of duty. Midane has said: "Go to the *oued*," and such is their esteem for the gentleman that they are determined to achieve the prescribed task of fetching firewood.

Midane is right. How could he be wrong in this his own milieu? The plateau drops suddenly into a deep valley, along the bed of which grow some desert thorns and grasses with heavy fibrous roots. A gazelle gallops up the far bank, slim shy creature of the desert, which lives for months on no more water than it can obtain from the sparse grazing; adapted remnant of the abundant wildlife that once flourished in the Sahara. Six thousand and more years ago, the Sahara was a well-watered country comprising grassland, rivers, marsh and forest. Innumerable primitive rock carvings and paintings found in the Sahara, show lively scenes of hippo, giraffe, elephant, antelope, horses, oxen, deer and also men who lived and hunted on this fertile savannah. Over the centuries, climatic desiccation has cleared the land of man, beast and vegetation. All that remain are a few plants, insects and animals, which have adapted to lack of water; for instance insects, snakes and rodents, which live underground keeping alive by avoiding water loss. Desert people such as the Tuareg who habitually cover all but the eyes, likewise reduce the area of skin exposed to the evaporating air and heat.

Now, in 1972, an immense wasteland, the Sahara occupies one quarter of Africa, is as big in area as the United States of America, the word 'Sahara' implying nothingness. Rainfall is erratically sparse, from 1 − 5 inches (2.5 − 12 centimetres) a year. After months or years may come a storm bringing torrents of rain, which rush over the baked non-absorbent land, filling the dry *oueds* with floods of fierce destructive water. Some *oueds* have a signboard forbidding travellers to camp on the invitingly soft sandy floor. Isabelle Eberhardt, a European-born woman who at the end of the nineteenth century sought fulfilment in the Sahara, was drowned in such an *oued*. More fearful than the deluges are the sandstorms: twenty five years ago, a sandstorm in El Golea killed 1,500 goats and 2,000 sheep, and 150 years ago, a sandstorm overwhelmed a caravan of 2,000 men and 1,800 camels.

In the *oued,* John and Anne find a well with water some 20 − 30 feet down, but no rope or bucket: presumably one carries one's own rope and container. Pulling up tough roots and brittle prickly plants, to carry back in armfuls to the bus, they spot a lovely big onion lying in the middle of the *piste*, flotsam of the Sahara, and take it along for lunch: a *chorba*, the spicy Algerian soup. It is delicious. After lunch they enjoy language classes with the Algerians, learning a little Arabic and teaching some English. Three of the lads are on their way to school in En Saleh, the schools in El Golea being overfull.

Another evening passes, and so to bed on the third night. In the small hours all are awoken by a lorry jarring to a halt within yards of the sleeping forms. It is the rescue vehicle sent by the Mayor of En Saleh to bring in the bus passengers. Some go. Some stay, including Anne and John:

it is far too cold to make the journey lying on the metal floor of a ten-ton tipper.

Daybreak of the fourth day and a count shows only nine passengers left. Needless to say, the schoolboys remain. A southbound lorry stops to offload cigarettes, dates, sugar, tea and firewood sent down by the cleaner in El Golea. John and Anne go off again in search of firewood and fossils. Ahead they can see a mirage of the bus, four-square and plum red but suspended on air a few feet above the desert surface; looking back at reality it resembles a henhouse in an allotment garden but it is, temporarily, home. By now the wind is rising and the afternoon is spent inside the bus, which rocks with the rhythm of an express train.

Midane passes round photos of his two sons, teenagers with assured but modest bearing.

"I am paying extra money to have additional teaching after school hours. I want them to have a job in an office or else a profession such as mechanic: I don't want them to be long-distance drivers. It's not a good life, always away from home, always moving on." Midane lifts a fold of his *chechi* to sip tea. Someone nods in agreement and tosses in an opinion. "You are right, Midane, but our youngsters are now becoming full of importance and have no manners. They interrupt, make too much noise, ask for cigarettes."

"Yes, yes," agrees Midane, "It is the fault of the parents who do nothing when the boys are young, never punish them or teach them manners. My wife, now, is always after the boys with a stick."

These desert philosophers, shrewd, confident, devout men tempered by an unforgiving environment and distance, are witnessing their Sahara undergoing a metamorphosis. Investment in education, roads, mineral technology, agricultural research, inspires but disturbs them. "The young men are putting off their *djelibas* and their discipline; they are going away to the cities and many will never return," mourns Midane.

The wind is still strong and they remain inside the bus for supper, thankful to have a retreat from the howling desert. At eight o'clock a pale glow of white light is seen on the horizon. It extinguishes, emerges and fades again. Suddenly powerful headlights swing into view and relief rushes in; new radiator, mechanics, oxygen welding equipment and all. After celebrating with more mint tea, all go to bed content: soon the henhouse will be rolling again, a powerful machine, the equal of the giant lorries and articulated trucks that pound up and down the *piste* carrying vital supplies to the oases towns, to the miners and drillers searching for water, oil, gold, uranium, zinc and copper in the merciless nothingness that is the Sahara.

Dawn comes on the fifth day and the chief mechanic who had rolled up in his blanket beneath the relief bus for shelter from the wind, opens an eye. Suddenly he gives a startled shout.

All the U-bolts on one side of the axle of the relief bus are broken.

They press on regardless – the new radiator is installed, the broken back axle of the relief bus is bandaged up with a length of chain and welded to the spring. *Insh' Allah.* Each bus goes its own way and soon the Tamanrasset express is bounding across the plateau like the startled gazelle seen in the *oued*. The *piste,* reaching the end of the Tademait Plateau, drops over the edge, winding down the 1/5 *Hadjhadj* Pass, whose lower slopes are scattered with the corpses of incautious *camions*. So at last they reach the lowest level of the Sahara, a sea of silt finer than sand, and at five o'clock in the evening, come into En Saleh, palmerie and caravanserai among the dunes.

Choosing to sleep in the hotel that night, John and Anne are reminded, by sporadic brouhaha in the corridor and not infrequent knocks on the door, that every port has its prostitutes, En Saleh being no exception. On the sixth day the bus leaves the oasis in an apricot-coloured dawn suffusing a golden bowl. The route passes across a slight depression of marsh grass and powdered salt, the bottom of the Sahara, soon to stop at a micro-oasis. It is a one-family settlement, with twenty palms, three vegetable plots, some goats, one cow, two calves and a few chickens. Today is the first day of Ramadhan, so the Algerians do not take a ceremonial tassie of mint tea but merely exchange news. The driver receives a handful of tomatoes and an empty can for cooking oil: no doubt he will bring the filled can when he returns in a week's time.

The day becomes hotter, the jolting more penetrating; forty gallon drums and the metal tool trunk do an Irish jig, jump, jump, slither forward, jump, jump, jump, slither back; one's body is slowly tenderised in ten places at once. The landscape becomes more monumental and bears traces of former grace and beauty: there is a ghost of rolling parkland and sunlit savannah in the few stunted casuarina trees and acacia thorns that straggle along the floor of an *oued*. The bus stops to allow passengers to gather firewood in a once wooded valley where John and Anne lunch on half a melon each and a big helping of tepid water tasting of chlorine and warm plastic. Delicious! It is not a long halt as it is Ramadhan and only a few passengers are eating anyway.

"I much prefer the month of Ramadhan," observes Midane. "We are away early because the eating must be finished before daybreak, we waste no time on the route, we are there by noon and I can sleep until it is time to eat."

Thus, in the desert it is no great hardship to go without food for long hours, rather it is the habit of the desert people. Water, yes: it must require a degree of self-discipline to resist water if it is available. Perhaps the most disagreeable abstinence is having to forego cigarettes from daybreak until sunset. Although the Ramadhan fast may be a reminder of the desert's inclemency, it is also a month of prayer and meditation. Moreover, it serves as a laudable exercise in self-denial compared to the Christian Lenten fast; a time for those who are far removed from the harsh struggle for survival, to identify with those who have an habitual hunger.

How different is Ramadhan in the city of Algiers where the advent of gastronomic treats is heralded with tinsel and gaudy window-dressing in shops full of special Ramadhan fare; almonds, raisins, prunes, honey and mounds of sweets and sticky cakes. If the citizens of Algiers cannot eat so often many can, and often do, at least eat better. Families save for a year in order to be able to afford Ramadhan treats and choice foods. Indeed for some, the monthly fast of Ramadhan is more of a gastronomic marathon, its hardships being indigestion, fatigue and no cigarettes during the day. For the unemployed, Ramadhan must cause the greatest misery because, with the bistros and coffee bars shut until sunset what else is there to do all day? Nothing. The streets and shops are crowded with people buying frantically, spending money feverishly on everything from flowers to furniture. "It is a commercial rave-up, like Christmas in Britain," observes an intellectual and well-travelled Arab. Ultimately, fatigue is the real problem during Ramadhan and with fatigue comes a rise in accidents of every kind, particularly the industrial accidents and road accidents. Nevertheless, one cannot but admire those that do fast. In the West, self-denial has almost passed out of daily life: more emphatically, many people are already slaves to indulgence.

Meanwhile for the passengers of the Ghardaia to Tamanrasset bus, comes another session of nerve-shattering, body battering, until suddenly the bus turns off the *piste* into a sandy-floored cirque among towering rocks. Three times round a *marabout's* tomb for luck and then stop in front of the custodian's house. The custodian, a very holy man, his head shaved, is dressed all in white. His wife escorts the Algerian ladies and babies into the house where they will pass the night. Hours later comes the Sunset (Maghreb) call to prayer, given by an *imam* among the bus passengers travelling to visit his son who is a merchant on the Algerian-Niger border and lives in Agades on the Niger side. Prayers finished, a tray of dates is brought out and offered to the Algerians to break their fast before the evening meal. After supper, everyone pulls round the fire, drinking mint tea and smoking.

It is tranquil lying in a sleeping bag in the cirque, a natural nave whose vault is the night dome wheeling slowly overhead. In this spacious firmament on high the stars, near the Tropic of Cancer, are as brilliant as stage footlights. One cannot help but be touched by vertigo, infected by space, exhilarated by silence, inspired by serenity.

Here the Moslem concept of Islam demanding total submission to the Will of Allah, complete submergence of the ego, becomes comprehensible. Here in the Sahara, Charles de Foucauld, French aristocrat, one-time playboy, atheist, soldier and scientist found himself so drawn to God, that he put away his wealthy, snobbish dissipated past, took monastic vows, was ordained priest and built a hermitage near Tamanrasset.

Comes the seventh day since leaving Ghardaia and the bus is approaching Tamanrasset, passing among the weird mountains of the Hoggar. This immense region 300 miles long and 200 miles wide, a volcanic cataclysm of peaks rising to 10,000 feet (3,000 metres), is the heartland of the Tuareg tribe: every few miles, blue-robed tribesmen, black turbans swathed over all but their eyeballs, stop the bus for a lift to market.

The Tuareg[22] are one of the earliest tribes to live in the Sahara and be known in present times. According to its own legends, the tribe came from the north under the leadership of an ancestress, Tin Hinan by name, whose tomb is at Abalessa near Tamanrasset. Most probably the tribe is of Berber origin. More certainly the Tuareg were fair-skinned and matrilineal: the children trace descent through the mother's family or clan, and the women have a

[22] Krebsen, Marcus and de Cesco, Frederica, *Touareg Nomads du Sahara,* Hachette, 1971

much more important position in the family than do their Arab sisters. In the case of divorce, the wife keeps the children and retains her share of the joint property: livestock is inherited through the mother and Tuareg women are usually more literate than their menfolk for theirs is the task of educating the children. The women sing, compose and recite poetry in their own language, *Tamahek*, a language spoken still but rarely written; Father de Foucauld, the French hermit, compiled a French-Tamahek dictionary published in four volumes in 1952. Tuareg women are certainly not veiled. It is the men who wear the veil: *Kel Tagilmus* they call themselves in *Tamahek*, People of the Veil. From the age of about fifteen, every male wears a cloth of white, blue or black wound round the head, leaving only a narrow slit for the eyes, and with loose folds over the nose and mouth so that he can feed without displacing his turban. Even in his home, he never unveils. Without doubt the cloth helps to retain moisture on the skin, in the nose and around the mouth. Perhaps, too, the veil affords some protection against unwelcome recognition: a Tuareg is recognised by his stance and stride, by the charms he wears, and by the camels he rides or herds. Today it is estimated that there are about 300,000 Tuareg in tribes extending as far as the Niger River, living still in an ancient feudal society where castes of nobles, vassals, serfs and slaves are rigidly maintained. Nevertheless the old order is breaking slowly as progress comes to the Sahara by aeroplane and lorry in search of water, gas, oil and minerals. The Tuareg are leaving their camels and finding employment in the mining camps, meeting other Algerians, also Americans, Russians, Japanese and Europeans. On the bus are several Tuareg going to Tamanrasset on leave from mining and surveying companies to which they contribute the benefit of their desert wise ways.

A geologist working on an oil survey in the Sahara relates that about eight years ago, there were two factions living and working in his desert base camp: there were the nomad tribesmen on the one hand and on the other, the young city-bred Algerians who had come south in search of jobs. The two factions just tolerated each other until one day, a *harattin*, member of the slave class in the Tuareg society, turned up seeking employment. He was not so young, his fuzz of wiry hair was grizzled. He was small in size but he was extremely agile and quite the best worker of the lot, obeying orders quietly and working faster than anyone else. He had run away from his master; apparently he had had a foot injury and found herding camels too much for his damaged leg, so he ran away. The two labour factions in the camp quarrelled fiercely over this man.

"He is a runaway slave and must be sent back to his master," said the tribesmen.

"There are no slaves in Algeria. The man is free to work where he wants," said the young men from the north.

When the two factions came to blows over the Negro, he had to be sent back to camp headquarters and the survey team lost the benefit of his experience and industry.

John and Anne arrive in Tamanrasset about midday, body and soul all but severed by the motion of the bus and the all-pervading dust. John's hair has gone quite grey until in the hotel shower, the grey washes off as layers of dust stream away. Lunch of *hors d'oeuvres*, lamb chops with lentils, followed by chocolate mousse is better than dinner at the Dorchester in London and that night there is the exquisite pleasure of sleeping in a bed.

Tamanrasset seems an unprepossessing little town, not much more than a frontier post, and in recent years, a tourist centre for sight-seeing in the Hoggar. In Tamanrasset one can book a landrover tour or a camel trip for a day or a week to visit the mountains, or stay in the tiny hermitage where Père de Foucauld lived.

Apart from his personal fulfilment, de Foucauld achieved another goal. His path had crossed that of General Laperinne's and the two became not only firm friends but lifelong partners in their explicit desire to further France's interest in North Africa. General Laperrine had the task of bringing the Sahara under French control so that explorers and surveyors could travel in safety. He recognised in Père de Foucauld a useful ally, a French *marabout* whom the devout desert people admired for his asceticism and trusted for his genuine sympathy and interest. As Ibn Khaldûn relates in *The Muqaddimah* in 1377, 'When there is a prophet or saint among them (The Bedouin)... they become fully united.'[23] Charles de Foucauld held the hearts and minds of the tribes people and without doubt Laperrine made use of the priest's observations and opinions: their work was all for the glory of God and France. De Foucauld was murdered at his hermitage in December 1916 by a group of tribesmen from Tripolitania, but there is evidence to suggest that his murder was a far-ranging result of the 1914 – 1918 conflict in Europe: France's influence in the Sahara was regarded jealously by other powers and it was men like de Foucauld who held the desert dwellers' loyalty. Laperrine died ten years later in his beloved Sahara as a result of a flying accident, his ambition achieved: France held sovereignty over a sizeable and promising piece of the Sahara. Boundaries were drawn, lines on a map of the vast nothingness, and when in 1962 France conceded Algeria, the 1918 French boundaries remained intact though not undisputed.

Two years later the tarmac will reach Tamanrasset, the black ribbon that bisects the Sahara: named the Road of African Unity, it will be carrying emergency supplies of food and medicine from Algeria to the drought-stricken people of Niger and Mali.

And so, Sahara, fascinating, challenging, frustrating, inspiring wilderness, *au revoir*!

---

[23] Ibn Khaldûn, op cit, p. 120

Chapter 12

The Two-Year Tourists

A further eighteen years are spent working in Africa, this time in sub-Saharan Africa. First exposure to the Dark Continent is pure delight. John and Anne fly into Nairobi, Kenya in 1975 from a cold, damp, depressed November Britain. They sit on the beautiful, manicured lawns of the Fairview Hotel, sipping afternoon tea brought by cheerful and subtly dexterous waiters; watch scintillant humming birds hovering at the canna lilies, and parakeets darting about the battery of lofty eucalyptus trees surrounding the lawns. Heaven has suddenly manifested itself on earth.

Their destination is Dar es Salaam, that Haven of Peace established by Sultan Seyyid bin Said, the Lion of Oman in the nineteenth century. Irritated by his quarrelsome wives and courtiers in the palaces of Zanzibar, the Sultan sought refuge on the mainland, finding there an excellent deep water creek where lay dhows from all parts of the Indian Ocean.

Dar es Salaam, grown like Tospy, is now a sprawling, shabby city, still spreading like a cancer as rural immigrants from all over Tanzania's vast area rush in to seek their fortune. Periodically Government officers, on a fruitless exercise, round up the incomers, pile them into lorries to be returned to their home districts. Unkempt as any frontier settlement, Dar es Salaam has witnessed waves of colonisers and fortune finders; the Chinese, Arabs, Portuguese, Germans, British and Indians have been coming for centuries. Many go away again. A few stay to leave their mark: witness the German railway station, the name of 'Kariakoo' (Karrier Korps) market and the landmark Lutheran church; ancient Chinese porcelain built into medieval mausoleums and a brand new Chinese railway constructed to carry copper to the coast from landlocked Zambia; the British port, Government House and hospital; the Indian commercial heart of the city. Add a rash of slums and a sprinkle of elegant, well-gardened villas strung along the breezy coast road, such is Dar es Salaam.

Temporarily accommodated in the Oyster Bay Hotel, once a British tuberculosis sanatorium built on the bracing shore of the Indian Ocean, watching long, lazy rollers crash against the reef, John's thoughts turn seawards. Compelling tide regimes, daily transits of the wind and a shining moonlight path on the night swell, combine to focus his thoughts on his navy days in the Pacific Ocean. First port of call is Dar es Salaam Yacht Club (DYC) where, fortuitously, an 'Osprey' 17 foot dinghy is posted on the 'For Sale' notice board. Days later John and Anne have no house, no car, no baggage but they do have an old boat, *Green Dolphin* her name.

The Oyster Bay Hotel, suburban, secluded and serene, affords a first close encounter with Africa's wonderful wild life. In the small hours of the night Anne, half-awake, hears a rustle in the bedroom cupboard. A snake? A rat after the packet of biscuits kept on the top shelf or lizards hunting insects, which have found a way into the cupboard? Without doubt there is something: alive. Anne sits up. The cupboard door swings slightly and a dark shape launches from the top shelf and hurtles through the jasmine-scented velvet dark to land on the headboard of the bed. A bat; a vampire bat? No: vampire bats belong to folklore, not to Africa. This creature, 'flying' from the bed head to the door of the bathroom unwittingly left ajar, vanishes through the open window onto a flat roof above the reception rooms below. Leaping from bed to bathroom, Anne can see it standing upon its hind legs, its huge eyes like moonstones, chattering loudly, indignant at the interruption of its midnight feast. It is a bushbaby, a meerkat not unlike a mongoose, practically a pet of the hotel and in the habit of finishing food left on the trays served as room suppers for small children and then placed on the upstairs corridors for later removal.

Dar es Salaam is a city which never quite wakes up. At dawn in the suburbs, mile-long car queues await their turn at the bridge over the creek into the city, dropping off children at various schools before crawling on to their offices. In the city where much of the retail business is managed by those of Indian origin who live above or near their premises, people saunter to work intent on keeping a low profile lest energy be interpreted as economic success and arouse suspicions of secret wealth, which a socialist government would deem unequal, therefore unlawful. Much of the city starts work at 7 a.m. By noon, the day is almost done and by one o'clock in the afternoon the business population is hurrying away, picking up its school children as it goes home, to eat, sleep and then till the *shamba*, the garden or yard, where maize and vegetables can be grown to supplement the meagre food supplies in markets and shops. Suburban gardens resound with the cries of goats or the lowing of cows.

It is a soporific city. It is hot, humid and seriously in need of more air-conditioning, which is, however, an expensive luxury in a third world country where electricity is always erratic and often absent. Dar es Salaam is a backwater struggling in a country where all aspects of life are conditioned by the creed of a socialist government. The city is quiet, its low-key sounds broken only by mosque calls to prayer. Nightlife there is not; it would be a manifestation of craven indulgence and Tanzania has no

207

time to waste on self-gratification. In short, Dar es Salaam is still a haven of peace and quiet, its population immigrant, whose collective mind is in the provincial towns and villages of Tanzania's huge hinterland or in India, or in Europe, or in North America.

Julius Nyerere, Tanzania's first President, is a worthy, righteous, honest, industrious man committed to establishing the rights of poor Africans as well as rich ones. His socialism is a specifically African Socialism. He cherishes his vision of a corporate government of the people by their elected council of elders such as is found in much of rural sub-Saharan Africa. Nyerere, repudiating western customs and culture, sought local traditions to preserve elements which appear truly African. His intuitive thinking found a measure of idealistic appeal in communist and co-operative methods and he allowed himself to be influenced by China and the USSR. In 1975 the State of Tanzania dictates, for the benefit of the people of course, the practice of education, health, work and community purpose. If this means forced "villagisation" of scattered gatherers and hunters into distant settlements around a school, health centre and government office – it is called *ujamaa* villagisation – so be it. But it also means that much of the population become civil servants whether they like it or not. It spells death to initiative, enterprise and development.

Tanzania's African Socialism was applauded by the governments of the rich, developed, influential countries as a worthy experiment; the way for developing African countries to leap, as newborn nations, out of the stranglehold brought about by a succession of colonial masters, into the late twentieth century. Accordingly, the rich countries sent in aid, planners, advisors, experts, educators, monitors and bags of cash. The armies of well-equipped technocrats also brought in exposure to the perceived delights of first world civilisation: shoes, bicycles, cars, tractors, radios, telephones, televisions.

Suddenly the have-nots came face to face with the haves of this world and it was heady food for thought. Nyerere and his Government strove to retain African values of corporate responsibility by banning imports of luxury goods; the televisions, cars for private use, tractors; restrictions which did not apply to the aid workers of course.

It is no surprise that some of the expert advice is entirely inappropriate. Some bright sparks in the Australian High Commission sell the idea that horses rather than land-rovers would enable local Agricultural Extension Officers to get around their areas. Horses do not require expensive petrol, tricky mechanical maintenance or driver skills, say the Australians, just a bit of hay now and then... Some months later when 500 Australian brumbies are gift delivered to Tanzania from the people of Australia, the circumstances of the deal are exposed. No one had mentioned that the horses should be broken, supplied with saddles and bridles, inoculated against East Coast fever, sleeping sickness or other parasites. And who is going to teach the agricultural staff to ride? For years, these wild horses live, die of disease or are turned loose to a feral existence terrifying the villagers. A handful of horses will be sent to Arusha where a skilled lady rider of German origin breaks them in and successfully teaches local army officers to ride. Meanwhile, the agricultural officers shout for landrovers.

Having spent six weeks in the galleried and gardened environs of the delightful Oyster Bay Hotel, Anne and John move to their now-vacant company house. Not for them the well-appointed villas and mature gardens with their flame trees and fragrant frangipani, their mature mango trees and deep, deep shade in the Oyster Bay suburb. No: their house in the company compound is on a former sisal plantation on a coral peninsula in the Indian Ocean, where the air is distorted by heat shimmer and the only height offered is that of the glaring tin roofs of many maisonettes. Never mind! The houses are, relatively speaking, cockroach-ant-moth-rat-and-snake-free. Bedroom cupboards have a light bulb built in at floor level to combat mildew. And the bedrooms have air-conditioning. Not the living room though; that has a soaring ceiling and high ventilation. The kitchen remains as an oven all year round.

Once installed in their compound house, mercifully near to the Yacht Club, Anne and John settle down to the local shortages. "Will you have a cup of coffee? I am sorry there's no sugar but here is a spoonful of honey to stir in. It's very good." Soon the Government bans all driving of cars on a Sunday after 2 p.m. Cars to go to church in the morning, yes, but not for pleasure in the afternoons. Dar Yacht Club is within walking distance so there is no need for John to claim a permit for essential business travel on a Sunday afternoon as many do. And, indeed, DYC proves to be a network nerve centre in this city of Can't and Don't.

"Do you want a *kikapu*?" a long-established resident asks. "Baskets of farm produce are put on the bus at Iringa at daybreak every Thursday and Dar families take turns at collecting them from the bus station and delivering them round to members of the group. You get an invoice each week and at the end of the month, you pay a cheque into Mrs Ghaui's account. Two families in the group of eight have just left so there are spaces. I'll phone Mrs Ghaui if you want to join. But you have to take your turn at delivery about once every two months. The Iringa bus should be in Dar by 2 p.m. but of course it may be late, and you could find yourself to-ing and fro-ing from Dar bus station all afternoon."

The *kikapu*, basket in Kiswahili, is a weekly treasure chest; unpacking it, pure pleasure. From a farm in the fertile highlands of Iringa district some 250 miles west of Dar, comes this green, woven, grass basket full of fresh seasonal vegetables and fruits. At the heart of the goodies is a *bon bouche*; a jar of cape gooseberry jam or lemon curd, a tub of cottage cheese or a punnet of strawberries with a jar of clotted cream. Every Thursday, it is Christmas. The

Iringa bus may arrive late, often does, but the moist grass packing is well arranged so that produce remains fresh despite the overwhelming heat.

In the meantime, Robbie starts at the International School of Tanganyika, Marion having chosen to remain in Britain's boarding school system and come out for holidays. There are compensations, of course. A relatively high salary tax free, annual home leave, help with children's school fees and fares, are welcome privileges to compensate for lack of amenities and social outlet but it is not everyone's cup of tea.

One of the compensations is a house help paid by the company. Anne inherits Esta from her predecessors in the house. Esta, who is perhaps 20 years of age and living in the servants' quarter behind the kitchen with her daughter Martha aged about eight, does all the housework, the washing, by hand of course, the ironing and will oblige with peeling and cutting vegetables and cooking rice. She cannot read or write but Martha can since Martha goes to school, as Esta never did. Now installed, rent free, in a small room of her own in the capital city, Esta lives on her native peasant wit. Her current young man, a soldier, calling regularly, is pleasant, courteous and speaks good English. Alas, he is involved in an army truck's road accident and suffers a broken pelvis but once mobile again, resumes his visits. Anne offers Esta some strelitzia flowers, lovely orange and purple bird-of-paradise blooms to brighten her room as a welcome to her man after his ordeal. Examining the gift Esta asks, "Can you eat them?" "No Esta you cannot: they are just for looking at." She accepts the flowers but her interest is not engaged. More important, is preparation of the maize flour. Esta has a hollow stump of heavy wood and two thick bamboo poles. She and Martha each armed with a pole, pound maize grain rhythmically up and down – down and up, arms power behind the thump.

For John, the job holds many frustrations. The project, this time for John with Mowlem and Company Africa, is to design and construct a road, Pugu Road, 13 miles of dual-carriage highway linking Dar es Salaam to its airport and destined to be a challenge for the motorists of Tanzania. Design work has been done in Nairobi, the African company's headquarters. The agent, a highly experienced white Kenyan engineer, is accompanied by a handful of tried and trusted Kenyan foremen, but other engineers, recruited by Head Office in UK, are new to sub-Saharan Africa, as is John. The labour force; plant drivers, clerks and the pick-and-shovel brigade are Tanzanian, all of them motivated by their unions which enjoy the full backing of a young socialist government operating avidly in its capital city. The *Chama cha Mapinduzi* (CCM) (a coined phrase literally translated as the society for overturning) is in every corner of the project.

Not only the CCM but local customs too, are an enigma. There is a heap of brick-hard earth left after the bulldozers and hand-shovel teams have finished levelling a stretch of *piste*. About one metre high and two metres long, the hump stands proud above the newly graded surface.

"Why is that mound there?" asks John of his Kenyan foreman.

"That piece no good, *sahib*."

"Well we must get it removed, it can't stay there. You get the gang onto breaking it up and I will send the grader back here."

Half an hour later, John returns to find the lump still in place. Irritated, he shouts at the foreman: "Come on, man, get this heap removed."

"No one will touch it, *sahib*."

"Why not? Is it magic? Is it an ancient *sidi's* burial site or something?"

"No, *sahib*, no holy man buried here."

In frustration, John seizes a pickaxe and swings forcefully into the mound. In a second, his head is swathed in a cloud of enraged bees. Swatting wildly with his hat, John runs blindly to a blue wooden door some ten metres distant. Mercifully it is not locked and he bursts inside slamming out the onslaught of bees. Staring at him in silent alarm, is a posse of Moslem schoolgirls, fear written on their dark shining faces. Suddenly there is a gale of giggles and the girls, pushing John down onto a chair, start picking with delicate, precise fingers the stings out of his skin. He is lucky to find such effective help, suffers no allergic reaction and the girls have an exciting tale to tell about their heroic moments of high drama, no doubt adding salt to the story at every telling.

Two years pass, marking time in a routine of heat and dust, heat and mud. On the credit side, Anne acquires the art of hanging out horizontal from the gunwales of *Green Dolphin,* attached at mid torso by a hook in a harness to a tightrope wire from the top of the mast and Rob learns the art of sailing, capsizing, recovering upright and racing his Mirror dinghy. There are picnics to reef-fringed islands and visits to wildlife parks of course, but otherwise there is not much to show for two years, except the nearly completed Pugu Road. There are no regrets about leaving the land of negative sanctions.

Kenya calls: Kenya, the land of milk and honey. John, having cut his teeth on Pugu Road, is posted to the 30-mile construction of the Kitale-Kapenguria Road contract, Kit-Kap Road for short, in Western Kenya. Packing the heavy baggage for the company to transport, selling the dinghies, Anne, John and Rob pile into their well-loaded Ford Escort and drive 600 miles north.

'Accommodation provided', says the contract, and enclosed is a long list of hard furnishings they can expect. Ensconced in a small bungalow of the Kitale Club, they tramp around the town trying to elude outrageous rents and unsympathetic landlords. "We can't live there. The landlord let slip he is intending to fell all the trees, divide up the garden and build another bungalow. Two years' of builders' rubble and noise is not on."

There is another house set in two acres of garden. It is magnificent: the master bedroom is as big as a tennis court and one could play squash in the dressing room. The curtain yardage would run into 5 figures. The only snag is someone else gets it the day before they decide to make an offer. "Thank heavens for small mercies," breathes John.

Then again there is a superb house: the verandah views of distant blue mountains would be food for the soul. Alas, the upstairs loo discharges up the outlet of the downstairs shower and the kitchen sink waste pipe is altogether missing. "And no one told us that the house next door is a police pistol range. Their popping, morning, noon and night, is driving us bonkers," say the subsequent tenants.

They eventually discover the perfect house: that is, it would be after painters have been put in. True, the previous occupant has recently kept two horses in the garden and there is not a flower or shrub left, but the fertility of the vegetable patch would more than compensate for the rough grazing round the verandah. But by then the company has decided to build temporary wooden houses in a farmer's field on the outskirts of Kitale. The obliging farmer, Ezekiel Okul, plants ten acres of Van Gogh sunflowers in front and the view beyond is 40 miles long and 20 miles deep. Their new home on stilts judders as John strides down the corridor: when a storm is raging their pillows are only a thin skin of plywood away from the violent, wet world outside. But it has a happy air of gay abandon; a long, long caravan holiday.

What to do with Rob, now ten years old? The English-medium prep school in Kitale having closed some years before, there remain a few more distant English schools and they select one called Pembroke House at Gilgil in the Rift Valley, some 250 miles from Kitale and about 80 miles from Nairobi, which has a large intake of boarders. Anne suspects that Rob does not really enjoy it and for her, it means driving a round trip of 500 miles at the beginning and end of term, but there is no alternative.

Kitale at 7,500 feet (2,500 metres), sits comfortably on the foot of Mount Elgon, an extinct volcano of enormous size now worn down to an agreeably symmetrical stub of 14,000 feet (4,500 metres). On the other side of the mountain lies Uganda, whence smugglers trudge across the windswept shoulders of stunted grasses studded with giant groundsel and lobelia standing 20-30 feet (7-10 metres) tall carrying massive, bulging bags of coffee beans to profitable Kenyan markets. Resident in the Kitale Club is a magistrate, a retired barrister, straight from Manchester UK on a Commonwealth two-year contract with the Kenyan Government. "These poor people appear before me almost weekly. What can I do? I can't fine them; they haven't got any money. I haven't the heart to lock them up because they are women with young children to feed. So I caution them, give them back their coffee and warn them not to leave any tell-tale trail of beans on the ground." Never mind; the compassionate magistrate makes a credible Father Christmas at the Kitale Club Christmas revels.

Remote Kitale may be from the fleshpots of Nairobi, but it boasts a rugger pitch, a polo ground, all-weather tennis courts, a challenging 18-hole golf course, a film club night and traditional hospitality to any number of people. Tournaments and Open Matches are well attended by Africans, Asians, Europeans, both native and expatriate alike.

Living at the Kitale Club is the resident doyen, 'Sammy' Weller. Now a cheerful 90 years of age, Sammy is a scrabble addict. "Do come, please; come over to my bungalow for an afternoon's scrabble," he pleads. Sammy arrived in British East Africa in 1910 to visit an uncle. "I was still here when war broke out so in 1915 I joined the East Africa Mounted Rifles and went to war." Sammy pauses, rheumy eyes focussing on a brigade of local farmers and settlers on their hunters and polo ponies, in bush jackets and shouldering their sporting guns. "And when my horse died of East Coast fever, I became an infantryman in the King's African Rifles (KAR). I marched all round German East (Africa), saw a lot of the country, got malaria three times." Sammy's mobile eyebrows shoot up through wrinkled brow towards balding scalp as gnarled fingers lay a cunning couple of tiles giving him three new words and a single score of 67.

"We never did catch the enemy; von Lettow was a wily old fox." Antique hands marbled pinko-grey and brown, pour tea from a tea tray delivered by a club steward. "Can't say we got on well with the regular army blokes sent from Britain or South Africa. They thought we were a lazy lot; we thought they were swollen-headed, worse than boarding school with their rules and regulations. But we knew the bush and they didn't."

Here is history served on a plate of biscuits with a cup of tea. When war broke out in Europe in 1914, no one in East Africa gave it a second thought. Dr Heinrick Schnee, Governor of German East, a keen liberal, was anxious to improve the native largely through the building of hundreds of primary, secondary and vocational schools. He did not want to go to war; a sentiment shared by Sir Henry Belfield, Governor of British East: both these gentlemen were to remain at loggerheads with their respective generals. Not so Colonel Paul von Lettow Vorbeck, a Prussian soldier with experience in China, in South West Africa and against fierce tribal opposition in German East. In 1914 he had command of the *Schutztruppe* with some 260 Germans and 2,500 native soldiers or *askaris* as they were known, the defence force of the German Protectorate. Immediately, he determined to disrupt the Allied European war effort, locking up as many of the allied forces as he possibly could by engaging them relentlessly in East Africa. His *Schutztruppe* were astonishingly successful. Masters of surprise, terrifyingly mobile in delivering a cobra strike, wizards at the disappearing trick, von Lettow's force fought a guerrilla war of the first order.[24]

If it had not been for three South Africans (two of whom had been against the British in the Boer War), Frederick Courtenay Selous, Pieter Pretorius both of them renowned big game hunters, and General Jan Christiaan Smuts who was primarily a politician, the end result of the East Africa campaign might have been a different story. As it was, Paul von Lettow Vorbeck, now a General, managed to lead the allied forces consisting of the KAR and troops from Britain, India, South Africa, Nigeria, Gold Coast, Nyasaland (now Malawi), Southern Rhodesia (now Zimbabwe), Northern Rhodesia (now Zambia) and the (Belgian) Congo, a merry dance between 1915 and 1918 all round German East into Portuguese East (now Mozambique) back into German East, out again through Nyasaland and into Northern Rhodesia. Here, an allied motorcyclist happened to be intercepted by the *Schutztruppe*. The messenger carried the draft of a ceasefire order announcing that an Armistice in Europe had been signed.[25] At this point, von Lettow had 155 Europeans and just over a thousand native *askaris*. The allied force had 2,500 European officers and NCOs and 30,500 native troops and carrier corps.

"And when the war was over," reminisces Sammy Weller, "I put in for some land under the soldier-settler Scheme. The piece I got was between Kitale and Kisumu. We worked hard and played hard; rugger, tennis, polo, golf. It was not a bad life. Worst bit I think was getting my grand piano from the railhead at Kisumu to my home on an ox-wagon. When a wheel fell apart, I had to ride 40 miles to

---

[24] Sibley, J.R., *Tanganyikan Guerrilla: East African Campaign 1914-18*, Pan/Ballantine 1973, ISBN 0 345 090813

[25] Miller, Charles, *Battle for the Bundu. The First World War in East Africa.* Macdonald and Co, 1974; Westland Sundries Ltd, Nairobi, 1976

fetch a wheelwright. Took a fortnight, that journey with the piano did."

In the neighbourhood of Kitale remain a very few white farmers, or else residents in retirement from the bygone Colonial Service. In general they are intensely individual, private persons who have chosen, despite the changed circumstances of Independence, to stay on in a remote but well-loved environment. Paraffin lamps; *piste* roads offering ruinous ruts and choking clouds of dust in the dry months and dire, deep mud in the wet season; families never driving without some packets of cigarettes, a box of biscuits and a bag of oranges in the boot of their car to distribute in gratitude to brigades of pushers who wait by the mud baths en route; do-it-yourself challenges on a daily basis, these are the normal circumstances of their life.

"Look at this chair," says Sep Meyer lifting the cushioned seat to reveal a stout leather webbing beneath. "I made it; leather from our own cows. I made all our beds too."

Escorting his visitors to the dairy, he describes his biogas installation. "I hose down the cowshed after milking and all the muck gets carried out to the digester where gas is released to that gas tank you see over there. That gives me enough fuel to run the sterilizer. And the slurry runs out the bottom into the vegetable garden below." He smiles a Hallowe'en lantern's smile.

"And this," he opens a wooden door into a large room, with walls of charcoal over one foot (half a metre) thick between wire mesh, and a ceiling of dense thatch sitting well above the charcoal walls "Is where I keep the milk churns waiting for the creamery pick-up truck. Spray the charcoal with water and the inside temperature will be 14° below the outside." Sep examines the astonished faces of his guests with delight.

These good people are more than kind to the 'two-year technical tourists', as those on contract to carry out specialist work that Kenyans are not yet qualified to do, are known by the locals. Anne's mother Sheila, in Kitale for a visit, is invited by Sep and his wife Helen to stay for a few days while mother does paintings of rare tree orchids in flower. Sheila, vividly reminded in Kenya of the old India she had known in her youth, is delighted but anxious. "Oh dear!" exclaims Sheila, recalling the antique etiquette of the Raj, "I've got nothing suitable to wear for dinner." The genial farmer roars with laughter. "Don't worry," grins Helen, "It is pyjamas and dressing-gowns here."

Another welcoming couple, Tim and Jane Barnley, are fascinated to learn that the Mowlem Company housing is being built on Ezekiel Okul's farm.

"That used to be Tim's mother's farm," says Jane. A sudden thought occurs to her.

"Do you want a cook?" When Anne nods vigorously, Jane continues, "We will get in touch with Owino, he knows that farm like the back of his hand. He cooked for Tim's mother for years. Just tell him at lunch time that there will be twenty in for supper that evening and he'll cope."

What a treasure! Soon Owino is happily installed in a 'quarter' of the housing block for domestic staff, well positioned of course by virtue of his local standing. Liaison officer between John Mowlem staff and the farm workers, acknowledged senior elder of the African communities living in company housing on the farm, trouble shooter of all *shauris* (problems occurring), and there are many, Owino cuts the nuisance in the bud, smoothes ruffled tempers, smiling serenely as he does so, for Owino has a secret weapon. His brother is a witchdoctor and everyone knows it.

The Barnley family lead unique picnics on public holidays, penetrating deep into the ridge-and-ravine maze of the Cherangani Mountains, armed with basketfuls of homebake and tropical fruits and dozens of small dogs. Tim, a walking encyclopaedia of wildlife, plant life, local tribal customs and lore, never fails to excite the interest of the two-year tourist, offering a rare, cameo glimpse of the old Kenya where early settlers could indulge enthusiasms, accept idiosyncrasies and enjoy the challenges of the big country.

One significant event occurs while Anne and John are in Kenya. In 1978, Jomo Kenyatta, the President, switches off his heart pacemaker in order to secure a peaceful political succession. There have been the rumblings of an incipient power struggle with increasing threats of violence and Kenyatta, regarded by many humble Kenyans as the father of the nation, wishes to ensure that the man of his choice, Daniel arap Moi, inherits the symbolic, ceremonial fly whisk. Mr Moi, a member of one of the Kalenjin tribes, rather than the dominant but divided Kikuyu tribes or the alert, assertive Luo tribes, is little known and possibly regarded as an interim lightweight: time will tell.

"How brave to turn off one's pacemaker," exclaims a middle-aged lady who has had one confrontation with cancer and must have glanced nervously at death.

But no. Africans do not fear death as many Europeans or North Americans do. Death is merely a change of state from the seen to the unseen: moreover Africans believe that some spiritual essence of the deceased is able to detach and enter infants about to be born. Many a Kikuyu mother will now name her baby for the late president, at the least giving her infant a sporting chance of being host to the spiritual eminence of the great man.

Both Moslem and Christian Africans have a fundamental desire to be buried in their family land-holding since the African family consists of the living, the dead and those yet unborn, a scattered family being deemed to lose its corporate strength. From the scientists' pens comes gene news that picks up the African wavelength about the corporate family, endorsing the view that an individual lives on in his/her offspring; 23/46 genes from each parent, random of course. Ancestor veneration is not so obsolete, but then truth is often stranger than fiction.

Meanwhile, in 1979, the Kenyan exposure is closing and it is back to Tanzania, John having decided to leave the contracting engineers, John Mowlem and Company and join the consulting engineers, Sir Alexander Gibb and Partners. After an interview in Nairobi with the senior partners of the Africa branch of Gibb, John and Anne weigh up the pros and cons. Engineering in Kenya has little to offer the expatriate: Kenyan engineers are increasingly able to fill the available posts. The job on offer in Tanzania is not in the hidebound capital city, Dar es Salaam, but upcountry in Morogoro, some 125 miles to the west and John's remit includes, liaison with the Ministries, Treasury and the funding agency, in this case the World Bank, all of them in Dar so that access to the sea will be available from time to time. On the credit side, they do know about the difficulties and shortages common to expatriates who are not in diplomatic missions and they have a coterie of friends with access to some of the food essentials. On the debit side, the border between Kenya and Tanzania is now closed, the two countries having abandoned their East African community in a fit of mutual recrimination. On the other hand, Sir Alexander Gibb and Partners Africa have their own small plane, so business communication will not be confined to the telephone and increasingly difficult postal service between these two feuding nations. What about Rob at a boarding school in Kenya? Well, there are five boys in Pembroke House from homes in Dar es Salaam who somehow manage to be transmitted through the closed border at beginnings and ends of term. Rob will join them.

Back in Dar in a rather seedy coast hotel, first port of call is, of course, Dar Yacht Club where, fortuitously, a 26-foot keel boat is for sale. It could be regarded as an expensive luxury for a two-year contract, its purchase requiring financial juggling, but a small cabin cruiser on the moorings can become a seaside cottage for a landlocked family in Morogoro. A considered decision to purchase *Ragtime* is made and with it comes the services, and salary, of a watchman named Osmani to occupy the cockpit during the night hours lest passing fishermen help themselves to fittings and equipment. A dozen or more boats of the club moorings have night watchmen and the club's dinghy is accustomed to ferrying them out at dusk and in at daybreak.

For some three months, John is occupied with rehabilitating Sir Alexander Gibb's Dar office. Having been left in the care of a Tanzanian of Indian origin some years previously, it has had no modernisation of premises, no new equipment, nothing. Hot, dusty, infested with cockroaches and silverfish, bookcases and filing cabinets filled to overflowing with antique documents and files, reports and invoices, it shouts neglect and decay. Situated on the second floor of a 1930s building, its approach is via the first floor where shapeless bundles of women and babies cocooned in black *bui-buis* (Kiswahili for spider's web) await a doctor's surgery although Dr Mtwali, highly respected skilful practitioner whose patients include native and expatriate alike, will not be in for another hour. On the ground floor of the building, euphemistically called Kelvin House, is a car and motorcycle spare parts sales room. It is empty of stock. At least its windows remain intact.

John's Project in Morogoro is Mindu Dam designed by Gibb to create a reservoir for the supply of both domestic and industrial water which will be needed for new industries coming to Morogoro such as leather and textiles, enterprises which demand quantities of water. The construction contract has been won by a Brazilian company. In addition, a treatment works and large gravity feed tank will be constructed for the domestic water supply, this separate contract being won by a Zambian construction company.

John has a foreboding about the Brazilian company who have nearly completed a job in Morogoro erecting railway engine sheds, Tanzania having lost access to the East Africa Railways and Harbours infrastructure in Kenya when the East African Community ruptured in 1977. The

Brazilians are rumoured to have offered MAJI, Tanzania's Ministry of Water, ten percent off the price of building the dam in order to get the contract. Meanwhile the Brazilians, already having a presence in Morogoro, are snapping up all available rentable properties there.

When John and Anne get to Morogoro some months later, they are obliged to stay at the Railway Hotel while searching for a villa to rent. The Railway Hotel, odorous of ancient grime but bearable for a week, renders up a bonus. A bush telegraph having buzzed around the town, the hotel manager presents to the *memsahib* a caller, Mustafa his name.

"How are you, *memsahib*?" he opens, the standard procedure for establishing a rapport.

"I am well, thank you."

"And how is your home?"

"It is well."

"Your children how are they?"

"Well, thank you."

"And what is the recent news?"

"Good news." This reply, even if one is sick or sacked, is the key to whether the rapport has been clinched: only a positive reply ensures further communication. Once the recommended questions and statutory responses of any Kiswahili introduction in Tanzania have been satisfactorily completed, the gentleman states his business.

"*Memsahib*, you are looking for cook. I am very good cook. Many years working on trains. I cook rosbif, pudden, yokshir, custad, bred, everything." The black tassel on his red fez bobs up and down as he nods to confirm his credentials. And with some misgivings about his age, it is agreed that he will start three months' trial as soon as they get a house, coming in twice daily, in the morning at 6 am and in the evening too.

A rentable house is found, overlarge perhaps but it will do for the next three months whilst the Brazilians are building six engineers' houses on a compound on a former sisal estate called Mafiga, houses which will eventually be turned over to MAJI maintenance engineers. Mustafa comes daily and produces great quantities of plain food. Shortages are less severe than they were in Dar and Anne, accompanying Mustafa to market, makes friends with various vendors. After some weeks, another Gibb engineer arriving in Morogoro with his wife and Labrador dog in the company plane from Nairobi, all move into the Gibb house, and Anne is thankful to have Mustafa's help. Mercifully, Mustafa finds a lad called Steven to help him with the heavy work of cleaning and hand washing. And yet another couple, this time recruited straight from Britain, arrive and move in to Gibb house since the engineers' houses are still under construction: a full house indeed. Still to come are Robert from school in Kenya and Marion from school in Britain. Fortunately, the engineers' houses are within days of being ready for occupation.

John and Anne take their turn at fetching schoolboys from the Kenya/Tanzania border at Namanga near Arusha, some 300 miles from Morogoro and 350 miles from Dar. On this occasion, there are only four boys to collect ranging in age from 7 to 10 years, since a couple of brothers are meeting their parents in Nairobi and flying to Europe for the summer. They drive up to a private Lodge near Arusha on the Saturday, stay there overnight and continue to the border next morning. Parking at the Tanzanian barrier and walking ¼ mile to the Kenyan side, they await the arrival of the Gibb car carrying its load of lads from Gilgil some 150 miles distant. They pray that the car will not be late, that there is no long queue of bus traffic going through immigration and customs since it is Sunday and one must be back to the Lodge near Arusha before the curfew at 2 p.m. They greet the arriving boys and quickly check through their miscellany of hand luggage, rucksacks, shoulder bags, fishing rods, comics, picnic pokes, water bottles, a plastic bag of stream water containing three tiddlers, packets of bubblegum, a small sack of marbles and proceed to immigration and on to customs. Generally the officials are well disposed to children but difficulties may occur when crowds of bus passengers fill the offices. The boys are masters at inserting themselves and wriggling forwards to the desk, watching for a moment to present their passports for stamping, and manoeuvring out again. Since their patience is none too great, they can be relied upon to draw the attention of the officials in immigration and customs: a fiddling with the rubber stamps and ink pads on the desk, a shuffling of the declaration forms, a relocation of pencils and pens or a ribbon of bubblegum across them or, at worst, fumble with the ties around the plastic bag of stream water containing three tiddlers now deposited on the immigration desk. Then Anne and John walk them across the no-man's land, urging them to hurry with their essential purchases of gum and goodies from the well-supplied Kenyan kiosks, before they enter the land of nothing, and repeat the pantomime of immigration and customs at the Tanzanian border.

At the Lodge at last, too late for restaurant lunch, they all eat a picnic Anne has bought in Arusha market and spend the afternoon in the small, game park surrounding the Lodge. At dinner, first into the restaurant ravenously hungry, they are delighted to see the platter of pasta placed on their table while the waiter disappears to fetch the casserole from the kitchen. By the time the waiter returns, Anne has distributed the entire platter among their six plates and is embarrassed to learn that it was intended for all the Lodge guests. Luckily, food supplies are more obtainable in Arusha area so near the Kenyan border and more pasta can be hastily prepared for the other four guests in the Lodge.

So back to Dar es Salaam: the road, in places, is appalling with deep potholes able to strip a hubcap or disfigure a wheel rim. Stretches stripped of tarmac, gravelled and rarely graded, have deep ruts worn by buses which pound along in a spray of flying stones, and where a saloon car must drive with one wheel down a rut and one wheel up the ridge or risk being caught and held on its chassis. Nevertheless, Dar is reached, the boys delivered to their homes and Marion is met off the London plane before arriving back in Morogoro.

In the Gibb house in Morogoro, the removal into the barely completed engineers' houses at Mafiga is discussed in detail. John and Anne and family will move first. But what about Mustafa? Will he want to walk over a mile out to the new compound twice a day or even once a day? It is probable that some site staff will have to be ferried to and fro from the town and no doubt Mustafa could join them. Anne is anxious to retain Mustafa who is a sympathetic friend, and wields a good iron even if he is a mediocre cook.

"Mustafa, will you come to Mafiga with us? We can arrange a lift on the staff bus from town and back in the afternoon for you until the staff accommodation is ready, and then you can have the first quarter."

"No, *memsahib*, I not coming to Mafiga. Too old for work now, I go back to my home and sit in sun." This is disastrous news. "I have young friend who is good cook. Ismai Ali his name. I bring him to you tomorrow." Mustafa nods knowingly and Anne must be content.

Ismai Ali, only marginally younger than Mustafa and anxious to prove his candidature, rolls up his sleeve to display strings of sinewy muscles. "Strong, you see," his grin is disarming. "I keep Steven in order," Ismai Ali suddenly leaps sideways with a stick-waving mime of discipline. "Steven my boy. He do what I say." A wide smile of high glee enhances his sprightliness, belying his grizzled hair and lean, stooped stance. Sad at losing Mustafa, Anne agrees to accept the change. Ismai Ali, 'Smiley' as he soon comes to be known by all the Gibb staff, will commute daily in the staff bus and will move into the staff block at Mafiga as soon as a quarter is ready. And weeks later it is not to be denied that it is Smiley who really wanted the job, putting in Mustafa to job-warm until he, Smiley, could serve three months' notice on a previous employer.

Chapter 13

The Land of Hamna

An inventory of the amenities of expatriate life in Morogoro is by no means slender. It is a university town accommodating the agricultural, forestry and veterinary faculties of Dar es Salaam University, wherein a cosmopolitan campus population enjoys shady, tree-lined, flowering suburbs on the lower flank of the Uluguru Mountains. The campus contains a viable English-medium primary school, but to age eleven only. In addition to a large Dutch Aid compound for the families of groundwater specialists, with tennis courts, swimming pool and *banda* club/bar facilities, there are a number of other smaller enterprises. These include some Swiss-managed sisal estates, a British tobacco company holding, an Italian restaurant and some engineers building a leather-dyeing factory, an Israeli presence about to build a New Morogoro Hotel and, of course, a sprinkling of missionaries of all stripes and creeds. The magnificent Uluguru Mountains offer delightful scenic walks, with some trout fishing for aficionados of the dry fly and a mountain rest house, known as Morningside, for overnight lodging. For the sporting gun enthusiast there are opportunities to participate in deer culling and vermin control to protect villagers' crops from the ravages of warthog and even elephant. Soon, when Mafiga gets going with tennis court, swimming pool and club *banda,* which is a palm-thatched awning by the pool, Morogoro promises to be a stimulating experience for a couple of years. On the debit side must be entered: no television, since the Government has declared it to be a corrupting influence, no telephones in the Gibb engineers' residences, no city shops, no cinema and no supermarket.

While the Gibb staff drafted to the Mindu Dam contract from Kenya are seriously unimpressed with the posting, those straight from Britain are more willing to accept the challenge of making a home and creating a garden. The University Forestry Department promises unlimited hedgerow seedlings to divide the compound, fast-growing trees, fruit tree grafts, banana pups and various flowering shrubs. A hot climate barely south of the equator and adequate water for irrigation should do the rest. Papaya seeds, sour sop pips and avocado stones planted, and having germinated, grow like weeds, a profusion of papaya fruit being picked within the year.

Besides the hard work of establishing home and garden, there is the community; a DIY community of course. Wives, including Anne, may be drafted in as teachers in the campus primary school. Play-reading, and indeed the production of a bloodthirsty Victorian melodrama, choir practices and concerts, quiz nights and competitions, besides tennis matches, swimming regattas, barbeques and various club feasts at any excuse for a party, exercise time and ingenuity to their limits; everything must be homemade. Basic foods and necessities are all available in Morogoro but nothing that is processed such as jams, canned fruits and vegetables, condiments and preserves. Forget about cheese, exclude all chocolate from the gnosis. But there is, in 1979, locally canned corned beef and local instant coffee, that is until the coffee factory in Western Tanzania blows up due to an electrical fault.

John begins to yearn for a bacon and egg breakfast but bacon is *hamna.* Kiswahili is specific in its negatives. *Hapana* means no, it is not; *hakuna* signifies there isn't any hereabouts, while *hamna* means most emphatically there is nothing, anywhere. As Smiley serves up his breakfast egg in one form or another, John thinks aloud to the cook.

"*Sahib* want bacon," Smiley reports to Anne. "We make bacon. Get pig and make smoke."

"How, Smiley? Do you know how to make bacon?"

Smiley turns, cuts some bread, toasts it in the grill, a mechanical task easily done while a memory search takes place.

"Yes, *memsahib*, I know. I do this with *memsahib* long time ago." Smiley, who is about 65 years old now, has in the past, worked in domestic service. And in the 1920s and 1930s, settlers to the then British Protectorate of Tanganyika brought rural skills garnered from their mothers and grandmothers; skills that are now curiosity exhibits in the Museum of Rural Life at Reading University.

Getting a pig is not a problem. The lady who supplies fresh eggs to a number of families, also rears pigs. Yes, Mrs Mshendwa has a suitable pig ready for slaughter. The main constraint is lack of freezer space, Anne, having the use of half a freezer since Gibb only managed to obtain three freezers for six households, so a university campus family is found to take half of the pig. The next hurdle is obtaining saltpetre to cure the fresh meat, and here university staff with access to chemicals, very kindly help out. In future, Anne will have to bring it out from the UK in her air luggage. In the Zambian company that is constructing the treatment works at Mindu Dam, is found a friendly mechanic who supplies a 40-gallon oil drum complete with lid, and tailors it to Smiley's specification. Two steel bars are welded across the top of the interior, rails on which to hang the meat, and near the bottom, a small hole is cut in the side of the drum and about ½ metre of steel pipe is welded into the opening. The drum is then set about 30 cms into the ground, its steel pipe leading into a metre-long trench covered with corrugated iron, *mbati*, and mud well tamped down. Firewood can be bought in Morogoro market.

All is now set for action. Into a saltpetre brine bath go the sidepieces of the pig: two days' immersion then turn for one more day. Drain meat and pierce with string for hanging on rails in drum. At dawn, light a fire at the outer end of the trench and sprinkle with water when it burns well. The lid of the drum is the smoke control: lift more or lift less to draw smoke through drum continuing for 12 or 14 hours. This is Steven's job though Smiley and Anne check on his efficiency at intervals. The result, eventually, is delicious, better than wafer-thin supermarket bacon. Soon Smiley and Anne are obtaining impala, reedbuck and warthog for smoking, the ultimate accolade being an invitation to smoke a 33 lb sailfish (like salmon) caught by Dar friends and commissioned for their wedding feast.

It is perhaps the boat, *Ragtime*, at Dar Yacht Club, which provides the greatest pleasure, and challenge. John must drive to Dar es Salaam about once a fortnight on business and instead of staying at an indifferent hotel, they go to the Yacht Club where, a secure car park, good food, drink, friends and changing rooms guaranteed to have working loos, hot water for showering, mirror glass and electric fittings which work, are sure to be had. At bedtime, dinghy out to *Ragtime* for a quiet night in comfortable bunks and at daybreak, John can catch the night watchmen's dinghy back to the club changing rooms before going to a city hotel for breakfast and on to the office for 8 a.m. Anne can either join John's routine for town or laze on the boat. The weekend is given to sailing *Ragtime* and on Monday, John resumes his office routine before driving back to Morogoro in the afternoon.

There are idyllic islands of coral strands and coconut palms to visit for swimming and snorkelling in pellucid water both near the yacht club and further afield around the south of Zanzibar Island. Pale jade seas studded with indigo, channel waters sheltered from exposure to the vast

Indian Ocean by an offshore chain of islands, where are warm, translucent waters and many coral reef anchorages for safe snorkelling in the teeming tide reach world of the tropics. And DYC sailors being avid racers, not only in the dinghies every Wednesday and weekend, must race the keelboats too; day races round an island or a shipping buoy (which may or may not be in place). Weekend races round Zanzibar Island or north up to Pemba Island or to the mainland coast at Tanga, where Tanga Yacht Club offers hospitality, and back, are normally held at or near the full moon.

Of course, not all is straightforward: sailing never is. Trade wind shifts can be anticipated but sudden squalls which obliterate visibility as surely as a stage curtain, windy night sailing in shipping channels marked with unlit buoys or, worse still, no wind at all for boats without engine, are hazards. As are the many reefs where hand-bearing compass work and close attention to the echo sounder are a must, if the green waters indicating shallows and submerged reefs, not always picked out by white breakers, are to be avoided. It must be said however, that grounding in such sheltered waters is more likely to cause repairable damage than total loss; injury to a skipper's pride rather than to the boat. Unlit fishing boats are a risk and tangling with an extensive fishing net is a time-consuming penalty when racing, vigilant watch keeping being essential.

Longer holiday cruising having been temptingly discussed, plans are made to take some leave and accompany another 26' yacht, *Kusi*, for ten to twelve days down the Mafia Channel. Late September to early October is chosen, a season between the strong southerly trade winds (the *Kusi* in Kiswahili) and the even stronger northerly trade winds (the *Kaskasi*) when the wind is often from the east and thereby pleasantly helpful for a North-South passage. Victualling a 10-12 day yacht safari is a nightmare since almost nothing in the way of tinned goods is available: luckily, the corned beef factory is still operating and the instant coffee factory has not blown up yet. The brother, Henry, of *Kusi's* skipper, Don, has a coconut farm on Mafia Island, 100 nautical miles south of Dar: the boats can each carry stores for up to five days plus 100 litres of fresh water and 20 litres of boiled water, it being the plan to reach Mafia Island by the fifth day. On day three, *Kusi* catches a bonito, allegedly at 8 knots under spinnaker, and the two boats pull in for the night to a five-mile-wide horseshoe reef, which looks like a jade green taffeta tablecloth with a deadly white lace frill, to enjoy fresh fish steaks with lemon juice and black pepper; delicious. Onwards next day to another island twixt the mainland and Mafia where, skilfully cutting the water, are dozens of passenger ferries, dhows and *ingalawas*, native canoes with a stabilizer plank on each side; a sort of trimaran: local boats which have not changed in a millennium. The sailors, spare of frame but strong, are able seamen handling expertly their unwieldy vessels beneath vast expanses of canvas.

They sail to Mafia Island on the fifth day. Henry meets them with his car, driving them to his house at the far side of his coconut plantation where his herd of dairy cows is grazing in shady comfort. Unable to transport fresh milk to the mainland markets, Henry's resident manager has set up a cheese factory. Having loaded bread baked at Henry's house, cheese, a sackful of unripe coconuts, *madafu*, which yield the 'milk', hands of nearly ripe bananas, replenished the fresh and boiled water and having re-frozen the cool box ice blocks, the boats are ready to sail. Visiting various favourite haunts of *Kusi's* skipper Don, the two yachts swish and slap, glide and gurgle their turquoise way through shallow seas amongst warm green water and tiny islands with tricky anchorages. One particular island, a lump of coral embroidered with coconut trees and fringed with gold, where the swimmer snorkels among shoals of small, jewelled fish accompanying every movement, has a plume of smoke rising from the beach. This could be an answer of what to do with too many bananas ripening all at once.

"Take them ashore and trade with the fishermen," advises Don.

They row ashore with a basketful of golden bananas, the fishing camp taking remarkably little notice of the white strangers in their midst; merely offering a polite greeting. Very strange. Generally, local people want to know who, why and from whence; exchange of news and views being the spice of life in communities living without benefit of television, or indeed local newsprint in their camp. Perhaps they have a radio but batteries are currently so scarce that it seems unlikely.

Walking along the beach, Anne and John notice every small hut has a rail of drying squid like skeins of fossilised yarn, and racks of sun-curing fish spread flat as pieces of newsprint and about the same colour. Some fishermen are cooking fish or lobsters on sticks over a campfire, boy scout fashion. They are relaxed and quite indifferent to their visitors. Are they the strangers, *persona non grata*: have the militia brainwashed these simple people that all strangers, and particularly white ones, are potential spies and must be treated as subversive until interrogated by the local political representative? It is sinister and not unlikely, having occurred thus at a remote anchorage on Zanzibar Island recently.

"How are you today? A big fisherman falls in beside them, his English excellent, idiomatic and fluent. Spotless yellow *kanga* (striped cloth wrapped and tucked at the waist) and tailored cream shirt cover his ample, therefore prosperous, frame in contrast to his fellow fishermen whose figures could best be described as skeletal. Who is this man of property playing at boy scouts?

"I am enjoying a camping holiday," says the man of substance, indicating his *kanga*. "I am employed in Dar es Salaam in the Harbour Authority as a diver." He produces from his shirt pocket an identity card with photo showing the same gentleman in crisp, white naval uniform complete with crested buttons and epaulettes. "I'm having a busman's holiday" he chuckles. He is delighted to accept the bananas. "Help yourself to fish," he enjoins, pointing to a pile one metre high and two metres across, newly gutted. "Only four fish? Come on. You can manage eight surely. Take ten, I insist." Persuaded to take rather more than they can comfortably eat, they remain baffled by his total lack of curiosity about them. "You are going home tomorrow." It is an informed statement rather than a query. "I saw you at Mafia Island," he added. "See you again next year. Goodbye." He shakes hands all round.

So, he has seen them at Mafia, and everyone all around the Mafia Channel knows Don's family, knows of Don's annual sailing holidays in the Mafia waters, knows about Don's sailing cronies, in fact knows all there is to know.

But what is this lordly fisherman doing on his camping holiday? They wonder whether someone having recently arrived into the urban lifestyle, would wish to revert to primary industry for their holiday; go 'walkabout'. Perhaps? Or is he engaged in some family business - purveyor of dried fish to the mainland – or smuggling? If they discourteously persist with questions, they will not be given a true answer anyway.

For yachtsmen on the East African coast, a visit to Zanzibar is a must. Remote or rustic; whatever one may choose to call it, Zanzibar has compelling allure. Land of sultans, slaves and spices whence significant explorers such as Richard Burton and David Livingstone equipped and started their historic quests into Africa's interior. From Dar Yacht Club to Zanzibar town is about 30 miles. Long before the mainland shore has vanished, one can see a lighthouse denoting reefs to the southwest of Zanzibar Island. Then becomes visible the needle of another lighthouse ahead, this marking the start of the Great Pass, Zanzibar port's principal channel. Other passes to the port;

Eastern Pass, Northern Pass and Inner Pass being self-explanatory, English Pass and French Pass carrying deep, historical, colonial implications, all of them screaming of reef-infested waters. In the not so distant geological past, this area was a land bridge between the mainland and Zanzibar Island; some of the land bridge is not far below the surface. They need to keep an eye on the echo sounder.

First glimpse of Zanzibar town is as a white inscription on the endless grey pencil that separates the sea from the sky. At closer range, the town divides into two about a tree-crowned point: to the south is the residential quarter dominated by the ex-British Government House and the hospital; to the north lies the business district with dhow harbour, port wharves, palaces, fishermen's quarter and the ancient coral ragstone fort.

There is much to see and do. Zanzibar old town, being a maze of narrow alleys, excludes motor vehicles but a tourist must be wary of sudden collision with busy bicycle traffic in Stone Town, now dilapidated but still occupied by the ghosts of former oriental splendour and quaint antiquity. The neo-Gothic memorial grandeur of the huge Protestant Church built in 1875-77 on the site of the former slave market, reflects the collective guilt of Victorian Britain, and its interior walls are lined with historic plaques. In the dhow harbour, often redolent with the aroma of cloves, native boats are being unloaded without benefit of cranes.

Nearby, a museum piece sits in the marine research station boatshed, forgotten but not derelict: 15 metres long with seats for twenty oarsmen, the former sultan's state barge is canopied, carved and built in Cowes, in Britain.

Anne and John board an uncertain country bus to the other side of the island and later hire a taxi for a tour past the house where David Livingstone planned his last visit to the interior, and on to the ruins of Beit el Mtoni palace which Sultan Seyyid bin Said, the Lion of Oman, built for his wives and children in the 1840s. It is a pretty spot with grey stone Moorish columns in a cool green grotto of coconut palms. Sultan Seyyid married among others, a Persian princess for whose pleasure he built a bathhouse, some 12 miles distant from the palace. Imagining the princess in her litter accompanied by ladies in waiting, eunuchs, slaves and picnic provisions, Anne and John travel by old and battered taxi on a mud road now rutted and ruined by rain. But the baths defy the ravages of time and climate. Going in through a gloomy cavern of overgrown shrubs, descendents of scented, flowering species, turning a dark stonework corner, Anne exclaims: "Someone has forgotten to switch off the light!" What a silly thing to say about a one-hundred-and-fifty-year-old ruin! The late afternoon sun, directed like a laser beam through cunning slots cut in the dome, one slot for each hour of the day, illuminates the glowing whitewashed walls of the boudoirs and bathing room. Sensationally green frescoes of entwining trees and creepers wherein perch graceful birds, remain vivid against silver walls. Green: the Islamic colour of paradise, vibrant after all these years.

Having anchored *Ragtime* opposite a useless edifice euphemistically known as the Gateway to Zanzibar and the wind during the night having backed to an undesirable quarter giving an uncomfortable swell, they decide to move to the lee of an adjacent island for breakfast. Here the ebb tide is revealing a golden strand and miles of naked reef which invite a visit. Among the island's tangled vegetation and lianas, is a sudden neat box hedge, recently clipped and tidy. What on earth is a topiarian garden doing on an uninhabited coral island? Inside, the garden is a war graves cemetery wherein lie the graves of 27 sailors from the cruiser HMS *Pegasus*, sunk in Zanzibar Harbour in 1914.

At the outbreak of War in 1914, the German cruiser SMS *Königsberg*, in the East African waters showing the flag at Dar es Salaam, quietly made her way to the British shipping lanes serving India where she sank SS *City of Winchester* off Aden. *Königsberg* then vanished, to the dismay of the British, until some six weeks later she sailed into Zanzibar harbour to sink HMS *Pegasus,* which was riding at anchor, a sitting duck undergoing boiler cleaning. Thereafter *Königsberg,* running low on coal, and herself in need of boiler cleaning, was forced to hide and did – up one of the tidal creeks of the Rufiji delta on mainland German East Africa. It was a daring and skilful manoeuvre in a deadly game played out in East Africa between 1914 and 1918.

The final round of hide-and-seek was a match of ingenuity and dexterity. *Königsberg's* commander, van Loof took off the ship's big guns mounting them at the main mouth of the delta to deter intruders. The British meanwhile had not even a clue as to where the *Königsberg* lay until one day, a German order for the delivery of good Ruhr coal to the port of Lindi for the Rufiji delta was intercepted. Coal! To a fetid swamp of mangroves, mud and mosquitoes? But exactly where in the vast delta morass? The hunt was up. A British cruiser commander operating a sweep of the coast noticed through his binoculars, a palm tree rather higher than the rest. It excited his curiosity, further examination indicating that the over-tall palm tree was tied to the top of a mast. *Königsberg* had been camouflaged. Having discovered where she lay, the problem remained of how to get in and get at her, but that is another story requiring good detection work from the intrepid Pieter Pretorius. The *Königsberg* was eventually sunk, but not her big guns. Mounted on wooden carriages, they were hauled around East Africa with the *Schutztruppe*.

Also in the cemetery were the graves of British seamen killed in dhow-chasing skirmishes in the nineteenth century, when Britain attempted to prohibit the slave trade not only by treaty with the Sultan of Zanzibar but by patrolling the slavers' sea routes. The Arab shipmasters went to any lengths to preserve their human cargo. When the British frigates got up steam to give chase, Arab shippers dressed the captives as deckhands, pointed to the smoke and told their gullible cargo it was the boilers being got ready to cook them. Presumably, the British navy did contribute to the eradication of slavery but, judging by the account of one sub-lieutenant, G.L. Sullivan, in his book *Dhow-Chasing in Zanzibar Waters* (first edition 1873, Cass 1986), few or no slaves were retrieved. The dhows vanished under cover of darkness, and if they failed to escape, they ran their ship aground in the surf and swam ashore, most captives perishing in the shipwreck. Sullivan relates more about cruising among and camping on the coral islands. When a friend, snorkelling off one of the Zanzibar islands, comes up holding an antique bottle with 'Ross Belfast' embossed in the glass, it is quite possibly a naval throw-out since it is later identified as a Hamilton bottle first patented in 1814, Ross of Belfast being a mineral water manufacturer which closed in 1911.

***

There is a Swahili proverb, which says: 'Hide your good fortune lest an evil eye falls on you'. Many Africans carry an eye-shaped amulet of blue glass, with inner white circle enclosing a black spot, through which is a hole to thread a hanging cord or leather string; Joseph, the company driver, has one in the Gibb Peugeot 505, buses always have them. These charms are to be had in every market for a small sum of Tanzanian shillings. Perhaps it is not too late to hang one in the house. Certainly fruit trees in Mafiga gardens wear a talisman tied onto their trunks, a stone or an empty maize husk.

"Smiley, why are these objects tied onto the trees?"

"It is the custom, to stop people from helping themselves. If a thief takes fruit when the empty maize cob is tied on, he will find his teeth falling out. If it is a stone on the tree then he will get an abscess." Smiley shrugs his shoulders, taps his temple. "All in the mind," he grins his engaging smile. A young leopard raiding chickens at the neighbouring farm, is killed at Mafiga's water pump station, its tail and one paw missing from the corpse. One of the university scientists observes that these will have been taken for the purposes of magic.

Wildlife is indeed all around. White ants are busily eating the house's wooden door and window jambs, leaving an empty shell of paint; struts which will eventually have to be replaced. Hundreds of bats roost in the roof, flying out at dusk in fits and starts so that the hovering falcon has a less than sporting chance of dropping upon one. A pair of wire-tailed swallows, having built their mud and saliva nest against the verandah ceiling above the front door, are busy coaxing the young out for a first flying venture, the real test being when the chicks have to regain the nest for the first time in their life.

Siafu, the carnivorous warrior ants, marching across gardens and through houses will attack anything, man or beast in their path; a late night carouser coming home in the dark and stepping in a trail of *siafu*, will become a jumping bean, slapping and tearing at trousers, wrenching off underpants as dozens of ants simultaneously dig razor-sharp pincers into his flesh. A chained dog, rabbits in a pen, a baby in a carrycot can be stripped of flesh to a skeleton if intercepted on the route of marching ants. *Siafu* are known locally as the '*moto*' (literally, 'hot') since the synchronised grab of myriads of pincers feel akin to burning by fire.

Mice are all over the gardens and houses too and there is no alternative but poison. Rats and mice being a serious problem to local farmers and families, eating up to a quarter of the stored harvest of grain, Danish Government Aid set up a Rodent Control Project. Alas, the Tanzanian staff are not co-operative, stealing the grain allocated for coating with chemicals.

"In Tanga region," says Sam, an American scientist on the Project, "They gave up poison and imported 100,000 traps!"

"What is needed, rather, is 50,000 cats," Anne volunteers.

"What is needed is to change the eating habits of the locals," snorts Sam.

"You mean, eat rats?"

"Why not; good source of protein. In the Philippines, where I have been working, there's not a rat problem, or rather the problem is, shortage of rats to fill the saucepans."

One morning, Anne, standing on the verandah with a mug of coffee, is suddenly aware that a maddened buffalo, having broken through the perimeter five-strand wire fence as if it were cotton thread, is pounding up the garden towards the verandah. Too stupefied to react, she is rooted to the spot, but fortunately the terrified, wild creature swerves 10 metres before the verandah, rounds the house, crosses the drive and bursts through the five-strand back fence into the fields. Alfred, one of the *shamba* men (gardeners) downs tools and joins the chase, shots being heard about 20 minutes later; it is another 40 minutes before a weary Alfred comes, panting, back, carrying over his shoulder ½ metre of rib bone on the end of which is 5 cms^2 of meat and hairy hide, which he strokes triumphantly.

In Morogoro, food supplies are becoming more and more scarce. John negotiates with the Client MAJI, the Ministry of Water, to receive an allocation of flour, sugar, cooking oil and soap powder for Gibb staff. Anne's job is to go with the Gibb driver, Joseph, in the Peugeot 505 estate to the Government depot, wait for hours in the hot sun to receive a 50 kg sack of flour, sugar, soap and/or 20 litre drum of cooking oil, and then ask all personnel to bring plastic bags and empty bottles to the house where Smiley and Anne weigh and measure. Soon there is no bread in the bakery. Well, the *Malawi Cook Book*, vital Christmas gift from a friend in that country, has a recipe for a bread using half maize flour, still available in the market, and half wheat flour. When the market runs short of maize flour, buy rice flour to eke out the wheat flour, or cassava flour, or even mashed potatoes to spin out the precious wheat flour. Occasionally, good friends up country at the Brooke Bond Tea estates at Mufindi arriving for a stopover coffee or tea, or a bed and breakfast on their way to Dar es Salaam, bring a welcome sack of wheat which Anne must take to the local flour mill for grinding. When the Gibb Partners from Nairobi come and stay, a toilet roll is cut in half, all of 5 cms width hanging in the loo: for the rest of the time, it is squares of newsprint and a litter bag.

Hearing that the Morogoro canvas factory has opened, Anne, needing to make new covers for *Ragtime's* fenders, goes to the factory shop in search of canvas. The quality is good but at £11 per metre by official rate of exchange, it is too expensive and Anne chooses a cheaper, local cotton drill. "I will have one metre of this please," says she pointing to the drill. The three staff of the National Co-operative Retail shop shake their collective heads. "We do not know the price of that cloth."

"Can you ring up your regional headquarters and discover the price?"

"No telephone; it does not work," they say glumly. "You can, if you want, go to regional HQ and find out the price." But if Anne goes to get the price, would they accept it?

"No, definitely not."

Such ennui, such insolent contempt for their jobs as employees of a Parastatal company, such enterprise elusion is painful. Irritated beyond measure, Anne decides to calculate by the unofficial exchange rate, bringing down the price of the quality canvas to a reasonable £2.30 per metre, and returns to the factory shop.

The shop is empty but for the three salesmen lounging in listless pose. It appears that they suffer from an affliction of the eyesight since Anne fails to gain any attention at the counter. Not to be denied her canvas, she lifts the weighty roll of cloth and plonks it on the counter in front of them. "One metre, please." Six eyes are directed towards her.

"You cannot buy any cloth."

"Why not? The price is marked." So it is, in purple marker ink all over the first half metre of the cloth: *Ragtime* would forever wear that price on her fourth fender.

"We have no scissors."

No scissors in a fabrics and materials store! A salesman indicates a limp line of once-white tape dangling from a nail in the counter; nothing attached to the tape tail. Not to be defeated again, Anne drives home to fetch her scissors and the purchase is completed.

Anne has broken a tooth; not deeply painful, but the sharp fractured edges lacerate her jaw and tongue when she talks or eats and something must be done. She shuns Morogoro regional hospital dental clinic after hearing what befell a British woman friend recently. The friend, suffering raging toothache for some days, was seen by a courteous white-coated African dentist who inspected her mouth and, exuding confidence, pronounced emergency extraction to be necessary.

"So he gave me an anaesthetic and pulled the tooth," she retailed, "But the toothache was as violent as ever next day." She returned to the clinic where she encountered quite another white-coated dentist.

"The other dentist here treated me two days ago," she explained.

"What other dentist? I am the only dentist here."

"But he pulled my tooth. And I have still got toothache."

"I cannot think who did this job, but nevertheless let me look."

He did so and pronounced that the wrong tooth had been taken out, that the adjacent one was badly infected.

"I am sorry, but I will have to take it out." Anaesthetised again, the lady had another tooth pulled. And still the toothache raged. Distraught, she went to Dar es

Salaam, to the African State Hospital, where an x-ray indicated a severely inflamed, swollen sinus. Treated with penicillin, the toothache subsided as the inflammation retreated but she did not get back her two teeth.

Signally failing to get an appointment at the African State Hospital in Dar, Anne accepts the offer of the Indian clerk in Gibb's Dar office to get her an appointment at the Aga Khan Hospital; it would suffice for a temporary filling until the next home leave. The dentist is so enshrouded in Sikh turbans, sterile gauze masks and surgical long coats that it is difficult to judge his age and experience. His voice is of the lowest key, wearily patient, faintly hypnotic; slim, girlishly slender even and probably young, more to the point is he experienced? Anne cannot tell. "I have broken a tooth and would like a temporary repair filling until I next go back to the UK" Anne knows that crowning a tooth is not available in Dar since only the year previously, she had had to have a cast and crown done in Nairobi for lack of facilities in Dar es Salaam.

"We can do crowning here."

Already irrationally exasperated, Anne, reiterating her intention to have the crowning done in the UK, is reluctant to admit that she views entry into the Aga Khan Hospital, even the dental department, with deep mistrust. She hedges her suspicions with excuses; lives 125 miles up country at Morogoro, cannot easily get into Dar for a series of appointments such as a crowning job requires.

"That is no problem. I can do the preparation of the tooth now and take the cast. You can come back at your convenience to have the crown cemented." Anne hesitates and the dentist recognises the pause as the victory it is. "The only problem is that you will have to find the gold."

She clutches at this new straw to acquit her of the decision they both know she is about to make. "I haven't time to go traipsing round Dar searching for gold," she explodes. "My husband is a busy man; he can't hang around while I hunt for gold." She is free of the awful dilemma, saved from fear and pain.

"There is a possibility we could obtain the gold for you but it would cost more."

"How much?" Anne is almost committed: the harder the bargain to conclude, the harder it is to back out of the deal. She is fighting a rearguard action. The price he quotes is favourable but what if she ends up with an abscess, septicaemia at the hands of an inexperienced dentist. "Let me phone my husband," she plays for time: time to reassess her chances of survival.

"Certainly. I will anaesthetise you in the meantime, it takes a few minutes to act."

Anne leaps from the chair. "I'm not going to be anaesthetised."

"Don't be alarmed." A fragile hand descends upon her shoulder, "I mean only to give you a local anaesthetic."

Again Anne leaps. "I'm not having a local anaesthetic."

"But it will be painful. The vital parts are protected, I think, but the drilling must hurt."

"Never mind about hurting me. I'll let you know if I need any anaesthetic."

He laid down the pen, which had been scratching hieroglyphics on a small card. "Are you quite well?"

"Quite well." Anne's response is automatic.

"The heat perhaps has affected you!" As he speaks, Anne begins to consider the awful implication of his suggestion. Is she indeed looking white, or red, grey, green or yellow; hushed, flushed, feverish, spotted, mottled, warbled, tumbled? The indignity of his inference drives her to regain the dental chair.

Some fifteen drill-filled minutes later, he lays down the tool. "You are one of the few, indeed the *only* patient I have ever had who permitted me to work without the use of anaesthetic." "You know," he continues, "I will spend up to fifteen minutes of the appointment trying to persuade a patient not to have an anaesthetic because one makes a more satisfactory job without it." Anne writhes at the bare-faced hypocrisy but with a gaping hole in her molar she could hardly quit the surgery now.

"Rinse out," he orders.

"I can't," she lisps. "You've left a swab in my cheek." As he extracts the offending cotton wool, he observes that had he done it in his finals examination he would certainly have failed. She knew it: indubitably young and inexperienced, he is desperate for patients on which to practise. Thank heavens she has remained fully conscious throughout: it needs no imagination to think what might otherwise have been perpetrated upon her sleeping teeth. Much later, the crown he fixed is found to have an unfortunate 'positive edge'.

At Christmas, Anne is given an *Atlas of Tanzania*, 1974 edition; not bound but in sheet form – *hamna* binding, but no doubt that can be done in Britain. One can now see the significance of the Uluguru Mountain range which is one of five high 'islands' of good rainfall and luxuriant forest in northern Tanzania; islands rising far above the scrub and thorn bush savannah of the mainland as it dips from the eastern rim of the African Rift Valley to the Indian Ocean. The Ulugurus have emotional impact, "They remind me of my Cyprus Mountains" sighs a Greek; "Just like the Trossachs but a bit bigger" enthuses a Scot. Not only emotional, the Ulugurus have elemental impact; "I will lift up mine eyes unto the hills from whence cometh my help," in the shape of rainfall and fertility: certainly the region around Morogoro is conspicuous as a cornucopia of agricultural production and a pool of population. However, Pre-Cambrian rocks some 500 million years old, fractured and crumbled, do not offer the ideal basis upon which to build dams. Parallel to the Ulugurus lies a ridge known as the Mindu Hills and the intervening lowland carrying the Ngerengere River, is as flat-floored as a rift valley; indeed, parts of the valley form a vast swamp, a natural reservoir onto which a mile-wide earth dam across the river will pond up a sizeable lake.

The Brazilians, having spent the advance monies for Mindu Dam on completing the construction of Morogoro's railway sheds, proceed not at all with the dam, causing John intense worry. The Zambian company building the treatment works advance with their work and the Client MAJI, blinded perhaps by the progress on the treatment works, are not persuaded that the Brazilian company are incapable of building the dam. Unable, or unwilling, to recognise the no-go circumstances developing about the Brazilians, no one in MAJI is prepared to gainsay them, kill the goose that may lay a golden egg. Tension between the consultant, the contractor and the client is spreading like a virus, its symptoms, heated words and veiled intimidation. Amidst the growling and snarling, another distemper is manifesting itself. Some six of the Brazilians and two of the Zambians are confined to bed with hepatitis. This is indeed serious but there is not a lot anyone can do about it: it appears to be confined to the site staff, all of whom come and go in the site offices. Later, it will be inferred that the office tea boy is a carrier though not a victim, and he is banned from the office block, confined to the bucket and spade brigade, not before time.

John, suffering from stress and insomnia, coming out in a series of boils and tropical sores, lacks energy, is permanently fatigued and running a slight fever. Consulting the Arab doctor in Morogoro who is treating the hepatitis sufferers, a blood test for malaria is ordered and when the slide is said to prove positive, an injection of chloroquine is pumped into him. Improvement is marginal but he is no worse until some two weeks later, his scant appetite degenerates and he is sick, signally sick. Hepatitis, no doubt about it, and another of the Gibb staff is ill with suspected hepatitis, along with four more Brazilians.

By this time, John is not always lucid; dozing more and more, answering irrelevantly, refusing all food. Anne confiscates his false tooth on a plate, result of an old rugger injury, lest he swallow it and choke. "I want my sweetie," he insists, "My sweetie. Give me my sweetie." Gibb staff in Nairobi are contacted about his condition, which is now alarming, and after discussions, the company plane is promised for tomorrow. But on the morrow, the plane has an engine problem which Paul, the company pilot, must get fixed. It will be tomorrow, yes definitely, and they will send Cathy, Paul's wife, who is a registered nurse to attend the patient. So it is and John, now in a semi-coma, is flown out and to Nairobi Hospital. Later the message comes through that he is none the worse for the journey, sitting up in bed eating a jam sandwich, and in the care of Dr Phillip Rees.

Two days later, Nairobi head office informs Mindu site office that they would like Anne, and also Marion and Robert who are out for Christmas holidays, to come up to Nairobi immediately; for tests, they say. What tests? Anne is curious but not concerned. Gibb Nairobi further adds that Paul, the firm's pilot, flying to Morogoro airfield, will buzz Mafiga compound. Upon this signal, Anne and the children will be driven to the airstrip. The plane, instructs Gibb Nairobi, will be on the ground for only five minutes so boarding must be quick. Exit visas, tax clearance and entry permits, the lot, can be dealt with on arrival in Nairobi.

"I'm so sorry about this confusion," says Paul as the plane flies up through the cloud layer and sets course for the north. "I didn't have time to file a flight plan for Tanzania so I told them I was going to Amboseli on the Kenyan side of Mt Kilimanjaro. Then I went off the air, nipped down to Morogoro for you, and will come back into contact with Nairobi when we reach Amboseli."

This seems to Anne irregular, if not illegal. However, she knows that Paul is a pilot of long standing in Kenya and is highly respected by the Kenyan authorities at Wilson Airport in Nairobi, so she gives the matter no further thought.

Flying up through the cloud layer and over Mt. Kilimanjaro, looking down on the crater's cone and its lesser twin Mt. Kibo, an Antarctica of lava in a snowy cloudscape, Anne remembers that Queen Victoria gave the mountain to her grandson Kaiser Wilhelm II as a birthday present because poor dear Billy had got no snow peak in his African domain. Anne recalls driving Marion and Rob up to Moshi where they would attempt to climb the mountain. Before Moshi is reached, Anne stops the car for she has seen it, white-ribbed, sun struck, floating as if by magic above a distant layer of stratus cloud. The youngsters search the horizon in vain. "Look up, look higher," she exhorts. Suddenly they see it and stunned silence follows. "I had no idea it was that high," says one of them and the tone of awe implies that they had had no idea what 6,000 m altitude meant.

At Wilson Airport, the two Partners directly concerned with Mindu Dam, Brian Lindsay and Stewart Roberts, are waiting to meet Anne. Paul goes off to deal with the passports at immigration.

"Dr, Rees wants to see you, Anne, at two o'clock," says Brian. "We are going to drive you to the hospital now. We'll pick up some sandwiches on the way and you and the children can eat them in the hospital gardens."

In the waiting room at the hospital, Marion and Robert find a selection of magazines and journals and a pack of well-used playing cards which they take into the garden to while away the time. Anne goes to see Dr. Rees.

The doctor greets Anne; "I did my clinical training at the Westminster Hospital in London with your brother, Colin. Give him my salaams when you see him. And of course, you know that Anthony Bryceson is here in Nairobi." Yes, Anthony, another Westminster Hospital trained doctor, and a long-standing friend of Anne's family, is setting up a hospital research unit in Nairobi.

When Anne is seated Dr. Rees pauses. "I am afraid the news about John is not good. The results of blood tests just back show that his liver functions are poor and the blood is not coagulating properly: it is already seeping out of the veins into the urine. As you know, there is very little treatment for the hepatitis virus, just good nursing care and time. He is getting injections of vitamin K to bolster up the liver but I am sorry to say, I am not very hopeful. His coma will deepen and he'll feel nothing. Thirty-six hours or so is the time it will take." He rises, puts a hand on Anne's shoulder. "Now, I am going to phone Anthony and get him to come over to you."

Walking with Anthony along the wide hospital corridors to John's room, Anthony cautions Anne, "John is in a coma, I'm sorry to say. But it is important to behave normally, speak naturally, because it is possible that he can hear and register the presence of people."

Having entered John's room, Anne sits down on a chair by the bed and slips her hand under the covers to find John's hand. There is a slight responding pressure of the hand and a grunt which might be "Hi," from John. His eyes are shut. Anthony talks about his work and his family living in the Karen suburb of Nairobi. Young William, his son, goes to a local preparatory school and loves it: Maia, his daughter, attends a kindergarten. Ulla, his Danish-born wife and a trained architect, is looking for work in Nairobi. "Now I must get back to work," says Anthony. "I'll see you tomorrow, John."

Anne continues to sit as near John as his bed will allow. She concentrates on the exercise of sounding normal, describing the flight from Morogoro in 'Tango Charlie', the Gibb plane. She mentions Marion and Rob playing card games on the lawn outside. But she is entirely aware that John is leaving: his mysterious withdrawal into unconsciousness is the beginning of a journey to… Where? That is the ultimate question.

"I'll be in tomorrow," she says cheerfully as she goes to the door. "See you then." Anne is numb; empty and weightless. She feels disembodied; as if she is floating near the ceiling, watching a movie film of Anne walking alone in the hospital corridor. In this passage there are dark cavities filled with doubt and corners curving into fear. Her mind focuses on how to impart this disaster news to Marion and Robert.

In the waiting room, Brian Lindsay, who has returned to the hospital for Anne, puts his hand under her elbow. "This is dreadful news for us. We are so sorry for you and the children. In the meantime, we will do all we can to help you: leave all the practical arrangements to us. And I want you to think who in your family you would like brought out from the UK for John's funeral.

Chapter 14

The Damned Dam

It is good to leave the jet aircraft with its plastic food trays and air-conditioned discomfort, descend the gangway into the soothing sauna of Dar es Salaam, greet Gibb's Asian clerk and climb into the now much-tried Peugeot. Boneshaker vehicles are as much a part of Tanzania as are the limitless landscapes, imponderable cloudscapes and disorderly assembly of vegetation.

From Dar on the Indian Ocean, the grey band of tarmac sets out for Morogoro, Zambia, Zaire and the Atlantic coast. The flying miles give a sensation of speed as one swoops down the empty highway, a speed which is merely a satisfying illusion since it omits the surfaceless sections, the gravelled ruts and the deep potholes. A bicycle or two, a short crocodile of women bearing loads upon their heads, the occasional bulging burden on four donkey legs, some lorries gaily painted with vividly coloured palm trees, purple mountains and blue, blue skies, juggernauts for Zambian copper, and a rare bus; these are the norm between Dar and Morogoro. The buses are always named in bold writing above the windscreen. There is Queen Victoria, an old friend; and the well-known William the Conqueror; then comes one not seen before, Carl Peters. Carl Peters! Oh no! Carl Peters, a sadistic bully with an outsize appetite for colonial expansion, who scurried around East Africa in the 1880s 'persuading' illiterate tribal chieftains to put their mark on a 'treaty' accepting German protection, would eventually be dismissed from Germany's colonial service for cruelty to Africans. But not before he had sneaked around the backside of Lake Victoria with an eye on Uganda, an expedition that alarmed Britain and prompted action on the plan to build a railway from Mombasa in British East to Kisumu on the Lake, thereby claiming Uganda as a part of British East. Uganda held the Nile headwaters, which flowed to Egypt and Egypt embraced the Suez Canal, which was the route to India, ergo Uganda was vital to Britain.

It is now 1981 and Anne is back home in Morogoro at last. It is over five months since she left, illegally, by 'Tango Charlie', Gibb's own aircraft to Nairobi hospital to hear of John's imminent change of state from the seen to the unseen. But a miracle occurred. Anthony Bryceson appeared and perhaps his presence penetrated John's unconscious psyche, giving him a gleam of hope. Anthony's coming certainly gave Anne optimism: he, and his wife Ulla, were a tower of strength, gathering up the witless, empty Anne and the two children, taking them to their home to stay, reassuring them with sage medical criteria and Dutch courage. By morning, John was no worse and a day later he had turned the corner. Recovery was slow; five weeks in Nairobi hospital, two weeks on holiday in Kenya staying with kind Kitale friends and three months in Britain, during which he had extensive medical tests and appraisal before being pronounced fit to return to work in Africa.

At Mafiga, the ceaseless chatter of Africans replaces the aimless banalities of radio disc jockeys in Britain. The garden is a profusion of flowering colour. In the freezer is a gift of impala but sorrowfully, Smiley is not there; the ills that flesh is heir to, old man's problems, a vexation of the spirit, any or all of these afflict the old man. Anne visits him in his home with a golden handshake and a gift of candy and it is not many weeks before Steven informs them of his passing.

One last kindness done by Smiley is to introduce Issa, who resembles nothing so much as a leprechaun, the wily dwarf-sized Irish brownie who helps with domestic duties. But his diminutive form is made of sprung steel. He is a true peasant, entirely capitalist in his outlook, and has no time for the luxury of socialism, holding a scornful view of his Government's political strategy. "I can sell my good, white maize at fifteen or twenty shillings for a kilo and then go to the market and buy government maize, American yellow stuff, for four shillings a kilo." If the government realises his ruse and refuses to release staple foods then the peasant may go a little hungry – until the government relents.

And yet, Jim and Val Whittle, having retired from the Colonial Service twenty years ago and speaking fluent Kiswahili, observe a big improvement in rural Tanzania. "Country people are better dressed; many have shoes now. They look better fed and generally brighter."

Morogoro market, after five months' absence, has changed: prices have doubled. But the variety of headgear remains the same: crocheted skull caps, embroidered Moslem toques, Andy Capp caps, pixie hats, knitted cosies, tam o'shanters as heavily striped as any football fans', jelly bags in multicolour, non-denominational toques of wool, tweed and plaid. Hats being a status symbol, a *mzee*, a venerable elder, always wears headgear; a *kijana*, a youth, does not. At age of about thirty, a man may start wearing hats on occasions since he is a *mzee kidogo,* a junior elder. In this season, the start of the harvest after the rainy months of March to May, the market has plenty to offer. Sacks of maize, rice, pea flour, cassava flour, millet flour sit under a pall of pale dust and a mealy scent. Basket and string craft with rolls of plaited matting is redolent of new-mown hay and aromatic of sisal; in tobacco corner, with its twists of umber, hazel and liver-brown leaf, there is a spicy odour.

Swatches of brown wrapping paper squares for rolling the tobacco, are in evidence.

Friends among the vegetable and fruit sellers, with their mounds of tomatoes, oranges, limes, cucumbers, green and pearl onions, peppers, yams and shapeless lumps of cassava root, are the same as ever.

"Mama Sears where have you been? We have not seen you for so long time."

"In England, for some months," Anne explains.

"Did you bring me a present?"

"No, no presents."

"But clothes are so good in England. You could have bought me a shirt. Between friends a gift is customary." An inevitable audience is now gathering.

"So sorry. I had no money to buy presents." Little shrieks of laughter erupt from the burgeoning crowd as the show gets under way.

"But clothes are cheap in England. And your husband is a rich man." A cloudburst of giggles. The audience swells, those at the front genuflecting courteously so that the back row may participate.

"My husband may be rich but he is a hard man: he doesn't give me any money."

"Ah-hh-hh!" A ripple of sympathetic sighs and knowing grins passes round like wind over a barley field. The breed of hard husbands is something they all understand, even join on occasions. Their mood changes to compassion. "Never mind! Here is a present for you, instead." Two cucumbers are pressed into the hands of a victim of tyranny. Amid a gale of guffaws, the audience disperses to retail, with the peppers and potatoes, suitably embellished accounts of the drama.

John, returning to a dam barely started, sweet nothing having been done in his absence, resumes vexatious discussions with the client, MAJI, about the capability of the Brazilian contractor ever to build Mindu dam. MAJI, suffering the ennui and inertia of all government offices, quibbles and prevaricates, flits from one argument to another, passes the buck and evades with a mesh of fabrication. The World Bank, donor agency of the Mindu Project, fares no better with the client. The Tanzanian Treasury, also part of the equation, misinterprets and misinforms. Meanwhile, the Brazilian contractor, with endless enthusiasm and incorrigible optimism, persists with ingenious reassurances in raising expectations. It is a cat's cradle, a battle of wits between the protagonists to maintain the status quo, John being the cat caught in the middle of the farce.

The *Guardian Weekly* has run an article on the Queen, probably after a Christmas Day Speech, which contained a moral defence of Her Majesty as a dedicated disciple of the Commonwealth. This does help restore Anne's slipping ideals in connection with working in the Third World. She sometimes asks herself why they are there. Is it that they wish to assist in the development of East Africa, or Pakistan or Algeria? Do they kid themselves that since there are no new frontiers left to pioneer, they must be content with what challenge and adventure they can find in the less developed countries? Or is it purely materialistic; that they can earn more money overseas and pay private school fees?

President Nyerere claims that the Third World has a right to be aided in recompense for all the years of exploitation. And in translating the word 'exploitation' the President has coined the Kiswahili word for 'sucking', as of old men sitting around a gourd sucking *pombe*, home-brewed beer, through long straws. Tom Clausen, head of the World Bank, prophesies world chaos and disaster if the rich nations fail to help the less developed countries. John and Anne realise that their own further employment depends upon rich countries' largesse; but they suspect this aid may profit the developed countries more than it does the Third World's poor. Perhaps this is termed Capitalism cloaked in Philanthropy, which is probably as old as mankind.

Essays, memoirs and stories of the old Raj in the Indian subcontinent, stress paternal benevolence manifested by an incorruptible and dedicated administration. Dedication, even by habit, is a hard taskmaster and undoubtedly yesteryear's conditions were a great deal tougher than now. Anne is astonished: staying at the home of a North American missionary in Tanga, recently, she marvels at the air-conditioned house, the deep pile carpets and Sanderson-style chintz furnishings. She is stunned by so much imported food; is astounded by the two monster deep freezers, each the size of a Morris mini-minor estate car, the more so since she only has three shelves in a shared freezer. Her first reaction is one of sympathy for the North American congregations whose church collections furnish such luxuries for their evangelists. How many sackfuls of pensioners' dimes would be needed to bring North America to Africa? Why should the rich nations flaunt such affluence; after all, Christ was born in a stable, symbol of poverty. On the other hand, many Africans, being all too familiar with poverty, will admire affluence, covet it and regard the missionaries with respect.

It is said that one can give a man a fish and he will eat for a day; give a man a fishing net and he'll eat until the net breaks; show a man how to make a fishing net and he'll always eat fish. Although this particular *bon mot* is hardly appropriate, since coastal and riverine Africans are skilled fishermen, it should be added that if the fisherman starts to prosper, some political bully will harness him and his industry, thereby reaping the fisherman's profits. What is more, they will blow the reefs to pieces with dynamite. But, of course, the developed countries must be charged with destruction too: pumping sulphurous smoke, factory effluent, and toxic sludge into the air, the sea and the underground.

A young Briton called David, just finishing Kiswahili language school in Morogoro, is expecting to be posted to Babati, a semi-arid area, famine-threatened, depressed and a worthy case for Christian aid. David is assuming he will work on small-scale projects directly among the villagers but the Bishop of Kilimanjaro, Bishop Alpha, in whose diocese the deprived area falls, thinks otherwise. He wants a big, prestigious Episcopalian model farm with David as farm manager. David is anticipating a clash and numerous resounding engagements with the Bishop. Certainly, the Bishop will win; David will either have to accommodate the Bishop, and the Bishop's pocket, or move elsewhere.

While David's convictions are worthy sentiments for a thinking man, child of contemporary concepts on 'direct' development, could it be said that the Bishop's method will be the more effective? The model farm technique is how Kenya put over much agricultural technology. To give Kenya its due, the direct development method was repeatedly recommended: for instance in the 1920s through Jeannes Schools. But these failed to inspire the local farmers. "Why should we have to use primitive (local) tools when what we really need is mechanisation? Give us tractors, not *jembes* (hoes)." And the *Tanzania Daily News* of 12/9/1984 in an editorial writes: "If we can handle cars, how much better should we be able to manage tractors."

In Morogoro, the Chamber of Commerce has been instructed by the Ministry of Agriculture and Food to DO something constructive about the dire state of domestic production. President Nyerere now endorses the need for self-reliance. "We must stand on our own two feet," he tells Tanzania.

When Anne next goes to Mrs Mshendwa's to buy eggs, the lady, after the normal procedure for establishing a rapport, asks a favour. "Would you please ask your husband if he would kindly come and talk to my husband about setting up a hydraulic ram on a farm he has been given near Kingolwera Prison farm, with frontage on the Ngerengere River?"

"Of course, shall we call on Sunday morning about 10.30 or 11 a.m.?"

Having agreed this, Anne and John, allowing for 'African time', get to the Mshendwas about 11.30 a.m.

"Yes, he is in," says his daughter. But he is not actually *in* the house, arriving some half an hour later to find his guests seated in the parlour drinking coca cola. Mr Mshendwa, an intelligent, energetic civil servant and member of the Morogoro Chamber of Commerce, is a printer by profession, speaking good English. A rapport is soon established since John's father was in the printing profession.

"How many acres is this farm?" Anne opens the discussion.

"Eight hundred acres, near Malela. It is an old abandoned sisal farm."

"Near Malela?" John queries. "I thought it was on the river near Kingolwira."

"Ah yes, that one will be a thousand acres; it is virgin forest still."

What? He is in the process of acquiring two farms! Then there is no hope of progress or development; one would have taxed him beyond his capabilities, two is lunatic.

While Mr Mshendwa outlines his plans for installing 'tanks' and shallow wells on the sisal plantation and converting it into a dairy farm, and for clearing the forest, introducing a hydraulic ram to lift water out of the river and breaking in the virgin land for dairy farming – dairy farming again – John and Anne listen with sinking heart. They know that Mr Mshendwa will never build a hut on his land, live out there and bully a gang of labourers into raising a weir across a gully to form a water 'tank', or into digging shallow wells; would never ring-bark a single tree and hire a team of oxen to haul out the timber and the stumps.

"And it will take a long time and be very expensive," finishes Mr Mshendwa. "And the problem is I have no tyres for my car to drive out to my land."

Of course, Mr Mshendwa will sit and wait, talking, planning, arranging but never doing. When one recalls the magnitude of development occurring in South Africa, Kenya, North America, Australia and a number of other places too, one must admire the restless energy of the European settlers, intrepid pioneers all of them. Disillusion sits in the car with John and Anne as they drive home.

John takes Mr Mshendwa to the Malela farm to help him identify on his large-scale Ordnance Survey map suitable gullies for small earth dams. The hot season is starting with the onset of drought. On the disturbed ground of this abandoned sisal estate, the torrid earth offers a listless landscape, labouring under a searing sun in colours of ivory, ash, coral and bleached bone; faded weeds, withered grasses lend albescence like banded agate: a heat haze hangs over the burned land, with a blinding shine of glare, and dust devils spiral sporadically across the skyline. It is an incandescent death of the land, relieved only by the citrine sheen of a mango tree in full flower heralding a promise of new life.

"And what happens" explodes John when he returns home, "When Mr Mshendwa finds squatters on his land and peasant neighbours who think this is a government-sponsored project and help themselves to anything they can lay hands on. He will need a bloody good farm manager," finishes John, and it is obvious he is thinking in the manner of a European; a forlorn thought.

In the fullness of time, MAJI and the Treasury, having been finally convinced that the Brazilians have not got the resources to build Mindu dam, make up their collective mind to dismiss them and call in the second lowest bid of the original tender, a Canadian contractor called

Marientette Brothers Ltd, MBL. Details of the eviction are planned with the utmost care of a military operation lest the Brazilian staff sell off equipment supplied for the dam, from tipper trucks and bulldozers to domestic cookers; lest personnel scarper with gold or ivory in their hand luggage, having omitted to obtain tax clearance before they flit. Eight o'clock on a Saturday morning is selected for the balloon to go up, John the only individual supposed to know of MAJI's swoop. At about nine thirty, the army rolls into the site office compound, weapons showing and, putting a cordon around, collects up or drives away all moveable equipment, taking it to the safekeeping of Morogoro Police yard where the plant is subsequently used to build a football stadium. Meanwhile, the local police force surrounds all the villas occupied by the Brazilians and, just in case, all the Mafiga British bungalows too. Police descend upon the houses from their vehicle, fully armed with spare ammunition stashed in their springy spiral hair. Such is their zeal and speed in leaping from their minibus that bullets tumble out into the flowerbed among the canna lilies and they must stop and scrabble in the earth before they can take up their stand by the front door. Many cigarettes and not a few coca colas later, Issa is happily squatting on the verandah with them, chatting away, and everyone is friends again.

Now, in 1982, begins a year-long argument about money to pay the Canadians, whose bid is considerably higher than the Brazilians'. Moreover, only some of the advance monies paid to the Brazilians four years earlier is recovered in the form of plant and equipment. Inflation has occurred. The World Bank is not well disposed to lend more to Tanzania since interest on earlier loans is not forthcoming; the projects the Bank has funded being unable to generate the anticipated financial improvement in Tanzania's budget. As the wrangling, discussion and counter discussion rolls on, the Gibb Africa Partners are becoming more disappointed: several Gibb staff at Mindu are withdrawn to other postings. The Canadian Government, being importuned by MBL to invest money in Tanzania, is reluctant. John is frustrated: there is talk in Gibb of pulling out of the Mindu Project altogether, and his name is on the submitted tender for a treatment works in Mwanza. But that is some two or three years away, still.

***

Mwanza! It is miles from anywhere, at the back of beyond, in the middle of Africa, on Lake Victoria. Anne groans at the prospect of such a penal posting in the middle of nowhere, an exile comparable to that of Napoleon Bonaparte on St. Helena Island in mid-Atlantic; without benefit of television and naught but a few chosen books and some desert island discs. She amuses herself deciding which six books, besides the Bible, she would take to Mwanza. Lytton Strachey's *Eminent Victorians,* Douglas Adams' *The Long Dark Teatime of the Soul,* Dorothy Dunnet's *King Hereafter,* Lawrie Lee's *Cider with Rosie,* Joseph Thompson's *A Journey through Masailand* and Edward Gibbon's *Decline and Fall of the Roman Empire,* all six volumes; or just the *Oxford English Dictionary* and write her own book.

"We will go and look at Mwanza," promises John. "Drive up, spend a few days there, see the place." Well and good; it is some 600 miles so they take a land rover and Joseph, the Gibb driver, stopping midway at Singida in a Lutheran hostel found in the town centre. It reminds Anne of the film *The Inn of the Sixth Happiness.* In the early twentieth century, Gladys Aylward (played by Ingrid Bergmann), an evangelical called to China, concluded that the only way she could spread the Gospel was to set up an inn for caravaneers which offered an extra happiness above the five essentials expected from an overnight lodging. In addition to shelter, warmth, food, a bed, and a pound for their mules, she offered story time with thrilling Christian tales of miracles, treachery, bloodshed and resurrection. She must have been a compelling storyteller because her inn was always full. The Lutheran hostel has a clean room, laundered sheets, mosquito-proofing, wholesome simple food, an *askari* or watchman, for the vehicle and a bookshop full of good Christian literature.

Destination is Kamanga, 'across the water' from Mwanza, three quarters of an hour in the vehicle ferry across Smith's Sound, where Gibb's man in Mwanza, Klaus Gaetje, lives with his family. Approaching Mwanza town, the landscape is sporadically rocky: it is as if a kindergarten of giants had tipped out a box of rocks and were busy playing at building with their toys when they were called away. Klaus, having stayed with Anne and John at Morogoro once or twice, welcomes the travellers off the ferry, introducing them to his wife Waebke, their three-year old son Mark and Klaus' mother, Mama Gaetje. Klaus' parents, originally from Germany, had settled in Kamanga, which is on the Burundi Zaire side of Lake Victoria, many years before, Klaus being born in Tanzania and educated in Kenya before a marine engineering training in north Germany. Waebke, whom he met whilst a student, is still hankering for Europe and north Germany, struggling with boredom, the isolation of up-country life, mother-in-law problems and uncertainties about the future for the family in East Africa. They live in a very beautiful setting, Mama Gaetje having spent decades planning and planting her lawns and flowering shrubberies about a rocky knoll by a lakeside beach, at the same time growing or processing most of their food requirements, as is the habit among the old settlers. They have various boats, of course, Klaus having built and managed Kamanga Ferries for many years. If it were not for the fish eagles wheeling and screeching in the trees around, Smith's Sound might be western Scotland, Sound of Sleat for instance. Kamanga Ferry cuts off many motoring miles as does the ferry from Mallaig to Sleat and southern Skye. The Gaetje gardens could easily be the lovely, near-tropical gardens found near Ullapool. Smith's Sound, ten miles long and four miles wide with its surrounding hills and islands, is indeed a drowned river valley, but drowned recently, only some 25,000 to 30,000 years ago in Pleistocene times when the East African Rift systems were forming. This accounts for the extreme cragginess of the landscape around Mwanza.

Back in Morogoro, there is still no progress on the fate of Mindu Dam, and Gibb prepares to withdraw the rest of their staff as the third and last deadline for the client, MAJI, to reach a final decision on whether to appoint MBL approaches. Packers are booked and tentative plans for evacuation to Nairobi made. John is in Dar es Salaam for a week at a time attending meetings and more meetings with MAJI. The boat, out of the water on a cradle, is up for sale so they stay at the Kilimanjaro Hotel in the city. The hotel, a matchbox-shaped edifice built with many floors, small rooms and low ceilings suitable for now non-existent air conditioning, is not too unpleasant in the cool season. From the bedroom balcony, one can look out over formal gardens to the coruscating creek with its distant din of boat repair yard, a ballet of wooden legs, now filled with port shipping where 130 years ago, Sultan Seyyid bin Said decided to build a peaceful palace, far from the clamorous intrigues of the Zanzibar court. A curious plume of smoke hangs over the city.

John returns to the hotel at lunchtime. "They have burnt down the Bank of Tanzania." He uses the active tense, factual and accusing; not the Kiswahili causative tense phraseology, "The Bank of Tanzania has been caused to burn down." John's reaction is incredulity. "They couldn't possibly: they wouldn't be able to." But maybe 'they' did! Indeed, on the BBC news that evening, the event is announced in conjunction with the observation that penetrating corruption investigations were about to start.

A week is a long time. The final deadline for MAJI to award the contract for Mindu Dam to MBL has several times come and gone, the gangplank of the ship of time is being raised for good when suddenly, the flying figure of MAJI leaps on: Mindu Dam can go ahead; MBL to build it. Hoorah!

Anne picks up her teaching again at Morogoro's university campus, this time for a small group of three girls who have now outgrown the Sokoine University Campus primary school and whose parents are reluctant to send them away to boarding school. The Worldwide Education System, WES, part of the long-established Parents' National Educational Union, PNEU, has been researched and the girls' parents decide to set up a schoolroom in one of the campus residences and embark on a WES correspondence course with Anne to administer much of the course work. Most interesting and quite a challenge! One aspect is physical education: there are available tennis courts and a swimming pool, so tennis and swimming are selected. These girls, however, already swimming like trout, are ready for water survival and rescue skills, so Anne writes off to the Royal Life Saving Society in the UK for their manual and their award syllabus, she herself having achieved those skills at school some thirty years earlier. Soon, other campus children are clamouring for swimming lessons too and, with the Mafiga pool committee agreeing to have both beginners' and advanced lessons held in the pool, much fun is had by all.

The Canadians breathe new enthusiasm into the site; new equipment for the dam and office, and, oh luxury, more freezers, one for each household. There are, too, six new cookers each as big as a prairie: Issa can scarcely see into the saucepans on the back rings.

Morogoro, coming to life after a chronic hibernation, witnesses the long-awaited opening of the New Morogoro Hotel. The conceptual inspiration not matchbox but rondavel is avant-garde, a metamorphosis for dormant Morogoro. Around the principal rondavel, housing reception, bar and restaurant, are grouped smaller accommodation rondavels each with eight rooms arranged in segments around a hollow core. At the thin edge of each wedge, lie the bathrooms abutting the core hollow which, as a giant organ pipe magnifying a hundredfold, picks up every hiccup, aeration, gust, hiss and blow: the din at seven o'clock in the morning is said to be horrendous. Presumably the acoustics of ablutions are the architect's responsibility and some poor Israeli will be asked to find a solution to the unfortunate situation. Plant papaya trees in the cores, perhaps.

Among a number of small European enterprises dotted around Tanzania, is the Brooke Bond Tea estate near Mufindi in Western Tanzania, where the tea being grown at 8,000 feet altitude is of very fine quality although of lesser quantity. Here, some 600 miles from Dar es Salaam, eight or ten British families in a tiny corner of colonial life, live like Alice in Wonderland, in bizarre, larger than life mode where fact may be stranger than fiction; or else half dead from boredom. Anne and John and the children are invited here for Christmas.

"I'm afraid you will find us at Mufindi over-familiar and overindulgent," says their hostess, Kim. "But do come. It will be fun." Kim's family includes not only her husband and two daughters but also a Belgian sheepdog, all 400 lbs of her, a lad of 19 betwixt school and the army and a young wood owl which had been brought to Kim as a fledgling with a badly broken wing and which she has raised; in the sitting room mostly. The owl is brought to the table at the end of lunch where it 'kills' the tinsel and pecks avidly at red jelly. Later, some 20 people play silly team games, charades and liar dice round a roaring log fire. Without benefit of television, of course, these small isolated communities have a distinctive eccentricity; horseplay with the soda siphon, owl droppings on the sofa, an overwhelming quantity and variety of alcoholic drinks: these are part of the up-country compensation. It is delightful to be participating rather than just watching others acting it on the television as is likely to be the case in the UK.

They return to Morogoro to find the Ngerengere River, normally all of three metres wide under the trunk road bridge, is now an awesome half-mile across after day upon day of heavy rain. So named from an Arab phrase meaning 'river of rivers', the Arabs either having had their tongue in cheek or seen the trickle in its rare flooded state, it is the lifeblood of Morogoro farmers. A local lorry having missed the bridge and overturned, is submerged. But the peasants are jubilant. Every year they plant in November -December an out-of-season crop, a gambler's crop, but perhaps one year in five affords enough rainfall to harvest anything. The rain is not such good news for Mindu Dam. With the river still rising, the emergency spillway, designed to accommodate April to May's 'Long Rains', is brought into action rather than risk a breach in the mile-long earth dam. The swamp upstream of the dam is filling well, creating a lake; the reservoir to be Morogoro's industrial resource, its water supply for the new industrial greater Morogoro stepping forward towards the end of the millennium.

The coming of the lake brings an unplanned embryo fishing industry. For want of a boat, polystyrene tiles lashed together, a log of felled timber, anything that floats to carry local lads out across the water with their bent pins on a length of sisal string. Of course there are accidents but the drownings deter no one. Women suddenly gifted with adjacent abundant water, go to wash their clothes; with their wetly clinging *kangas* (colourful cloth wraps) impeding movement, they fall over, thrash about in panic, tangle in waterweed and drown. The drownings deter no one. These are people who should have basic water safety, rescue and resuscitation skills. But how? There is no way Anne can approach them.

"There is a place near Morningside in the mountains," says Issa when Anne mentions the drownings, "Where the boy scouts and girl guides go for weekend camping. They swim in a pool of a small river up there. I know the Scoutmaster in Morogoro. I will talk with him."

The Morogoro Scoutmaster has, alas, almost no English and Anne's Kiswahili, adequate for shopping and family affairs, is unable to cope with water safety. However, it is a beginning and in time the Scoutmaster contacts the Chief Scout in Dar es Salaam, who is willing to give Anne an interview at the Scout Headquarters. John is increasingly in Dar es Salaam at this moment in time, his work being to continue persuading MAJI and the Treasury to release necessary payment to both MBL and Gibb. *Ragtime* is again out of the water on a cradle during the wet months, so Anne and John house-warm friends' houses in Dar for six or eight weeks at a time while the incumbents are away on leave. The Chief Scout is a portly, pompous middle-aged gentleman with good English but an uncompromising manner. He glances through the Royal Life Saving Society manual, taps his teeth and nods. "I will think about it." His voice is noncommittal. "Phone me next week," he says as he rises to shake hands. It is a disappointing interview but disappointments are a way of life in Tanzania. When Anne phones him the following week, he is away: no one knows when he will be back.

Meanwhile back at Mafiga, they find their house has been broken into; much of the bed linen has gone and some kitchen equipment. The police, being informed, have a shrewd idea where to look and it is not long before Joseph, the Gibb driver, is called to the police station to drive them to raid a suspect's house. There they find only the linen for one single bed plus two kitchen items; the mincer and the plastic jug from the electric liquidiser. The rest of the stolen goods having vanished, the police take the recovered items to the police station, there to await the court case.

Weeks later the court case has still not been heard. Anne, requesting an appointment with the magistrate, is astonished to be ushered straight into the office. A very attractive young Tanzanian lady rises from behind the desk to shake hands. "I am so sorry, Mrs Sears, for the delay in returning your recovered property."

"I hate to bother you, Madame, but I need the recovered items urgently. You see, I have to prepare a decent house for a business guest from Nairobi."

"My name is Fredrika, by the way, and I can see you will need things for your guest."

"These visitors from Kenya think Tanzania is a poor place to live. I know it is not and I can offer excellent hospitality. But without my bed linen and kitchen equipment, I am handicapped."

The young lady nods her graceful head.

"I am embarrassed not to show Tanzania in its true colours." Anne presses the point as firmly as possible.

"That is right!" says the lovely magistrate, "I must help you." This goddess of wisdom sits thinking for a minute, calls for a file on the case, dips into it with elegant hands. "There is no problem. All we have to do is get the accused, the owner of the goods, that is yourself, and a witness of the recovery of the said goods from the accused's house, that is your company driver, together and we can have an instant hearing. It will only take a minute or two." Her well-modulated voice and impeccable English is a delight to hear, as is the message it extends. "It is a straightforward case and the accused is likely to get five years."

"Five years; poor man! He was bullied, bribed or intimidated to act for one who the police say is a known and convicted criminal."

"Ah yes," explains the beautiful magistrate, "But we must have sentence as a deterrent to others."

The mastermind thief deserves a stiff penalty but surely not this middle-aged peasant parading as a night watchman. It is possible of course that the accused will welcome a spell in prison with free meals, free clothing, free roof over his head. In old colonial days, the 'Hoteli King Georgi' as prison was known, could offer respite from the ceaseless grind of survival: many worked hard to get in. On the other hand, it seems unlikely in this case: the accused is out of prison on bail, and has gone to tend his *shamba*, farm holding, during the growing season.

Joseph knows his address so it is arranged that the Gibb driver will call upon the accused to inform him that his presence is required at the courthouse for a minute or two next day. But on the morrow, no accused appears. "We should get the police to arrest him," suggests the magistrate. This proposal is vetoed since it is likely to cause the accused to take to the bushes. "We must ask the man who stood bail to go and bring him along," the magistrate instructs. So Joseph and the man standing bail set off to find the accused: two hours later, having had a puncture and run out of petrol, they return empty-handed.

"Oh dear, that is a pity!" sighs the magistrate when Anne reports next day.

"Never mind; I will arrange for the police to lend you your recovered items for the duration of the guest's visit. But," says this rare African orchid inclining her beautiful head, "You don't really have to return them for the hearing. You might never get them back."

Anne is in Dar es Salaam again, housewarming for a month or two at a time for various families on leave, while John battles with growing inertia in the Ministries. Anne finds no joy in looking after other people's dogs or establishing a rapport with other people's domestic staff. The various families have differing household and kitchen appliances with which Anne must familiarise herself. Meanwhile, John is struggling with increasing difficulties in obtaining meat, sugar, beer, petrol and diesel. It is all disheartening.

Ultimately, they are housewarming for a British harbour pilot. His house, which is provided and maintained by the Commonwealth Office, is neglected and in a state of disrepair: the telephone does not work, the electricity bill has not been remitted and risks being disconnected. What is more, the rains have started and the mosquito netting at the windows is broken. Anne is in limbo having left the home in Morogoro after six and a half years there, the longest period she has ever spent under the same roof. Reason tells her that this is a part of the alluring challenge of Africa. There is an unending chorus of frogs during the wet nights and of pie dogs baying in the small hours; one starts, others take up the chorus in unison, in harmony, in counterpoint and in descant but always *fortissimo, vivace* and *vibrato*. At this moment, Africa palls. When the space shuttle *Challenger* explodes on take-off killing all aboard in 1986, Ronald Reagan, that movie idol of yesteryear and now President of the United States of America, who must be speaking off the cuff, puts a rational perspective on the disaster. "Pioneering is not for the faint-hearted," he asserts. Wonderful words, which are therapeutic and spine-stiffening to Anne in Dar es Salaam as well as all round America.

"There's a message for you at the office, from the Chief Scout. He wants you in his office at 11 a.m. tomorrow." John's intelligence is a shot in the arm.

The Chief Scout, uncommunicative as ever, introduces a young man, Stewart Kiluswa, a scout executive officer in Dar, and the interview is over. Stewart explains that he is employed in the Public Library and is interested in the RLSS Manual. "I nearly drowned when I was a youngster playing about in the sea. I can swim," he assures Anne, "As long as I have one foot on the bottom." He grins, a disarmingly charming smile. "In the junior section of the library we can put up some of these life-saving pictures and simple methods of survival." He taps the Manual, now tucked under his arm. "You know, here in Dar, a primary school teacher will take his class to the beach, boys in shorts, girls in skirt and blouse, to 'swim' in the sea. The teacher, in shirt, trousers, shoes and socks, on the beach, has no control over the children, just waves a stick and shouts. It is asking for accidents. Now we in the library are

271

in touch with schools: we can reach them with elementary water safety.

Stewart's infectious enthusiasm inspires Anne to write to the RLSS representative in Harare, Margot Webber of the Zimbabwe Life Saving Society. She sends a copy of her Zimbabwe-printed and produced code for universal water safety; not just for the swimming whites and elite black populations but for everyone. Margot has circulated to 157 local schools and persuaded 107 teachers to sign on for a teachers' training clinic in basic survival, rescue and resuscitation; she has simplified the UK and the Australian manuals to produce the English language Zimbabwe code. It is a mammoth undertaking. In Tanzania, however, the task must be as a pre-school preparation, an attempt to switch on awareness to water hazards. Accidents are *shauri ya Mungu* (the affairs of God) and number one project must be to break through that barrier; survival and rescue, being more distant concepts, can wait a while. And it must be in the Kiswahili language.

In this nutritious gel in the petri dish of the mind, an idea of a *Tanzania Water Safety Code* begins its earliest growth. In Tanzania, Anne has been blessed with the gift of John's life. She vows to do her best to help reduce the many water accidents occurring in the country. Suddenly, Mwanza on Lake Victoria offers tantalising opportunities.

Chapter 15

The Lake on the Roof of the World

Incredible! The Gaetje's guest house is built atop a rocky crag on the shores of Lake Victoria. It is level with the upper branches of a false fig tree below and Anne finds herself virtually living in an aviary. Multi-coloured birds of all shapes and sizes dart about; hundreds of them. It is disturbingly noisy and hyperactive but for some weeks while the tree is in fruit, it promises to be interesting. The rooms are full of roses. Roses! Waebke, Klaus's wife, cultivates half an acre of roses to sell as cut flowers in Mwanza. What a pity she cannot get her roses by air to the bigger markets of Dar es Salaam. But at this moment, in 1986, Mwanza airport is operating only a 49-seater Fokker Friendship aircraft since the runway is too neglected and damaged to accommodate the 180-seater Boeings.

Mwanza is indeed cut off, at the end of the world, a further outpost of Africa. Australians might call it the Outback. And Kamanga is the back of beyond, connected to Mwanza by ferry four and a half miles and forty-five minutes across Smith's Sound. Anne stands on Kamanga jetty watching the loading of a bus the roof of which is piled high with ripe pineapples and a swarm of bees and flies, and three landrovers one of which is pushed on by

273

people power. There are also innumerable bicycles and full wheelbarrows, a bull on a rope, several crates of chickens, a goat or two, and some three hundred people disgorged from buses serving the ferry station, plus a dozen lads selling chewing gum, cigarettes, and soft drinks. Anne realises that this could be regarded not as the end of the world but its beginning. She sees on Kamanga jetty more energy and enterprise than in Dar es Salaam but of course, it is 600 miles from the constraints of the capital city and its government sanctions, and 3,000 feet higher in altitude with a climate more akin to the Mediterranean lands than to the equatorial littoral of Dar. Some of Kamanga's ferry traffic is connected with a gold rush to Geita alluvial gold field some 60 miles to the West: every Tom, Dick and Harry carrying a spade and a tin dish is rushing to pan for gold, accompanied by a host of camp followers.

John's project in Mwanza is the construction of a new treatment works to serve a city of three quarters of a million people and edging weekly towards the million mark. A deep water intake off a high granite headland known as Capri Point will draw water free from the bilharzia cyst which is universal round the Lake shore's surface water. Besides the treatment plant there is a massive distribution pipe system to be installed to all quarters of the city. A contract with a French Construction Company, SCEEM, is being signed in Dar es Salaam and John must commute to Dar frequently because a lot of contractual discussion is still outstanding: the Client, MAJI, keeps changing its mind.

Meanwhile, the six resident engineers' houses are being built high on Capri Point with stunning views over the two Capri Islands, over Smith's Sound and out across the Lake to its horizon. Some 200 miles away lies Uganda to the northwest and Kenya to the northeast. This virtual inland sea, as big as the Aegean, is but a giant freshwater puddle filling a shallow depression on the crystalline primeval plateau of Africa. The various relatively recent earth movements which have shaped the Rift Valley, have changed lake water levels, drowning long arms of inflowing rivers, forming spectacular fjords and islands. The weather, entirely local and quite divorced from the global trade winds experienced at Dar, has a reputation for nasty storms and total windlessness.

The community is an interesting mix of Scandinavians, Dutch, French, African and Asian. What is more, there is a Mwanza Yacht Club with a number of lasers and wayfarer dinghies which race regularly around a fine bay or out into Smith's Sound and around the islands to Kamanga. Excellent, safe sailing grounds for small dinghies, yes, but a shock squall can capsize the entire fleet and indeed, tragedy strikes when one of the Danish crew, who had divested himself of his life jacket because it was a hot windless day, is drowned.

Now is the time to bring *Ragtime* up country from the Indian Ocean to Lake Victoria, John and Anne having already installed an inboard engine for the windless Lake before leaving the Morogoro contract. They join the mad band of yachtsmen who rail or road haul yachts from the ocean to Africa's several inland seas. Loaded on a rail wagon with boat tender, John's laser and Osmani the boatman, the freight arrives a week later at Mwanza's deepwater port, Osmani being much exercised to find lions prowling the dockyard by night. Cruising the roof of Africa is largely a pleasure for the few posted there, but with time, intrepid entrepreneurs may be able to offer skippered cruising or bareboat hire. Who knows?

There is plenty to see. Ukerewe Island boasts golden beaches with forestry reserve behind, pine-scented and silent but for the fish eagles screeching; the stuff of Robinson Crusoe adventure. Rubondo Island some 70 miles distant, offering pleasant lee shores for night anchorage, is a game sanctuary with tracts of primeval forest where Frankfurt Zoological Society places endangered species. Admiralty charts of the Lake are accurate, having been surveyed from 1901 onwards, when the railway which became known as the 'Lunatic Line' reached Kisumu and surveyors rushed around the Lake establishing wooding stations for lake shipping; and thereby laying political claim to Lake Victoria and the Nile headwaters.

Although the Lake is tideless, seasonal fluctuations do occur with associated hazards. Papyrus islands of towering grasses and hundreds of tons of matted root having broken adrift from the margins as water levels rise, are randomly windblown. There is trouble with *Ragtime* now moored at Mwanza Yacht Club which is bound to occur while John is away in Dar es Salaam. At dusk, the yacht club Commodore's landrover screeches up to Capri Point. "Come quickly. There is a huge floating island bearing down on *Ragtime*." The club committee meeting is suspended while all stand by to help; it is an eerie, twilight sight resembling a clever boat show stunt at Earl's Court London, with the yacht moored by tropical island. The only snag is that yacht, mooring and hundreds of tons of island are moving inexorably towards the shore. Osmani stands on the beach petrified like a rabbit before a python's open jaw: these islands are allegedly alive with poisonous snakes and rapacious insects. Commodore and committee jump to action. "We'll back the boat off and go across the bay to the Port. Anne, you drive Osmani round to the Port, picking up one of the Danes working there as you go so that you can get in the Port security gate. See you there."

All is well and next day, the Danes arrange some useful tug manoeuvre practice for the Tanzanian crews, pulling the island off the yacht club beach and out to the bay mouth. *Ragtime's* mooring is recovered in knee-deep water and replaced before *Ragtime* is brought back to the yacht club.

"You are lucky," said one of the Scandinavians working in forestry on Ukerewe Island. "I got my propeller snarled in an old fishing net stuck in one of these islands and was towed for miles round the Lake before I could cut it free."

Having moved into the house on Capri Point and found a treasure of an old cook known as Mzee (Kiswahili for venerable elder) and also a girl for the housework and hand washing who is pleasant, partly trained, strong, mission-schooled and liable to become pregnant, it is necessary to start making a garden. On an acre of noble rocks varying from one metre to 20 metres high what else but a giant's rockery, pools of canna lilies, busy lizzie, marguerite daisies or geraniums and a few shrubs dotted about. The whole is easy to plan since the rocks dictate the size and shape of flowerbeds. The surrounding 'lawn' is kept short by SCEEM's garden handyman, a dozy drudge wielding a slasher implement.

Now is the time to turn to the water safety project. But how? The first idea, of approaching the regional authorities in Mwanza to ask for ten minutes' time with the Regional District Officer, get his sympathetic ear and show him the Zimbabwe Life Saving Society literature, fails. Anne tries the Regional Chief Scout and the Chief Girl Guide but after two months, there is still no response to her overtures. That dour fellow, Disappointment, dogs the notion of water safety.

Mwanza yacht club has a new commodore, Richard Rugarabamu, and the committee has been debating whether to build a swimming pool on the premises. Richard is keen for his children to learn to swim. "I could teach them, perhaps." Anne proffers Richard the Australian Royal Life Saving Manual.

"This is impressive. But there is a problem" ventures Richard, the trained lawyer of many years' practice. What problem? Is Anne missing some vital constraint?

"What about – er – swimsuits?" he queries with delicate embarrassment.

Anne perceives the ghosts of old colonial *memsahibs* gossiping among themselves. 'They (the Asians and

Africans) can't join our club; they'd want to swim in our pool and they haven't got a swimsuit between them.' Anne exclaims with relief: "That's not a problem. They can swim in their underpants and the girls can wear a vest or sleeveless top as well, if they want."

"I don't think any of the girls are old enough to need that," grins Richard.

Two days later, Richard has arranged for lessons to start in Mwanza Club pool, what was the Gymkhana Club in days of yore. 'Club pool' is a euphemism for what is an extension of dirty lake water fed in from the city domestic water supply: it is evil green at the shallow end with black depths. True, there are no hippos or crocodiles in it, and it is assumed that chlorine is sometimes added, which may kill the bilharzia cysts.

"Richard, what about a boy scout or girl guide to help with the language barrier?"

"Good idea. I will arrange for you to meet the regional Commissioner of Scouts and of Guides, Mr and Mrs Ithuli." These are the very people Anne has been trying to contact. It is the old adage; not what you know but who you know. "And," says Richard, "The Asian members of the yacht club are going to donate plastic jerry cans to use as teaching aids; 'personal flotation devices' as your manual calls them."

A week later, Anne meets her Scouts - Mosa, Nelson and Mchela - and from the guides, two lovely girls just finished school and awaiting exam results; Pendo who is the daughter of Mr and Mrs Ithuli, and Aiyesha. They all seem interested, enthusiastic even. It is most encouraging.

Housekeeping and catering in Mwanza are much easier than in Dar es Salaam. In Mwanza where market forces operate freely, there is plenty of grain, fish, meat and vegetables in the market; sugar, cooking oils, beer and soap products are available from Kenya if need be. The Gaetjes supply milk, butter, cream and pork through their shop in Mwanza. This is just as well since Anne must cater for visits from Gibb personnel from Nairobi in Mwanza *en mission*, the 'flying circus' as they are known. She must welcome representatives of the European Economic Community, which is the funding agent of this treatment works project; also the British High Commissioner and his wife while they do the rounds of Tanzania. And on one occasion, the national Manager of British Airways and his wife grace Mwanza Yacht Club with a visit to present prizes in the B.A. Regatta, among many others. Fortunately, there is a guesthouse for their accommodation but Anne must supervise it.

The convent-trained lass who has been engaged on three months' trial for housework and hand laundry, proves to be incompatible with Mzee the cook. So in comes Pascale, a teenager working as a handyman 'gofer' on the Gibb compound gardens; strong, willing and trainable, he becomes an excellent houseboy. Soon, Anne installs her appropriate technology smoker in the rock garden for meat and for Nile Perch, which abounds in the Lake, and Pascale learns to read the wind, that fickle diurnal wind which commands the lakeshores, adjusting the lid of the drum, applying more wood shavings from the local cabinetmakers or else damping down the erratic fire. The rich, oily smoked Nile Perch adds gourmet interest to the Capri Point cuisine. However, Anne stalls at experimenting with lake fly recipes gleaned from the *Malawi Cook Book*. Bimonthly, at the new moon and the full moon, zillions of tiny flies hatch from the warm lake water, rising in dense opaque clouds, which drift randomly on the wind. If a swarm has enveloped the house, lake flies piled half a metre deep on the far side of the fly screen of the verandah door could, if one wished, be gathered, compressed and dried. These minute insects are reputed to be nutritiously rich in protein and calcium, delicious in a tasty sauce of fried onion, tomato and groundnuts! Rather, let the fly larvae feed the teeming fish resources of the Lake.

The vexation of Mwanza is its inaccessibility: it is a dictatorship of distance affecting personnel, produce and post. Connection with Dar es Salaam is sometimes two small planes daily, sometimes none at all; and too often those that do fly, carry a freight of fresh fish plus its attendant aroma. This leaves only a ruined road or a thrice-weekly train service, both of which cost two and a half days' time. Not infrequently, John fails to reach his meetings in Dar or becomes stranded in the capital for days at a time. Worse, from Anne's point of view, is that business visitors become stranded in Mwanza. Public transport between Mwanza and Nairobi in Kenya, some 250 miles apart, is nil since the two countries are not on speaking terms. The alternatives are the very infrequent availability to some of the public of the Missionary Air Force, MAF, or a two-day drive across the unmade, mud-bedevilled tracks of the Serengeti National Park, sometimes winching landrovers through acres of ooze, or else a thousand miles by tarmac round the Lake to Kisumu and thereby onward to Nairobi. Thanks to the Gibb Partners' sympathy for the plight of their Mwanza personnel, their own small plane may be occasionally available for family and close friends.

Yet, such is the grandeur of Africa's size and space around Mwanza and such is its astonishing beauty, that practical problems become reduced; the psyche shrinks agitations of the mind to manageable proportions, to the commonplace. Thus, a plague of savage *siafu* ants, or a dearth of beer at the yacht club, is more alarming than the stress of trying to attend a critical business meeting six hundred or a thousand miles away from a remote region with a chaotic air service.

And yet. There is a modicum of satisfaction in arranging a Christmas party of consummate complexity. Klaus Gaetje's ferryboat *Uzinza*, normally in service across Smith's Sound carrying a lorry or two, a bus, some pick-ups, bicycles, wheelbarrows, hundreds of pedestrians with their head-loads, sacks of produce, goats and babies, is washed down and fitted with an awning. An abnormal cargo of tables, chairs, tents, fridge, freezer, charcoal brazier, a Christmas tree, boxes of drink, turkey, plum puddings, cakes, pies, sacks of fruit and avocados, armfuls of roses, two laser dinghies, fishing rods, bedding and deckchairs is put aboard. Klaus with his wife and small son, John and Anne with their two children and various friends out from the UK for the holiday, set off at eight a.m. from Mwanza Yacht Club, destination Rubondo Island. They light the charcoal and serve bacon and egg breakfasts as they cruise. At midday they stop for a swim. Then it is drinks with nuts and crisps followed by lunch of pies and sandwiches. By six p.m. arriving and slithering down the ramp to hurriedly equip the two rondavels on the island and erect various tents, it is time to switch on *Uzinza's* lights, decorate the tree and set up the traditional Christmas dinner – candles on the table, roses of course, crackers, wine, toasts to absent friends – it is all there on an uninhabited island in the middle of Lake Victoria on the roof of Africa.

Meanwhile, swimming lessons in Mwanza Club pool continue, and despite the disgusting state of the water, none of the youngsters want to give up. Anne begs the Club Manager to change the water frequently since they are without proper pool chemicals. "An accident is waiting to happen in opaque water like this."

A tragedy does occur; next day to one of the club staff's children. The manager, convinced that Anne has the gift of prophecy, has the pool drained until the essential chemicals can be obtained through the kind offices of a Swedish aid organisation.

"While the pool is empty would you like me to give a course in resuscitation, 'The Kiss of Life', to your club staff?"

"Yes, yes, we are very glad for you to train them."

And of course the scouts and guides join the training sessions, both to cope with the language barrier and to learn the basics of resuscitation.

It is while talking about the elementary physiology of airway, lungs, circulation and the heart during the resuscitation sessions, that the name of Dr Yongolo is mentioned. He is, apparently, a government dental surgeon in Mwanza and also chairman of the local branch of the Red Cross/Crescent, which runs courses in basic physiology. Anne writes to him with a brief summary of her attempts to introduce swimming, water safety awareness and resuscitation and asks if he can spare her fifteen minutes of his valuable time. When the answer is positive, Anne goes to his surgery to meet a man who will remain forever in her memory bank.

Dr Yongolo spends five minutes glancing through the UK RLSS Manual, the Australian Manual, which is more focussed on open water safety, that is sea and river, than is the British; and also the Zimbabwe Water Safety Code which has an universal relevance. Well into middle age, portly, he engages with the direct eye contact of the professional businessman.

"Yes, yes," he pauses. "It was just as the manual says; with a tied rope and a stone." He looks up. "You know about the tragedy which happened last week in the Serengeti Park?"

Anne does know; it has been lengthily reported in the national press. After days of heavy rain, the Grumeti River in the western corridor of the Serengeti National Park was in full spate, its ford closed to all vehicles, which must queue on either bank to await the torrent's passing. Eventually, a number of heavy lorries managed to go through while light traffic must remain waiting. But an impatient driver of a landrover full of eleven youngsters from three Mwanza families on a Serengeti outing, decided to risk the turgid ford. The vehicle was swept sideways off the causeway into deep water and overturned, trapping all under the water. A group of holidaying Europeans, grabbing a tow rope and a stone, tied the rope end round a tree trunk and holding it tight, making a human chain, managed to wade out towards the vehicle where they broke a window with the stone. Only five of the children were saved.

Dr Yongolo shakes his head. "These families are my friends, these children friends of my children. It is terrible, terrible." Grief creases his countenance; his empathy is palpable. A buzzer rings on his desk.

"My next patient!"

"Dr Yongolo, may I call on you again some time when you have a moment to spare? I am thinking about a possible Tanzanian water safety code, in Kiswahili."

"Yes, indeed. You know, the island people can swim and are more thoughtful of the dangers of water but the townspeople here in Mwanza have no idea and there are thousands more in the towns than on the islands. I have an Ukerewe Island man in the Red Cross here. He is a nurse at the Mwanza general hospital and he gives voluntary time to teach a Red Cross course for me. He is a good swimmer; I could get him to introduce water safety into his resuscitation course. Now I must go. Thank you for calling."

It is a privilege to meet and talk with Dr Yongolo. Overworked and underpaid, a dignified paterfamilias and pillar of Mwanza's social community, his humanity is inspiring and his co-operation intoxicating.

Discussing the idea of a Tanzanian water safety leaflet in Kiswahili with the scouts and guides, Anne finds them enthusiastic, more than willing to help put it together, translate into Kiswahili and do the drawings. And when Anne has assembled all the items she needs; translation, drawings, estimate of costs and supporting letter from the Red Cross, she begins drafting begging letters to worthy charities such as Rotary Club, Round Table, Lions' Club and others. She is sure she has a good case to make.

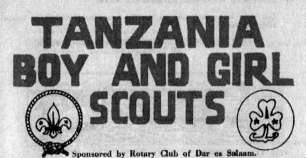

TANZANIA BOY AND GIRL SCOUTS

Sponsored by Rotary Club of Dar es Salaam.

KANUNI ZA USALAMA WA MAJI

Uwe salama karibu na maji

WAZIJUA HATARI?

Kuzama kunaweza kutoka katika mito mikubwa, mito midogo, vidimbwi, baharini, tanki la umwagiliaji, hata katika debe la maji katika bustani au nyumbani. Boti za uvuvi zaweza kuanguka na kuzama.

Kanuni tatu ziwezazo kuokoa maisha yetu.

BAKI UMETULIA, UKIELEA NA KUPUNGA JUU MKONO.

OGELEENI PAMOJA, MARUFUKU KUOGELEA PEKE YAKO.

(1) USIENDE PEKE YAKO

Cheza au fanya kazi ndani au karibu ya maji pamoja na rafiki yako. Ili kama utapatwa na matatizo rafiki yako ataweza kukusaidia.

(2) KAMA UKIANGUKIA NDANI

a) Tulia.

b) Lala chali huku ukipunga juu mkono mmoja.

c) Funga mdomo isipokuwa wakati ukipiga kelele uombapo msaada.

284

(3) **KAMA MTU MWINGINE AKIANGUKIA NDANI**

Lala chini katika nchi kavu na kumfikia kwa kutumia fimbo au kutupia kibuyu au dumu.

KAA MKAVU USILOWE. KATIKA KUOKOA TUMIA FIMBO AU TUPIA DUMU.

VITU VYA KUKUMBUKA

Ajali katika nyumba au bustani

1. Ndoo au debe za maji lazima zifunikwe.
2. Weka juu ufunguo wa bafu wasikoweza kulika watoto wadogo.
3. Maji yaliyohifadhiwa bafuni lazima yafunikwe.

Karibu na nyumbani

1. Angalia watoto wadogo.
2. Wafundishe watoto wakubwa namna ya kuokoa kwa kutumia fimbo au kanga na hata kutupia kibuyu.
3. Wasikae pembeni mwa mito; wanaweza kuzirai.
4. Wasikae karibu na mimea iotayo pembeni mwa ziwa; yaweza kuwa imefunika kina kirefu.
5. Kaa mbali na vidimbwi na madaraja wakati wa mafuriko kwenye masika.
6. Usijitengeneee boti kwa kutumia taka; zinaweza kuanguka na kuzama kirahisi, pia si rahisi kupiga—makasia.

Ajali katika maji wazi

1. Usiende peke yako.
2. Toka nje ya maji mara usikiapo baridi.
3. Usiogelee kwa muda wa saa nzima baada ya chakula; unaweza kutapika na kuzibwa koo au kujisikia vibaya.
4. Ni marufuku kuogelea karibu na feli au boti zenye injini.
5. Mtu asiyejua kuogelea asiende umbali kupita kina cha mabega yake.
6. Kabla ya kuogelea angalia hali ya hewa; mara kwa mara mawimbi hutokea ziwani.
7. Angalia kama bahari imesafiri maana yaweza kurudi haraka isivyotarajiwa.
8. Angalia kasi ya maji uogeleapo katika mito.
9. Ogelea sambamba na nchi kavu. Usiogelee mbali na nchi kavu maana unaweza kufika mbali bila kujua na hivyo kushindwa kurudi.
10. Usiruke katika maji usiyojua kina chake. Tumia fimbo kupima.

Juu ya maji Kwenye Boti

1. Ukiwa ndani ya feli angalia wasafiri wenzako wenye tabia ya kujionyesha na mambo ya kijinga.
2. Angalia watoto wadogo.
3. Jaribu kuangalia na kuhakikisha vifaa vya boti vinafanya kazi sawasawa. Uwe na uhakika katika boti kuna makasia na kamba. Jitahidi kuwa na dumu au kibuyu katika safari yako.
4. Jaribu kufanya mazoezi ya kujigeuza kwa boti na mtu toka majini.

286

5. Kama boti iliyoanguka haizami kaa karibu nayo. maana wawera kuonekana. kirahisi; maana jinsi ufikiriavyo — umekaribia nchi kavu huwa sivyo.

6. Mfahamishe mwenzio mahali unapokwenda na boti na wakati gani utategemea kurudi.

Katika Bwawa la Kuogelea

1. Usikimbiekimbie pembeni mwa bwawa; sehemu zake zikiwa zimelowa zaweza kuwa na utelezi.

2. Usiruke ndani bila kuangalia; unawera ukagongana na mwenzio mwingine na hivyo kuumizana.

3. Usijionyeshe; huongezea namba ya hatari.

4. Wawezi lazima wawaangalie watoto katika bwawa.

5. Fanya kama "ASKARI WA MAISHA" waaemavyo.

Printed in Tanzania by **Inland press** Box 125 Mwanza

Some months later, with Dar es Salaam Rotary Club funding, Anne is able to go to the missionary printing press in Mwanza, the Inland Press, and place an order for 5,000 copies of the leaflet. When she returns to collect the leaflets, she finds that her order was inadvertently printed on the wrong paper, on 70 gram paper instead of the chosen

80 gram weight, so they have printed another 5,000 on the right paper. For a small cash supplement, which Mwanza Rotary Club kindly agrees to provide, she now has 10,000 copies; plenty for the scouts and guides and the Red Cross/Crescent in Mwanza and Dar es Salaam.

Armed with sample copies of the water safety leaflet, Anne sets out in November 1987 for Harare in Zimbabwe where an African region conference organised by the RLSS Commonwealth arm is being held. Kenya, Malawi, Tanzania, Zambia and Zimbabwe are all there, plus a presence from Sudan. Two senior tutors from the UK and the RLSS Commonwealth Secretary, John Taylor, arrive to lead the discussions and training sessions. Stewart Kiluswa, the Scout Executive Officer from Dar, manages to persuade the Tanzanian Government to give him a ticket to Harare. Apart from the general interest of the meeting, it is a good opportunity to get to know Stewart.

He is taller than most, lean as a goal post and originally from the shores of Lake Tanganyika in Western Tanzania, not far from where David Livingstone died at Ujiji. Stewart has the natural dignity of the professional diplomat but without the sophistry of that genus. The attraction of this young man is his integrity, and an old-fashioned courtesy so sadly lacking in Europe these days; in the words of Chaucer, a 'verray parfit gentil knight' is Stewart. Brought up in Dar es Salaam, he did well at school, participating in everything available. His energy and ability earned him his place on the staff of the national library and also of the scout executive.

But what of his family life? Anne hears him mention his wife, Judith.

"And what about children, Stewart? Any children yet?" He would make a fine father.

For a second his face is eclipsed. "Judith has had a very bad time recently." He looks bleak. "She was in the big general hospital in Dar; in labour for over three days; it was a breech birth and in the end they just cut the baby out. A little girl, she only survived a few minutes."

"Ah, Stewart, what a tragedy for you and Judith! I am so sorry for your wife. But there will be others, in time"

"The doctor says Judith must wait three years before trying again. She is with her mother just now."

Whatever his private anxieties, Stewart endears himself to all the delegates by his determination to defy his big frame and plutonium bones and to swim without one foot on the bottom; with final success. Hoorah!

Out of this happy meeting in Malawi comes the idea of twinning Tanzania's Life Saving entity with a UK club near Ipswich. Deben Swimming Club offers to organise swimming regattas and fundraise to buy equipment for Mwanza: hold a Swim Aid. Armed with this understanding, Anne begins to try to interest local fishermen in rescue and resuscitation, and the police in elementary water safety and rescue skills. Encouraging too, is a letter from a Rotary club in Mombasa, Kenya, enquiring about the Tanzanian Scouts' water safety leaflet for circulation in schools. And a Norwegian Aid Agency called 'Sport for All' wants to buy 500 copies to use in P.E. teacher training. And Dar es Salaam Rotary Club wants a second edition. That ogre Disappointment is giving way to an amiable friend called Optimism. What is more, Mwanza airport runway has been repaired and is now accommodating the larger Boeing aircraft.

Meanwhile the Mwanza Scouts and Girl Guides are arranging a course of basic water safety and rescue for 9 – 15 year olds to be held in the public library on a Saturday morning. The idea is to have sixty different children each week for six weeks, making a total of three hundred and sixty children, exposed to the idea that water safety and simple rescue is something they can act upon; that drownings are not always *shauri ya Mungu* (God's affair). This is spreading the jam very thinly but it is better than nothing. What the scouts and guides actually get, is three hundred and sixty children every Saturday for six weeks: a logistical nightmare. Such is the enthusiasm for these Saturday sessions, and so biddable, so patient in awaiting their turn are the children, that the sessions are hugely effective and great fun. The children's delight in acting the part of a drowning victim, lying writhing on a length of blue fabric Anne has spread on the library floor, is palpable: born comedians every one of them.

At the Red Cross/Crescent premises water safety and lifesaving have blossomed. Recruiting some island-born assistants who already swim well, they have located a place on the lake to teach swimming. Anne is determined not to interfere in their methods of teaching swimming: encourage them only. The role of facilitator rather than teacher appears something of a novel idea among Royal Life Saving Society colleagues, most of whom are professional PE teachers and assume that if the class cannot perform some given skill in the prescribed manner, they, the expatriate teachers, are the most suitable people to instruct the group in perfecting that skill. Anne sometimes finds it an uphill struggle to resist her colleagues' good intentions.

Life in Mwanza is not all jam. Robberies have been occurring on the compound and site office yet the police have in the past done nothing but list the missing items. Now a windscreen is cut out of a Project landrover during the night. Significantly, the compound dog Ton never barked so someone who knows Ton well must have at least been an accomplice. Some months ago, an identical robbery of a windscreen has happened, and when police did nothing positive, there followed a massive robbery in one of the engineers' bungalows while the occupants were away in the Serengeti Park on their once-a-month rest and relax long weekend. This time the police, under a new Regional Police Commissioner, just arrived from Dar es Salaam with a brief to 'clean up' Mwanza, are quick and efficient. They have taken away the watchman, the gardener and Pascale, Anne's house help, for questioning, no doubt in conjunction with a dose of corporal punishment.

The watchman, wiser and older suddenly, is back and resuming duties since a new watchman might be more of a risk than a well beaten one. But Pascale is still assisting police with enquiries and Anne must do all the hand laundry, help Mzee in the kitchen and prepare the guesthouse for the arriving 'Nairobi Circus' of Gibb Partners. The pilot, Paul, staying with the Gaetje family across the water at Kamanga, is late in coming back to fly them all to Nairobi, and John discovers that the Customs and Immigration in Mwanza city office have gone home, so he must drive furiously around the town to find them and transport them to the airport. And the telephone has not worked for a week, and no one can discover whether it is a fault on the line caused by recent heavy rain or whether the line has been cut off for reasons known only to the Post and Telegraph Office. To crown it all, at 10.30 p.m. there is John's pregnant secretary Rhoda knocking on the door to say she is in labour. So out Anne goes to drive her to the hospital where an examination indicates a straightforward case and Anne is spared having to search out the city for her doctor. Next morning when Anne returns to the hospital, a delighted Rhoda has been delivered of a daughter, a pale apricot-coloured infant called Angel whose sire is a Danish construction worker, long since gone.

Indefatigably the Mwanza Project moves on, the end in sight if opaquely. Meanwhile, a prospect of finality manifests itself; the Gibb Partners in Nairobi are not willing to seek further work in Tanzania after a decade of operational stress and financial frustration. John's name is on a project in Kenya, a massive sewage plant on the outskirts of Nairobi. With this in view, an offer to buy the boat *Ragtime* is opportune. Danish friends in Mwanza relocating to Dar es Salaam are keen to have her so a railway wagon is booked. Loading of the boat and its tender, a long long day's work in a hot railway yard hard up against a metal warehouse wall, is done by John while Anne runs around collecting the boat's ticket, Osmani's ticket, a ticket for his chum Charlie who has agreed to accompany the boat's watchman, and all their luggage and provisions for a week. At length, Osmani and his friend are left sitting comfortably under the boat's canvas awning, like Lord Muck and his man, awaiting the train's evening departure from Mwanza. It is expected that it will be a week at least before they arrive in Dar and contact the Danes who are buying *Ragtime*, John arranging to fly down for the unloading. But four days later comes the phone call. Alas, the plane is not flying from Mwanza for a couple of days, in for servicing, so they say. Not to worry; John is accustomed to the vagaries of Air Tanzania.

Another robbery has occurred at the site office on the compound; most of the window louvres have gone, an old typewriter and other equipment. Theft is not regarded as a crime in these parts; rather, it is a way of life, an occupational therapy of pitting one's wits against anyone else's. Again the watchman, the gardener and Pascale are assisting police with enquiries. One hopes the police will beat a bit harder this time.

A vicious invasion of *siafu* ants is coming in via the drains and must be smoked out with smouldering rubber.

"They swarm when a giant spider is chasing them," says Mzee. "Catch the spider and the *siafu* will settle down to normal." The spider can be seen at the back of the drain but not caught: maybe it will succumb to the rubber fumes.

Another characteristic Mwanza drama begins one evening as Anne lies contentedly soaking in the bath, with a rumbling and clattering, rising to a roar which shakes the house. Earthquake! Get out! Leaping up, dripping, naked, Anne's eyes come level with the small window and she finds herself face-to-face with the tailboard of a capsized 5-ton site lorry not 30 centimetres away. John is busy instructing the unhurt but shaken driver and his mate out of the cab.

"My brakes no good. Can't stop," mutters the unhappy man. "I go too fast from top of hill. Better turn here or I go down very steep slope."

He had accelerated from the summit of Capri Point and taken the level ground of the housing compound rather than the steepening hill down, rocked up a slight incline between houses, hit a rock and overturned. The French Contractor SCEEM, taking all day to recover their lorry, congratulate themselves that the damage is confined to a bit of panel beating. Brakes prove to be in adequate condition when tested. John wonders whether the driver's foot, wearing only a sweat-soaked sock, had slipped on the clutch: he failed to engage gear and panic had gripped him. At least he and his mate are not injured.

One of the Gibb Engineers has resigned: his wife is unable to cope with life in Mwanza. Another is in the UK on a month's leave; at least he and his wife, both born and bred in East Africa, can accommodate Mwanza's Gilbertian idiosyncrasies. John is increasingly busy commuting to Dar es Salaam to kick the client and the Treasury for monies owing to both the contractor and to Gibb. Despite the larger aircraft in operation, seats are still hard to get. "No, no seats available that day," says the lady clerk at Air Tanzania's Mwanza office. When John, by dint of cajolery and honeyed words, manages to secure a ticket, he finds the flight only half full. Staff in the Mwanza office keep half the seats in reserve for the urgent traveller prepared to bribe with 'tea money'. Of course, being a State enterprise they do not have to show a profit.

The view from the bridge of Mwanza is increasingly gloomy and by the end of 1988, John and Anne are ready to go. The dreaded ogre, Disillusion, returns to haunt them. It is hard to understand why because Tanzania has so many natural resources, not least its people. Poor they may be by western standards, astute certainly, devout, misguided, many are truly remarkable individuals achieving against all the odds. One cannot forget people like Smiley, Issa and

Joseph the Gibb driver in Morogoro, Mzee and even that happy villain, the sagacious scapegoat Pascale. Stewart Kiluswa and Dr Yongolo leave standing a great many men of eminent worth in the western world and Anne counts it a privilege to know them. It can be said, however, that these remarkable people may be achieving in their own fashion regardless, oblivious even, of western methods and targets.

President Julius Nyerere, who managed or mismanaged Tanzania for over twenty years following Independence, was perhaps trying to assert the different route by which an African might reach the same target as a European. In Nyerere's view, the African's way, enshrined in his theory of African Socialism, was more appropriate than that of his European counterparts. He saw the European as an advisor not as an instructor in the western manner, a materialistic manner which to him undermined traditional African values of co-operative achievement. When President Nyerere retired from Office, he went on a farewell visit to Kenya. It is reported in the *Tanzania Daily News* of the 10th of October 1985, that the President was taken to visit a Ministry of Agriculture model farm and shown a recently imported bull with an arm's-length aristocratic European pedigree to be used for upgrading local stock. Turned out in a field with a herd of interesting cows, the bull grazed placidly taking no notice of his harem. Nyerere, standing at the gate gazing at this paragon of modern science, laughed: "Just like the Europeans in my country who come only to advise." The President's vivid vision of African Socialism remains with him to the end. That said, President Nyerere's Government, based as it is on central control and negative sanctions, has done much damage to Tanzania and its economy. It remains to be seen whether the new regime will rule in a more liberal way. It is early days as yet. And the challenge remains as great or greater than it did at Independence in 1962.

Tanzania is a vast country of coasts and mountains, lowlands and highlands, seas and massive lakes, endless views of stupendous beauty or limited ridges of tumbled granite and grove of thorn. There are swingeing contrasts of climate and weather, devastatingly unpredictable. A few towns and many villages lie isolated by miles and miles of inscrutable wilderness: a wilderness never deserted. Stop for five minutes and the watchers foregather; silent inmates of hidden tracks and undisclosed dwellings, round grass-thatched cots camouflaged as any military camp. This is a secretive land living on fear and faith where the phrase '*shauri ya Mungu*' (God's affair) prevails and the causative tense is commonly used. If Pascale accidentally breaks a plate while washing up in Anne's kitchen he does not say, "This plate is broken," he says "This plate was caused to be broken," and shrugs his shoulders with an engaging grin.

"Who caused the plate to be broken?" Anne challenges Pascale to admit.

"Mungu caused it, of course." Remorse and apology are not in Pascale's vocabulary.

Perhaps it is exposure to the African's determinism, this avoidance of blame and claim and an escape from the responsibility of one's actions, which makes Tanzania so frustrating to westerners. Perhaps the task of development in Tanzania is too complicated, too intricate, for progress to be recognisable within a decade or two. Whatever the cause for their sense of failure, and for Gibb's defeat in Tanzania, Anne and John have no regrets about leaving this fascinating, frustrating country. Kenya, land of milk and honey, beckons again.

[Note: Anne and John had occasion to revisit Tanzania in the year 2000. Mostly in Mwanza to attend the launching of a new ferry boat by Kamanga Ferries, it was soon clear that in twelve years, much had changed for the better. A more liberal Government was allowing foreign investment: South African, Asian and European personnel and money were obviously helping to rationalise enterprises such as gold mining, lake fishing, beer brewing and ship building.

Mwanza city had a rash of big new homes and one or two modern hotels. Everywhere there was hustle and bustle; not least at Mwanza International Airport where Boeings full of local produce for export to Europe, were leaving nightly. Despite gloom about the ravages of AIDS, there was a sense of optimism about the place.]

Chapter 16

Land of Milk and Honey

Flying into Nairobi in 1989 at two a.m., staying with kind friends in Gibb, it is back to the same old game; find a house, find furniture, find a house help, find a car for Anne, retrieve baggage still remaining in the previous posting and indeed find a job, the contract for the sewage works being far from signed. A rented service flat for a month or two, suggested as an interim while house hunting, will be a poky little place but better than a hotel probably. Meeting with reliable house help will be more difficult than discovering a house one likes.

Anne, in the kitchen helping her hostess Margaret, is aware of a voice at the back door calling.

"Why, Ruthie!" exclaims Margaret, "How are you? And how is your family? What of the new job in the Embassy household?"

"I don't like the Embassy job" moans Ruthie, "They are not good people."

Anne sees on the doorstep, a middle-aged figure, round of form and short of stature, Mrs Tiggywinkle herself with the same twinkle in her eyes. In print cotton frock and short linen jacket, carrying her handbag as if she were Lady Thatcher, Ruthie is the very model of a modern Kikuyu housewife.

"Ruthie was working with a Gibb family for ten years." Margaret turns to Anne, "Until they returned to UK for good recently. Are you interested?"

"Ruthie, this is Mama Sears just arrived from the UK. She is looking for house help." Ruthie looks hard at Anne. Anne extends her hand. Ruthie shakes it firmly. The deal is done and Anne agrees to pay a retainer until a house is found.

Another friend has spotted an advertisement in the local press for 'farmhouse to let'. Anne and John follow it up, go to look and find a mellow chalet-bungalow, whitewashed with red-tiled roof. A tarmac road from Nairobi, marvellous views, three bedrooms, three bathrooms, plus a huge windowed attic, spacious living room with warm, golden wood floor and vast log fireplace and an ample verandah, all set in a lovely garden with lawn, fruit trees and surrounding herbaceous borders that adds to its charm. It is the sort of house Anne has dreamed of. Moreover, the owners, a Kikuyu family called Cege (pronounced Chegé), who live in the main house, have a farm produce business selling milk, butter, cottage cheese, yoghurt, cream, poultry, pork, jams and jellies, pâtés and pies and all sorts of frozen vegetables - a veritable land of milk and honey. No doubt there will be snags but, importantly, Anne responds with empathy to Mrs Cege when they meet.

A complement of furniture may be rented from an emporium in Nairobi so thither Anne goes to bespeak her needs, finding everything that would be deemed necessary for a state-of-the-art home in Britain's 1960s. Downtown Nairobi is nothing but crowds, car crawls, traffic jams, pimps, touts and thieves. The suburbs are being razed to the ground, uncontrolled construction erecting ten apartment blocks where one home stood. Fortunately, Echuka farm, where they will live, is some fifteen miles from the centre of Nairobi.

Three of life's essentials, a house, furniture and house help, are now met within a few days of arrival. It remains to secure temporary accommodation for one month, to buy a small car for Anne, to retrieve the household baggage from Mwanza and to secure a contract for the sewage works so that John's work may begin.

At their hosts' wedding anniversary luncheon party, the day after John and Anne's arrival in Nairobi, they meet a guest who remarks that two old ladies are thinking of opening their large house to paying guests. Is this the solution to the temporary accommodation? Anne, now mobile in a small runabout Peugeot, goes to visit them in their gracious old house set in mature grounds and agrees to rent two rooms plus a bathroom for one month: the arrangement includes full board but, since breakfast is staggered and lunch informal, it is only for the evening meal that Anne and John will join their two landladies. Networking in Nairobi is proving highly satisfactory. The household baggage, now in Klaus Gaetje's workshop at Kamanga, must wait until John has obtained a work permit and residence status for Kenya, both of which are said to be in the pipeline. All that is needed, then, is a contract to work upon, plus the prescribed site vehicle.

Staying with the two old ladies and meeting their elderly friends is something of an ordeal; at times, their communication sounds ungracious. Anne suspects that their energy resources are inadequate to extend an easy welcome to those who must appear as here-today-gone-tomorrow newcomers in old Nairobi. Lorna is eighty-one, intellectual and interesting about old Kenya; Daisy, Belgian-born and seventy-nine, runs a cattery business and tends the household dogs and parrot. The parrot mimics a catfight and echoes Daisy's 'Stop that noise at once' when she shouts at the caterwauling cages. John is away a good deal, in Dar es Salaam, arguing about monies owed by the client and the Treasury, and in Mwanza to check on various technical details disputed by the client. In addition, he is posted to Botswana for two weeks to help out when one of the Gibb engineers is accidentally drowned in an overturned landrover. John counts himself lucky to be out of the Gibb (Africa) office in Nairobi since it is swarming with Americans, following a merger of Sir Alexander Gibb and Partners with an Atlanta consultant engineering firm. Nevertheless, all this is an improvement on the early days of the Morogoro contract, staying in seedy hotels in Dar and in Morogoro.

It is not long before Anne's new home at Echuka farm, at 2,000 metres above sea level, is found to have some rural inconveniences; a track of mud from the main road, a quagmire in the rainy season, brown bath water, some suspect plumbing and no telephone; she must use the phone in Mrs Cege's house for essential calls only. But stupendous views over forest and tea gardens, two huge 'umbrella' thorn trees to cast speckled shade over the lawns and a surrounding garden full of flowers; lilies, agapanthus, bird-of-paradise, cosmos, salvia and amaryllis in all hues, more than compensate. From just up the hill can be seen, on a clear evening, Mt. Kenya in one direction and Mt. Kilimanjaro in the other. The lawns have – oh ecstasy – mower stripes and are ringed by sweet, heady orange and lemon trees now in flower. Jasmine climbs the house walls and moonflower trees, the deadly datura, is coming out in pink, lemon and ivory-coloured blossom. It is a feast of colour, all joy.

The landlady, Cecelia Cege, is a mine of useful information and practical support.

"Cecelia, we need a room for Ruthie. Could she stay in one of your farm workers' quarters?"

At the rear of the steading is a cantonment; lines of rooms for farm employees with water supply and ablution facilities. Cecelia pauses, glances towards her staff accommodation, mentally adjusting room allocation.

"Yes, I can give her a room. A house for rent like yours should have a servant's quarter. And she is a Kikuyu. I will arrange it."

So Ruthie moves in, immediate friends with the Kikuyu farm workers' families, full of gossip, never a moment without chit-chat in the Kikuyu tongue.

Cecelia was orphaned at an early age and brought up by Presbyterian missionaries. She was a bright girl at school, continuing to Dar es Salaam University, in the days before the rupture between Kenya and Tanzania, where she graduated in Social Science. Short of stature, plump, with well-cut wavy hair, Cecelia sparkles with a vivacity verging on radiance, her manner refined, conferring upon her a comely elegance. Anne pieces together many snippets of gossip about her landlady.

"Cecelia is a splendid person," says a good friend from the Algeria days whose husband is now working in the British High Commission in Kenya. "But her husband is a disaster." Anne has never met him; all she knows is his name, Peter.

"Cecelia! Extraordinary person!" exclaims an acquaintance. "There's a story about her school days. The missionary teacher decided to take her pupils to tea with an English lady, the lady in question dutifully getting out her best china, the silver tea set with silver sugar tongs. The *mpishi* (cook) baked scones to serve with strawberry jam and cream, cutting wafer-thin cucumber sandwiches and making a fine Dundee cake. On the given afternoon, the *mpishi*, now in white gloves, wheeled in the tea trolley beautifully laid with embroidered tray cloth, lace doilies and delicate porcelain. The girls gasped in wonder and chattered on like hens in a pen, all except Cecelia who sat unusually silent. So unprecedented was Cecelia's speechlessness that the teacher became curious, observing her surreptitiously. Cecelia bereft of opinions, was a phenomenon the teacher had never before met, as enigmatic as a black hole in the cosmos. Then slowly the penny dropped. Cecelia was engrossed in observing the features of the room, the vases of flowers, the silver-framed photographs, the Persian rugs on the polished parquet floor, the pictures and bookshelves on the wall; all of it. It was a race against time to notice, evaluate and mentally record each item. When they came out, the girls were full of enthusiasm for the lovely tea they had eaten: all except Cecelia. "What did you think of it, Cecelia?" The question hung in the air like a morning mist. "When I grow up and have my own house, I'm going to have all those things," announced Cecelia.

"And she has too." The raconteur finishes. "Extraordinary girl is Cecelia!"

Sitting in Cecelia's elegant Edwardian drawing room enjoying tea from the trolley, it is difficult to realise what a long way she has travelled from mud hut to manor house, what huge social changes have been undergone.

"I do like your Christmas flower decoration, Cecelia. They are most imaginative." Anne's genuine appreciation draws out Cecelia.

"I do so love flowers and gardens," she admits. "I hope to go to a Conference in Spalding next June. I should love to visit Britain."

"If you go to Britain you must come and stay with me. I should love to show you round"

But sadly she does not eventually go; says she cannot trust Peter if she goes away.

Anne's house, the guesthouse of the farm in days of yore, is attractive inside. Floors and ceilings are of red-gold cypress wood, windows are small panes set in black lead, rather Tudor in effect. Ruthie is in the kitchen singing and a second Kikuyu lady called Marida comes in from her home daily to do the laundry, cleaning and some garden tidying and weeding around the bungalow's vicinity. Anne is glad to have Marida, a young woman totally inexperienced but being trained by Ruthie, partly because the house is large with a lot of wood to polish and partly to chat with Ruthie, who would chatter to Anne all day if Marida were not there. Ruthie and Anne must often combine forces. This Kenya may be the land of milk and honey but in the shops, some things are sadly lacking; no mincemeat or marzipan for Christmas cooking so they must make it all. Never mind. Limuru Race Meeting on Boxing Day is a Kenyan traditional treat as is a Gilbert and Sullivan performance in Nairobi of *The Pirates of Penzance* by an all-dark cast, which burlesques more than the D'Oyley Carte troupe might have done but to good effect, and the audience roars approval.

On the farm there is intense activity: Cecelia has galvanised all her staff to clean and tidy the place in readiness for a visit from the British High Commissioner's wife who wants to bring her small grand-daughter to see the calves and pigs; milking shed and pigsty being hosed down, every pig scrubbed, rose garden dead-headed, perimeter hedges clipped. It is fatiguing to watch it all.

"Anne, the Kenya Horticultural Society are coming next week; please ask Marida to tidy the flowerbeds and deadhead everything."

"Anne, the Ministry of Agriculture are bringing the Prime Minister of New Zealand to visit Echuka Farm. I am obliged by Protocol to ask the Prime Minister to plant a tree and his wife another and really I have no place for any more trees, so I shall have to put them in the lawn by your house."

"Anne, please may I borrow your verandah and shady lawn to hold a lunch party for my sixteen guests from the East African Women's League; I have no shade and no verandah at my house. Oh! And will you please make mayonnaise for the salads and also ice cream to go with the fruit flans?" Cecelia's idea of a light lunch consists of platters of home-smoked hams, home-made sausages and meat loaf, vegetable curries, potato salads, green salads and pickles of every sort from her business kitchens, followed by peach or strawberry flans with whipped cream, and

Anne's ice cream. She is out to impress since the East African Women's League members, who include many of the diplomatic and business company wives during their posting in Nairobi, are among her best clients.

"Anne, I would like you to come and have lunch with us. I am entertaining the United States Ambassador and about twenty other VIPs. Oh! And will you make mayonnaise and ice cream and stew three kilos of peaches in vanilla for me. And get some peaches for yourself."

Grateful for Cecelia's friendship and for the many comforts of Echuka Farm, Anne can stay home during periods of political and social unrest that flare suddenly in the city and suburbs. Peter Cege is reported to have had a confrontation with rioters who threatened to overturn his Mercedes car unless he paid the Kenya shilling's equivalent of £5. Moreover, John is away a great deal, to Tanzania but mostly on temporary postings to Botswana, where a sudden new contract with emergency status has opened. There is still no signing of the sewage works contract for the project to which John has been posted. President Daniel arap Moi of Kenya has made it clear he will not have the Israeli contractors whose tender won the deal to build the sewage treatment plant, and the World Bank funding agency has stated that it is the Israelis or nothing. Relocation to Botswana is discussed. Meanwhile Echuka Farm is a safe haven for Anne.

Cecilia has four children; a well-mannered lad of nineteen called Thuo waiting to study agricultural economics at Reading University, UK; Julie, a charming seventeen-year old and in high school; Edward, twelve years old and with a severe mental handicap who is cared for by a family relative in the home; and Rebecca, Becky, a precocious seven-year old who has just started primary school. It seems a happy, confident family. Anne particularly enjoys the company of young Becky. But all is not well; undercurrents of conflict are being marshalled into a riptide of assault.

One morning at breakfast, before seven a.m., Becky bursts in. "I had to get away" she covers her face with her hands. "Mummy and Daddy are shouting at each other, then Daddy went outside with a gun and shot the tyre of Mummy's car so that she could not go to town." Anne comforts Becky and walks her back to the Ceges' house, where she finds that Peter has left for Nairobi and Cecelia is sitting hunched up over a mug of tea, deshabillé, her head in a turban scarf rather than its elegant wig.

"Join me for a mug of tea, Anne. Becky, run and get ready for school."

She is not despondent but bitterly angry. Peter has changed to his sole name the title deeds of another farm they have owned jointly. What is more he has sold this property unilaterally and bought land in Nairobi to be developed into service flats. Cecelia had gone to his town office to try and seize documents and papers relating to this deal and police had been called to restrain Peter and Cecelia from fighting. "Peter is moving out of Echuka Farm. He has a new household with his pregnant mistress. I don't trust him. He will try and get Echuka Farm from me but mercifully I have a Church marriage and rights to the family home." Not that Peter will be influenced by such moral niceties if push comes to shove in the future.

"It seems to me that women are more sensible and logical than men." This is whispered, cautiously, as if Cecilia is unsure of the assumption. "But how can women be content to marry and have a family if they are condemned to second place in society? My son, Thuo, asks me who on earth he will find to marry. He says he can't marry someone like his clever, confident sisters; they damage his self-esteem."

There is not much Anne can add to these revelations. Some words of sympathy, a suggestion that it may be necessary surreptitiously, to prop up male self-esteem, otherwise men turn to fighting. She can hardly report D H Lawrence's observation that as a boy, he had wondered how anyone could assume that God was male when it was clear that women always knew best and men didn't care. Poor Cecilia! It is hard for well-educated women in developing countries.

Ruthie, now, has managed her life differently but then Ruthie was not raised by Presbyterian missionaries, nor did she go to university. Ruthie has done without the social grace of marriage, her children being cared for by a relation while she exercises her profession in domestic service. But Ruthie has also done without many of the material advantages enjoyed by Cecelia. Ruthie's house in Kiambu is still under construction, has been for many years. When taken to see it, Anne finds a two-bedroom dwelling with central living, cooking and eating room and a small shower room at the rear, the roof going on now and plumbing nearly complete.

"I shall retire when you leave, Mama Sears, and live in my new home. I shall paint it myself."

Ruthie is great fun to be with on market day in Karuri, an outer suburb known as Banana Hill in days of yore. She has chit-chat with all the vendors seated on the grass leaning against sacks of dried maize, rice, beans, lentils, sorghum or millet with their small mounds of garden produce set out on sacking. Around the perimeter of the green, the lower boughs of trees are hung with lengths of colourful cloth, blouses, chemises and brassières, with numerous hay-scented braided grass ropes, baskets and floor mats. It is a vivid place saturated with the exchange of news, gossip, scandal and comedy drama. Ruthie must examine every item displayed for purchase, passing wry comments in the Kikuyu tongue on each as she goes, her body language communicating the gist of the dialogue. Pausing at a range of bras suspended from a branch, Ruthie fingers an outsize model meditatively. Then taking it off a bough, she slips this boulder holder over her dress and fastens it at the back. There she is, her generously-proportioned form encased above, her bottom like two bolster ends below, parading round the entire market soliciting opinions as to whether the garment fits well and should she buy it. She is a born comedienne.

What of Royal Life Saving Society interests? Anne is piecing together, like Sherlock Holmes, what happens in Kenya. There is a Kenya Amateur Swimming Association (KASA), which has successfully introduced swimming skills into some of the more prestigious schools and into corporate groups such as teacher training colleges, the navy and the police. Indeed, when Anne is invited to stand in and teach swimming for three weeks at a private primary school near Nairobi, she finds the older children can swim. "Yes, Miss, we've done Life Saving," they chorus. In fact, their syllabus is the KASA survival scheme, which does not teach water safety or casualty recognition. This is important. Anne has memories of a situation many years ago when strolling along the coast near Algiers one windy March day. Spotting from the headland something floating in the water quite close in, Anne recognised a body: dark blue/black with brown head, poor drowned *matelot*, obviously dead, quite bloated-looking. Suddenly it turned its head and stared. Not dead. Quick; Anne must rescue him. In a panic of haste, she began to strip off jacket, shoes... The not-so-dead sailor looked up again. Urgently, she measured the distance from shore to casualty. Could she haul him a hundred metres? And if she did how would she get him out on a deep, rocky, windward shore? At last, she was thinking. Then it was that she realised that this was no drowning sailor but a seal. How stupid can one be in an emergency? Anne will tell this story to the children but they probably will not believe it.

Meanwhile, Anne, flushed with her sense of achievement in introducing elementary water safety, survival and rescue in Tanzania, still has a mission to give back lives in Africa if possible. Kenya is, however, a different ball game from Tanzania, as she will discover.

Slowly Anne makes contact with one or two of the KASA personnel in Nairobi. There is Anne Kioko who is on the staff of a teacher training college, Shirley Maina teaching physical education at a prestigious secondary school and Daksha Patel, mother of keen swimming children. With an African Region Conference in Malawi being arranged for April, Anne invites Cecelia Cege to help her to host a charity lunch for twenty five, raising money to help delegates from Kenya and, once the ball is rolling, other monies and sponsorship are forthcoming so that Kenya can send three delegates from Nairobi and two from Mombasa. It is a start.

The Malawi Conference passes successfully and the Kenya delegates seem interested in adding Royal Life Saving Society targets to their Kenya Amateur Swimming Association syllabus. More importantly, personnel from the UK, tutors and head office staff, get to meet the Kenyans in the same way they have previously met Stewart Kiluswa from Tanzania. Stewart is at the Malawi Conference and generates informal discussion and rapport with the Kenyans. Some useful networking is achieved.

Arising out of the Malawi Conference is an invitation to the RLSS Senior Tutors to visit Africa later in the year. To Anne's delight one of them, Sheila Norman, accepts the challenge so there is much to organise in preparation for her visit later in the year.

Meanwhile, John in Botswana phones to say he believes the Israeli contractor, HZ, is slowly making headway in the political arena and a contract may follow.

Now is the time to try and establish some sort of organisation to Kenya's embryonic life saving interests. Asking Anne Kioko to call together anyone interested, the matter is discussed.

"You will be Chairman of this Kenya life saving group." They assume that Anne will continue to arrange and administer.

"No, no. We need a Kenyan to lead it. I am here-today-gone-tomorrow. I will do my best to support you, raise money, liaise with the UK Royal Life Saving Society."

It is Anne Kioko who is finally persuaded to front the gathering; her dismay is discernible, but she accepts it. Anne, proposing that the forthcoming visit of Sheila Norman should be marked by a Sunday lunch get-together with everyone contributing some typical Kenyan food, offers her verandah as the venue and this is welcomed.

Meanwhile, there is a KASA presence in Mombasa on the coast, four hundred miles of indifferent road away: if only Africa were not so large.

Earlier, while staying as paying guests with Lorna and Daisy, Anne had met another old lady called Audrey who has a very small market garden enterprise, delivering fresh produce to clubs and clients in Nairobi. Audrey lives at Tigoni near Echuka Farm and Anne, calling in on her, finds herself helping to pick strawberries for an emergency order. Soon a rapport is established, Anne often being asked to do the vegetable deliveries if Audrey is unwell or her car out of order. Audrey has a coast cottage at Kilifi, near Mombasa.

"I long to go to Kilifi but I dread the drive. It is a rotten road and my car is none too reliable. My tenant has just left and I ought to go and check on the place, talk to the *mpishi*, cook" sighs Audrey.

"Perhaps I could take you in my car. I wouldn't mind a few days at Kilifi so that I can call in on some life saving contacts in Mombasa."

This being arranged, it is a pleasure to get to the coast despite eight and a half hours of driving in sultry, sapping weather. Audrey's health is, Anne knows, indifferent, but the principal concern seems to be one of the two elderly small dogs on the back seat, which has a heart condition. The cottage, designed by Audrey's architect sister, is small but very well sited. Furnishings are poor but to be replaced now the tenant has gone. The cook is an indolent but jovial soul: his duties are principally caretaking and Audrey is happy to condone his indifferent cooking if he is reliable and cheerful. Anne goes in to Mombasa, meets Anne Freeman, an Englishwoman who has been teaching physical education in Mombasa for many years but is soon to be leaving, and Pauline Rubero, another PE teacher; Anne stands by an excruciatingly hot swimming pool all morning watching their students and discussing life saving. Returning to the cottage, Anne finds one of the dogs has had a heart attack and Audrey wants to cut short the visit, to get back to Nairobi the next day. Leaving at four a.m. to beat the heat and stopping in a car park at Tsavo Game Park to walk the dogs and eat a breakfast picnic, a large baboon strolls past. The dog with the weak heart jumps up and down like a yoyo, the lead breaks and dog takes off, pursued by Audrey shouting and panting, which cannot be good for either of them. Anne scoops up the other aged dog and stuffs it back into the car because baboons like a bit of small dog sometimes. Audrey returns carrying the errant, invalid dog. From Anne's point of view, however, the excursion has been a success: later, she and John will be rewarded with use of the Kilifi cottage whenever they want to go to the coast.

The Kilifi cottage comes in useful as a respite in Sheila Norman's busy schedule. Arriving and meeting a number of interested Kenyans at the lunch party on Anne's verandah, Sheila holds a busy training session in Nairobi at the school pool where Shirley Maina works, followed by exams. Then down to Kilifi and a bit of relaxation before another arduous training and examining session in Mombasa at the pool where Pauline Rubero works. It is all very encouraging. Sheila is an easy guest, appreciating the unsophisticated life of Echuka Farm and the Kilifi Cottage, enjoying picnicking en route to Kilifi and while going around Tsavo Game Park, coping well with the culture shock and the intensive schedule of life-saving training. The Gibb Partners kindly arrange a duty visit to Mwanza for John and their plane 'Tango Charlie', so that Anne can take Sheila there for another busy training session. Stewart Kiluswa has promised to come from Dar es Salaam by bus, combining library work with life-saving. Poor man, the bus breaks down five times and the journey takes four days instead of twenty-four hours and yet, coming in half way through the seminar, he immediately gives a lucid and charismatic talk about drowning and life-saving.

Back in Nairobi with the weather very wet, these being the 'Mango' or 'Grass' rains that precede the onset of the rainy season, a log fire is burning all day. Anne receives a request from Nairobi Hospital to teach a crash course of basic swimming, water safety and rescue to eight physiotherapists so that they can operate their new Hydrotherapy Unit. And about now, John receives his Dandora sewage treatment contract vehicle, a new Japanese four-wheel drive assembled locally, which the Israeli contractor HZ has managed to prise out of the hands of Nairobi City Council. It is now over eleven months since John arrived in Nairobi and work is just starting with the arrival of a team of Chinese, subcontracted to build the housing for the future maintenance staff of the treatment works. Time is merely relative in Africa. Never mind, the physiotherapists are now ready for Anne to devise initiative tests in casualty recognition and rescue, which will be fun.

Christmas again comes and goes. This time the family comes out, Marion with her husband Jeffrey, and Rob. It is all *la dolce vita,* with Christmas lunch on the shade-speckled lawn, Limuru Races on Boxing Day, a visit to the Kilifi cottage and New Year's Eve at a famous fish restaurant in Mombasa, then Tsavo Game Park, followed by the Kenyan production of *The Mikado* in Nairobi. At the theatre, they come across Anne Kioko who says her daughter, a dancer, is in the cast.

In the New Year, it is time to plan for the Royal Life Saving Society's conference, a centenary celebration in England in June 1991. Can Anne get enough sponsorship for Kenyans to attend the meeting in the UK? And Stewart in Dar es Salaam, how can he get there? RLSS has extended encouragement to its Commonwealth members in recent years; a dozen or more countries will be sending delegates. Why not Kenya and Tanzania? Anne puts the challenge to the Kenyan life-saving group. Yes, Anne Kioko would love to go if sponsorship can be found, and Daksha Patel thinks she may be able to raise funds for herself from among her community. Shirley Maina cannot get leave of absence for June. Pauline Rubero says she would like to go if possible. In Dar es Salaam, good friends at the yacht club undertake to hold a fundraising Regatta in aid of Stewart, and the International School of Tanganyika promises to help.

In Kenya, friends at the British High Commission agree to hold a reception for the life-saving group. So few of the invited guests respond to the invitation, that the High Commission pressgangs some of their staff and friends to make weight. But, in the event, about eighty guests turn up, coming from as far away as Kisumu and Mombasa. The press carries a photo of the High Commissioner presenting Anne Kioko with a cheque towards the expenses of attending the RLSS centenary celebration, and Kenya's television service conducts an interview with Anne Kioko, which shows next evening. The following day, a feature article on life-saving in Kenya appears in the press. Success has crowned the effort; the only disappointment being the absence of Cecelia Cege who was to present some embryonic ideas about swimming for the handicapped, people in special schools like her son Edward. Alas, her Mercedes broke down en route to the party.

Naivasha Yacht Club, to which John belongs, holding a regatta weekend, promises donations to life-saving activities. Alas, the first race starts windless, thirty-five small boats sitting around the starting line, sails limp, crews joking when along comes a squall, a gully-washer of rain pounding the deep waters of the crater lake. Some boats emerge briefly from the shroud of cloud trying to get back to shore, most of them upside down, the rest of the fleet having vanished. It is all part of dinghy racing in the middle of the African Rift Valley; nobody complains and the need for water safety and rescue skills is enhanced.

Lastly, the life-saving group organises a Gala Day to urge local engagement with water safety and rescue. It promises to be a total disaster when the marquees fail to arrive and a malevolent mantle of rain occludes the far side of the swimming pool as curtains cut off a stage. A fusillade of ice bullets follows and then a sudden sun, revealing the marquees being erected and some two hundred participants gathering, an hour late but happily hot under a cloudless sky: it is an encouragingly enthusiastic day after all. An embarrassment of success, however, is the interest now being demonstrated by the Kenya Amateur Swimming Association: this hard-line organisation might yet expect to dictate how the life- saving group is managed. Meanwhile, RLSS in Britain has decided it wants to make a film for video circulation, to support a teaching manual being prepared for the developing countries and what about making it in Kenya? Anne scurries round Nairobi trying to get costs and budget quotes.

"Yes, we can help with this," says the Director of the British Council. "I know the very man to make this film; Alfred is just back from Ouagadougou, where he has been showing his work at Fespaco, the biennial pan-African festival of cinema and television."

Anne Kioko is intrigued by the idea of making this film in Kenya. "You mean that I shall be a film star?"

"But of course. You, Shirley, Pauline, the children in their schools, everyone will be in it."

At last, most of the bridges to the RLSS centenary conference of June 1991 are crossed. Pauline decides she cannot go, which eases the financial burden of fundraising. Two delegates, Anne Kioko and Stewart Kiluswa, constitute a manageable number to be accommodated in the

UK; Anne Kioko will stay with Anne in her small Reading flat and a room for Stewart can be arranged in a university hostel just across the road from the flat. Daksha has friends and relations in London with whom she can stay.

Anne meets Anne Kioko at Heathrow Airport and drives her to the flat while Stewart, who has arrived two days previously to stay with a London friend and do some shopping, comes by bus, the two Annes together welcoming him to the flat.

"Come on in, Stewart. Shortly I will take you across the road to your university residence, then you will come back to the flat for supper."

"Thank you. But first I have an important task. I must give your telephone number to my friend in London. Judith is about to give birth and my friend will relay the news as soon as it comes through." Stewart's sangfroid is reassuring. His wife is going privately to the Aga Khan Hospital in Dar es Salaam this time after her dreadful experience at the national Muhumbili Hospital three years ago. Anne Kioko, mother of three grown-up children, is sympathetic. A calm, quietly-spoken woman with big, glowing, dark eyes, she is a good colleague to have and Anne looks forward to her company. And when the phone call comes, it is a boy.

"He is called Michael," Stewart beams, "After Prince Michael of Kent, who is the Commonwealth President of the Royal Life Saving Society." Anne rushes out to buy a bottle of champagne; she and Anne Kioko change into African caftans and all troupe down to the forecourt for a photo, a bemused passer-by being press-ganged into wielding the camera. Hoorah!

A London hotel is the conference venue, evening receptions at Buckingham Palace, and at the Houses of Parliament; dinner at a splendid Chinese Restaurant as guests of the Hong Kong delegation. It is all a flurry of meetings, seminars, workshops, changing for evening functions and informal discussions with a fervour of interest in developing countries, in an aura of Commonwealth animation on account of the truly African delegates.

Sheila Norman having invited Anne Kioko, Stewart and Anne to stay with her in Ipswich, Anne drives them to Suffolk, whence Sheila takes them to visit Deben Life Saving Club at Woodbridge, Deben having done much to raise sponsorship for Tanzania. Sheila packs a thermos of tea, a packet of cookies and a rug in the boot of her car, stopping spontaneously in a delectable meadow surrounded by hedgerow wildflowers and redolent of new-mown hay. The informal picnic charms the African visitors.

The last event of the conference is held at the RLSS Headquarters, Mountbatten House in Studley, Warwickshire. At this closing ceremony, HRH Prince Michael of Kent gives out awards, Stewart receiving a Certificate of Thanks. It has been Stewart's week. Thereafter Stewart returns to friends in London and the journey home, while Anne drives Anne Kioko north to stay a couple of days with Anne's mother in Melrose in the Scottish Borders and then back south to Heathrow and a plane home to Kenya, where she is plunged into a plethora of college commitments. It is mid-August before she has time to issue Anne with a long-promised invitation to lunch at her home.

Now is the time to start fundraising and planning for the RLSS film, which is to be made in Kenya next April during the school holidays. Appeals going out to banks and international companies working in Kenya receive a good response. Meanwhile, Anne and Anne Kioko meeting with the Director of the British Council, and Alfred the Kenyan film producer, find them both enthusiastic.

"Much of the filming can be done in and around Nairobi, which will save expense, but we should have a sequence on open water. I suggest the Kilifi Creek as a possible venue, and there are life-savers in Mombasa who would love to come over by bus to act out the open water techniques." Anne's suggestion is based upon Audrey's cottage, the use of which has been promised, upon the expectation of being able to borrow a boat during the filming period from friends at Kilifi Yacht Club and, a desire to include the Mombasa people in the filming.

"Yes, I know the Kilifi Creek," says Alfred. "What we need is a preliminary survey. I could get down to Kilifi and meet you there." A reconnaissance is arranged during the Christmas school holiday, when Anne Kioko is free. Shirley and Pauline are invited as well, Shirley affirming that she cannot come and Pauline wavering. "I will come if I can." With this uncertainty, Anne and Anne Kioko pack a picnic and a thermos of tea for stops en route and wait at the rendezvous in case Pauline turns up.

She does appear.

"A picnic! No, I didn't bring anything. I thought it would be much better to have a proper lunch at one of the lodges. After all, we have got some funds now." Pauline, tall, svelte and fashionably dressed with long plaits braided into her own hair tied in a ponytail, is elegantly dressed for lunching out.

"But Pauline, we haven't got enough funds for lunches in hotels. We are stretching our sponsorship as it is."

At Kilifi, Pauline views the cottage with distaste. "We always stay in hotels when we go on KASA business."

There is however a limit to funds, the cottage, if not luxurious, being adequate for three persons. Alfred makes his own arrangements, and one of the Mombasa teachers and a naval man come by the day. Discussions seem satisfactory, the limpid turquoise waters of Kilifi Creek appeal, and Alfred is confident that the nuts and bolts of filming can be done there.

Driving back to Nairobi, four hundred miles of road which has been overused by big axle loads and is in poor condition, Pauline wants to discuss the funding of this film.

"Who is paying for it and where is the money?" asks Pauline.

"The Royal Life Saving Society is paying for most of it, but Kenyan sponsorship is paying for the preliminary work like this recce," replies Anne.

"Is the money for the film going to be put in an account opened by the Kenya Life Saving Group or is it going into the Kenya Amateur Swimming Association?"

"The money will be administered by the British Council. The director is most enthusiastic about this project," responds Anne.

"I advise that we open our own account for the Kenya Life Saving Society, KLSS. We must, of course, get ourselves registered as such first," Pauline opines.

"Good idea to apply for registration but that is something for Anne Kioko, Shirley, yourself and the Mombasa personnel to do. And I doubt it can be completed in time for the film making in April. You would have to find a Patron who is interested in the life saving work and get support, sponsorship. It is a long road but worth doing. I will help as much as I can but you Kenyans must arrange it all."

Meanwhile, there is a delightful weekend interlude staying with Bruce and Paddy Nightingale at their farm near Njoro, where they breed horses for racing and polo; a foal being born during the night, the thirty-fifth out of forty-six expected this season. Paddy does a bit of life-saving with local children so she and Anne compose a syllabus for some preliminary badge awards, such as badge 1: 'Put yourself safely and carefully into the water', and badge 2: 'Put your head right under the water and blow bubbles'. These Nightingales, second or third generation Kenyan, are less prickly than some of the elderly, old colonials around Nairobi, who may express an aggressive assertiveness, due perhaps to frustration. Or fear?

'The world is full of tricks'. So says an old Swahili idiom.[26] Kenya Life Saving calls Anne to a meeting about the video film monies and accounts.

"Why should the British Council have the money? It should go to the Kenya Amateur Swimming Association." Pauline is abrasively aggressive.

"The Kenya Swimming Association includes life saving in their syllabus. They should supervise sponsorship of this film." Shirley, drawn late into the argument about funding, cannot resist a good confrontation.

Anne Kioko must say something. Her eyes deepen with disquiet, jet cameos of dolour. "We can administer the money properly ourselves. There is no need for the British Council to hold it." The distress in her demeanour is patent.

"Funds will be transferred from RLSS in the UK to the British Council here and all expenses will be claimed from them."

So acrimonious becomes the dialogue, so abusive the insults Pauline and Shirley fling at Anne, that she walks out. The assumption can only be that they want a cut of the money for the film they are making in April. Were making... Anne cannot risk exposing the UK personnel to the tantrums and rudeness now occurring, and provisionally cancels the film.

"Maybe I can sort it out. Let me speak to them." Alfred, appalled, may be able to find an African solution to an African problem.

"Ah! Kenyan greed," sighs the Director of the British Council. True, most East Africans expect for services rendered some '*chai* money', tea money, a tip, a *pourboire*: everyone does it, even those engaged in philanthropic work.

A fax arrives from the UK Commonwealth Secretary. He says, "The fault is mine. I am phoning Anne Kioko. Hold everything."

---

[26] Farsi, Shaaban Salah, *Swahili Idioms,* East African Publishing House, Nairobi, 1973

"Maybe they will do for the Commonwealth Secretary what they won't do for you," observes the British Council Director. "Kenyan society is so programmed to women *doing* what *men* say that they may respond."

Two weeks later, nothing has been heard from the UK and the film is off. Kenya Life Saving is a very fragile entity: Anne Kioko, the chairperson, is not a born captain, is under pressure, leading from the rear by corporate decision. Such rudeness and tantrums, the stock-in-trade of the bully, are reported daily in the media, insults in Parliament indicating vivid imaginations and unbearable social, economic and political pressures; pressures which may erupt in provincial and tribal violence. Having heard from Pauline about her excessive emotional and economic hardships over the past two years, it is not surprising that she is aggressive, competitive, and calculating.

Pauline relocated from Mombasa to Nairobi with her second husband, having obtained a divorce from the first husband and father of her two girls, who had flitted the family some years previously. In Nairobi, on Pauline's sole salary, the only housing they could afford to rent was twenty miles out. Travelling, stuffed into packed buses at all hours, Pauline was mugged on her way home. She gave up the house, dispatched her unemployed husband upcountry and applied for a council house. She could not afford the necessary bribe. Her elder daughter at Nairobi University dropped out, had a baby by a Sierra Leone student who refused to acknowledge the child. Pauline's younger, and brilliant, daughter got top marks in a German Government scholarship for further studies in Germany, Pauline having to fundraise to pay the child's ticket with cake bakes and *harambees* (literally 'all pull together'). In January 1991, the child, having arrived in Germany and settled well with the German foster family, was suddenly traumatised when her real father travelled to Germany to remove her. Fortunately, the foster family refused to release her.

Pauline pays half her monthly salary to the German Embassy for the child's upkeep and has recently been to Germany to share Christmas with her daughter and the foster family. What is more, she has recently moved into a good residential quarter to a friend's house for two years' housewarming. It was to be hoped that the upturn in Pauline's fortunes would mellow her, but it appears that she has turned her aggressiveness onto the Life Saving group. The fact that Kenya Life Saving functioned smoothly for two years in harmony with other regional life-saving organisations, says much for Anne Kioko's charm, enthusiasm and personal convictions. It is a pity that Pauline has emerged to challenge her pragmatic good sense with radical and parochial behaviour. It must be said, however, that the blame game is in the normal fabric of Kenyan life. When in 1993 the first ever general election had come and gone, various opposition parties finally clubbed together and proceeded to blame the British High Commission, the Commonwealth Organisations and the American Ambassador for their defeat. Anne consoles herself with this rationalisation; it helps to assuage her disappointment.

Inexorably, the work of Gibb and Partners in East Africa, now part of a US business conglomerate, is remodelling itself; in comes high technology, out goes the old hands-on design and construct. Colleagues are leaving for pastures new before the inevitable end of the *ancien régime*: as a Swahili proverb says, 'There is no medicine for death'.

As far as Anne is concerned, Cecelia is now under unbearable pressure from her husband and there is a risk of being caught in the crossfire. Anne Kioko has retreated behind a façade of overwork. The life-saving video film will eventually be made in Malawi. Time to go.

As far as John is concerned, the treatment works at Dandora is nearly finished. There is talk about a big project in Ghana but it is some way off into the future.

Chapter 17

Living in An Antique Land

Jordan!

The hopeful project at Kumasi in Ghana, having been off-again-on-again several times and again postponed, is now to be operated in a different way from that originally proposed. Meanwhile Head Office in the UK offers John a post in Jordan on the Karameh Dam. This big earth dam, designed years previously by Sir Alexander Gibb and Partners as it was then, is at last to be constructed in the Jordan Valley.

Head office is reticent about details of the project.

"It is very close to a political trouble spot. Only a stone's throw from the Israeli-Palestinian-Jordanian border, you know." John nods. "The project housing will be in the Jordan Valley, below Sea Level, not in the city, Amman. What does your wife think about living in these circumstances?"

The offer is discussed in detail. Anne has already experienced Jordan, albeit some forty years ago, and has a memory glow of friendly people and sensational scenery. Why not take their current Ford Escort car from Britain, as they did to Algiers when posted there? Yes. Accepting the Karameh Dam posting, they buy maps of the route. Anne purchases the six-volume series *The Decline and Fall of the Roman Empire*, written by Edward Gibbon in the late eighteenth century with an introduction by Hugh Trevor-Roper, to go into the air freight; life in the Jordan Valley promising time to digest this weighty work whilst living in a significant part of the erstwhile Roman Empire.

Thus in late March 1994, they set out across a stormy North Sea from Hull to Zeebrugge and south by car through cold, grey France to Arles, where Anne revisits her old sojourn on the Camargue; now touristy and expensive. They continue through the Po Valley in Italy to Venice, for a few enchanted days. Staying on the mainland, going into Venice by bus on the viaduct road to the tiny island wobbling on the lap of its lagoon, to them the city first appears as in a mirage, its scintillating skyline punctuated by domes and towers floating above a morning mist. Wandering among the piazzas and palaces, the tall, close buildings, and bridges spanning corridors of canal, it is sublimely sensuous to hear a swelling aria from Verdi or Puccini sung by a retired opera singer in mackintosh and trilby hat slowly poling a gondola of Japanese tourists.

From Venice to Izmir they go by the Turkish ferry, M/F *Samsun*. John, exploring the ship and finding the captain on the Bridge, asks if he may see the charts.

"Certainly. Here we are. We shall pass through the Corinth Canal late tomorrow."

The Corinth Canal: talk about a camel going through the eye of a needle! There is no way, it appears from the deck of the *Samsun* anchored off and waiting to go through, that this camel will get through that eye of the needle. But slowly and surely, the big ship is drawn by tug into the throat of the canal: there appears to be all of one metre from vessel to shore on either side where tall walls of rock seem to grip the ship. Breath in, says the rock face. It is an extraordinary coincidence that *The Economist*, issued 11-17 March 1994, should carry an advertisement for Morgan Stanley Bank in the USA under the banner caption 'Zero Room For Error," showing a wide vessel in the Corinth Canal filling it from wall to wall. Now, on the very same vessel, Anne and John long to show the advertisement to the Captain but resist the impulse since he would wish to keep the copy, and traditional Mediterranean and Turkish courtesy would require them to grant his wish if possible.

In the sixth century BC, the idea of digging a canal across the lowest part of the four-mile long Isthmus of Corinth, was first mooted in order to avoid the long, often dangerously stormy passage around the Peloponnesus Peninsula, the plan being revived at intervals until 1893 when it became reality. In the meantime, the ancient Greeks devised another way of moving their shipping between East and West. They built a stone track with grooves in which ran wheeled trolleys for the ships. It must be assumed that slave power hauled the trolleys, handling them round curves built to ease the gradient.[27]

So to Amman, to stay in a small, comfortable hotel for a couple of weeks whilst looking for an apartment to rent for three months whilst the site houses are being constructed. First impressions of Amman bear no resemblance to the small, crowded town astride a steep valley that Anne recalls from forty years ago. This is a city of modern motorways and sophisticated circle intersections to which the Canberra sobriquet of 'seven suburbs seeking a city' might be applied; a metropolis flung over seven hills, in that respect comparable to Rome or Edinburgh. Under a strong sun, the city wears a bright, modern ambience, a quality of incandescent light, a luminosity reflected from concrete, pale stone and stucco, from marble and ceramic tile. Each hill or *djebel* different, one must become skilled in orienteering by recognising significant skylines and silhouettes. Now, on Jebel Amman, near Fourth Circle the diplomatic and consular quarter, Anne is reminded of Algiers as it was some twenty years ago.

---

[27] 'How the Ancient Greeks Transported Ships over The Isthmus of Corinth'. Nicholas M Verdelis trans Eugene Vanderpool, *The Illustrated London News*, October 19, 1957, p649

An apartment is soon found in the Abdoun quarter near Sixth Circle. This area is brand spanking new: all manner of desirable residences may be seen, architectural imagination knowing no bounds. Such ornaments of opulence confer a cloak of wealth upon the district but among the modern mansions, on patches of yet undeveloped land, flocks of sheep and goats graze daily; their attendant shepherds, in long black robes and Arabic head-covers, brewing tea over tiny fires of collected litter, are perfectly biblical in appearance. The apartment on the second floor possesses real marble floors in the hall and living room, balconies at each window, plumbing and electrics that work, and is cleanly spacious. On the ground floor live an American family, and on the first floor live the owners, Mr and Mrs Mahjid. An efficient lift connects the floors but the marble staircase is too beautiful to shun. Above the flat, nearing completion, is a luxury penthouse into which the Mahjids will shortly move. The basement is a giant cistern, allowing Mr Mahjid's Mercedes to be washed daily in company with all the other Mercedes of the neighbourhood.

Mr and Mrs Mahjid are Palestinian refugees from the West Bank; rich refugees, typical of the Abdoun residents. These refugees are highly educated, qualified professionals; doctors, lawyers, engineers, academics who have worked as expatriates in Saudi Arabia, Libya and the Gulf States, earning enormous salaries which are then ploughed into real estate in Jordan. Now Jordanian citizens, they have contributed mightily to the country's economy. Not so the poor refugees from Palestine who have immigrated into Jordan at intervals from 1920 onwards, a running sore of refugees turning into a tsunami wave in 1948 when Israel was established, and again in 1967 when Israel defeated a concerted attack from its Arab neighbours. There are still vast refugee camps around the country, cramped, squalid settlements full of people with no status, no jobs, no hope, creating unimaginable difficulties for the small, struggling Hashemite Kingdom of Jordan.

This is a Moslem country, Friday the holy day, the day for families to empty out of Amman with consummate quantities of food seeking desert, wadi or just the wide open spaces for a day of alfresco life which strikes a vital chord on their environmental roots. The only picnic furniture they may take is a portable barbeque: for them, the ground is their seat, their recliner, their daybed.

John and Anne join the exodus, heading down a fine motorway built by the Americans and euphemistically named 'The Peace Road' since it leads ultimately to the King Hussein Bridge over the River Jordan and into Palestine West Bank, now under Israeli occupation. Down, down, down from Amman at some 1,000 m above sea level, snaking between ridge and bluff, traversing cautiously the frayed side of the Rift Valley, zigzagging from spur to spur across wadis that rend the slopes, to a monument marking Sea Level; and on down. At a military checkpoint, the road northwards along the Valley to Karameh leaves the Peace Road. Young, conscript soldiers stare with credulous gaze at the passenger side of the Ford Escort.

"You have no steering wheel!"

"But yes, on the other side" grins John. "We are going to Karameh Dam."

"Where is that? Karameh we know, but no dam."

"It is the Selini place," John gives the name of the contractors engaged to build the dam.

"Ah yes, the Selini Italians, we know them. Have a good day, friend."

The Jordan Valley, part of that stupendous split in the earth's crust which is the Great Rift Valley, is old in experience, having existed as a dwelling place since before the beginning of history. Menhirs, two standing stones topped by a horizontal slab that litter the landscape, are assumed to be burial sites dating from at least eight thousand BC. Tells, mounds made by the rise and fall of successive settlements, are everywhere and from every Age; some tells having as many as twelve identified layers of habitation, and other tells still waiting to be excavated. Undoubtedly, the valley floor is fertile, that is if water control and irrigation can be applied, and it is abundantly clear that the ancients made themselves masters of water supply. Both ancient and more modern aqueducts, canals, siphons, storage tanks, cisterns and irrigation channels have come and gone over the centuries.

Today's effort to amplify and extend successive accretions of water supply driven to emergency by the flood of immigrants from Palestine's West Bank, is on an unparalleled scale: the idea is to build a storage reservoir into which surplus fresh winter water from the upper Jordan basin can be pumped, via existing reservoirs and canals, the flow being reversed and pumped back to augment local and naturally toxic water supply during the long hot summers. The concept of a mile-long earth dam situated in a tributary wadi of the lower Jordan River, creating a sump in the bowels of the earth's crust, is daring. The Rift Valley is part of an active geological zone, an unstable fault in the earth's crust. What if the dam breaks? This dam is a conceit born of necessity and if the dam were to burst, it is calculated that the released flood would pass over saline pasture into the Dead Sea, there being little permanent settlement downstream of the dam. That is, at present. One can imagine future villages, towns springing unlicensed on underdeveloped land, if irrigation water were to be available in sufficient quantity to wash out the toxic salts and minerals occurring naturally in the soil. It is a nightmare scenario.

Along the floor of the Jordan Valley is an endless but attenuated carpet of citrus orchard, banana groves and date gardens; of horticulture mostly under shrouds of plastic. The housing site for Karameh Dam, identified by a couple of bulldozers, is a spacious wire-fenced compound on stony ground above the fertile green belt. John pulls out the Italian architect's plans; houses will face northwest, as they should in this sort of extreme climate. A swimming pool and a tennis court; good. The word 'Gazebo' sits comfortably in the centre of the plan. What is a gazebo? The dictionary says it is a 'belvedere', from the Italian 'bel' – beautiful and 'vedere' – to see. There is orchard and horticulture to view in the foreground, much of it hung with shredded plastic of yesteryear's growth. In the distance, the west bank of the Jordan River presents a formidable desert sculpture, a scarp rampart in colours of rust-red, yellow-ochre, bistre and battleship grey behind which the hills of ancient Judea, in colours of jasper, verd-antique and verdigris, are layered in a structural symphony of skyline silhouettes building, ramp upon ramp, to a plateau broken by a few conspicuous mountain remnants. It is an uplifting scene.

Meanwhile, in Amman, John and Anne go to the airport with the *korani*, clerk, of the Jordanian consultant engineering firm to which the British engineers are attached for building Karameh Dam. After five hours of trying to clear their landed freight, they get nowhere and the *korani* will go again on the morrow. Procedures are alarmingly bureaucratic in this country; far worse than in East Africa. The luggage, when it comes, has been tipped out, sorted through and stuffed back hitti-missi but it is all there.

There is no sign of the site vehicles yet; nor will there be at the rate the client, that is the Jordan Valley Authority, moves. It is reported that JVA want Toyotas, and only Toyotas, but it takes three or more months to procure them from Japan; Chevrolets off the shelf are available in Amman but Chevrolets will not suit. What a mercy Anne and John brought their Ford Escort, otherwise they would be using taxis everywhere.

"Ah! You will need to register your car if it is to remain longer than three months," says the administrative officer, viewing the Escort with disdain. "I am not sure about your steering wheel on the wrong side. It may not be permitted. And of course everyone will have to sit the driving test to get a Jordanian Licence. You will also need Residence Permits," says the Administrator, known on the quiet, perhaps erroneously, as Mr Fixit. "I will take you to the Government Clinic for mandatory blood tests to be submitted with your applications." Blood tests! It becomes apparent that all expatriate residents are tested for HIV and AIDS. So be it. The Clinic is hygienic but busy, necessitating a long queue wait.

Thanks to a bureaucracy not commended for its aptitude, it is months before the Residence Permits are issued, and more months before the driving tests are called. Mr Fixit arranges, firstly, driving tests for the engineers and as an afterthought, and after repeated prompts, for their wives. By then, John and Anne are living in Karameh, so the commute to the Government Traffic Centre for testing is doubled.

Anne and another wife, Kitty, are together taken, in Kitty's private Renault car, by a Jordanian company driver who has, one must presume, passed the driving test but does not necessarily follow best driving practice, to the Traffic Centre. It transpires that only the eye test and theory test will be administered today and, if successful, a practical test will be called in the following weeks (or months). Alas, there is but a single copy of the English language test paper so Anne and Kitty must take turns to fill a multiple choice answer sheet. The questions being no more than obvious common sense, they both pass.

The practical exam, which follows some weeks later, is more a test of English language comprehension and bladder control. Having arrived at the stated time, along with a number of other candidates, Anne and Kitty are directed to a distant waiting room for ladies only; a hen house. Two police examiners, in an ancient government vehicle, after putting each male candidate through their paces, prepare to go home until the company driver reminds them of the two ladies waiting. The ladies! Of course! Well that will be a matter of minutes since lady drivers are assumed to fail several times before achieving a pass and this is, after all, their first attempt. A woman police constable is found to chaperone them. Getting the jalopy used for testing to run smoothly is a trial of ingenuity, double de-clutch techniques learned on grandmother's 1937 baby Austin requiring instant recall by Anne. The three-point turn is tricky when first gear refuses to engage, the police inspector jamming it home with an apologetic shrug; and a 'reverse parallel park' in the English language is more than their fractured English can manage until by divination, the instruction to 'park as in a garage between the blocks of wood' is interpreted correctly. The whole event, from Karameh and back, has occupied five hours but Kitty and Anne have passed. "You are good drivers," say the police inspectors with kindly condescension.

So Anne, now armed with her official Jordanian driving licence as well as her UK licence, continues to drive the Ford Escort here, there and everywhere. But not for much longer; it fails to be accepted for registration in Jordan and goes back to the UK in a cargo vessel, Anne and John buying a Renault Clio in Amman.

Jordan is not a willing, cheerful host to expatriate professional colleagues. Diplomats, Aid Agents, International Representatives and Advisors, yes, they are tolerated, but the technical managers and executives seconded to their essential services, they would prefer to do without. As far as the intellectual Arab is concerned, better that their expatriates be menials and of a servile nature. The Jordanian consultant engineering firm with which Gibb is linked, manages to have scant rapport with its expatriate staff. On site, some of the Jordanian consulting engineers and many of those of the client, the JVA, are self-persuaded that their positions are sinecures, to function only from an air-conditioned office or vehicle. Not for them a sortie onto the dust-deep ground in the searing sun. Work boots, sweat-stained jackets and litre plastic water bottles for essential re-hydration are as alien to these engineers as is getting their nicely-manicured hands soiled. What a talent for absenting themselves from their office to the canteen, the toilet or the prayer room; what limitless capacity for tea and cigarettes in the cool of their a/c offices and what a bank of complaints against delinquent foremen and dozy drivers!

Abrasion between Gibb staff, the Jordanian consultants and the on-site engineers of the client, the Jordan Valley Authority, continues to scour and sour working practice. Mistrust mounts. Gibb manages to have transferred one of the client's engineers known to be a formidable, unmanageable person; meanwhile JVA calls in an international panel of experts to arbitrate on the design and construction techniques being employed by Gibb on Karameh Dam.

The report from the panel of experts is good; much more favourable than expected but the confrontation does not abate. Then the blow falls. The client, JVA the employer, says they are not satisfied; that in particular, two of Gibb's senior staff, one of them John, are not careful enough, not committed to JVA's interests; they voice exaggerated threats of dismissal. Gibb, bewildered and anxious, posits the notion that JVA, accustomed to operating in an atmosphere of tension, distrust and fear, in the habit of taking a pickaxe to peel a peach, judges Gibb's attitude as too complacent for JVA's normal business procedures. An alternative explanation is perhaps to be found in the Bible: this could be a case of an eye for an eye and a tooth for a tooth, the engineer transferred by Gibb, a tartar of the first order, having thought to turn the tables on Gibb. Whatever the cause of the red herring which offers a salutary insight into Arab ways of business, the affair does with time, blow over. If Karameh Dam is ever completed, it will be despite the Achilles heel of such engineers and thanks to dedicated and skilled foremen and plant drivers from such places as Pakistan, Sri Lanka and the Philippines and, to the determination of the Italian contractors.

This part of the world will take some time to get used to, both to understand the antics of the local people and to detect the reaction of expatriates to life in Jordan. It appears that people of the Near East hardly know who they are or what their future may be. Their histories are so woven with deception and mistrust, with seizing land or losing it from time immemorial, that it is no wonder they are suspicious, exacting and peremptory. As for the European expatriates, they come for as long as is necessary, make their money and go: come with a suitcase of clothes, not with a load of household effects and a grand piano. With regular, frequent home leave, ensuring they stay on the home professional ladder, they see little of the country and show no curiosity about Jordan.

As ever in a new posting, Anne searches for some domestic help. As spring migrates into summer, sudden winds from the south race through Amman, deterred by nothing, neither windows and doors, nor cupboards and drawers, nor hair, eyes and nose. Acres of marble in the apartment wearing a patina of fine silt need sluicing down; carpets, upholstery, bedding all need to be beaten and vacuumed.

"The ground floor flat employs a Phillipina," reports Mr Mahjid. "I will ask her to come and see you."

Linda agrees to help, proving herself a good friend. Married to a Jordanian, with two young sons, speaking good Arabic and English, she is a godsend.

"The Americans downstairs are leaving. You are moving to Karameh. I will come to Karameh on the staff bus for three days a week. I know the contractor's bus driver well and he will bring me from my house." It is a round trip of sixty miles.

Linda's offer is indeed a gift from the gods. Chris Richardson, whom John and Anne had known in Morogoro, and his wife Kitty living next door, are delighted to share Linda; taking the lion's share of time and wages since they have two young boys, Sean of four years and David of one year.

The move to the new-built house at Karameh occurs at a season when the scorching sun is a dreaded daily event, when the land quivers in a haze of heat and dust, when sudden, brutal hot winds fill the air with whirls of leaping litter and shredded plastic. Fly screens at windows and doors, while not deterring the grime of an arid land, do exclude swarms of flies attracted to untreated chicken waste used by farmers in the valley: swarms which could equal those visited upon the lands of Pharaoh as one of the ten plagues of Egypt. It is an indomitable environment, full of wild natural history, immense in its vistas, magnificent in its antiquity, intoxicating in its aura of continuity and disorientating in its remoteness. Here is nothing of the suburban and the bland.

It is a place, of course, to be tamed and treated to Man's excesses. Three thousand trees are being planted in the Karameh site compound; grass, grubbed up by the sackful from the banks of the canal, is being poked into the ground in front of each dwelling along with dozens of flowering shrubs and roses; and a massive high water tank, which a contractor's bowser refills twice or thrice daily, stands ready to water the infant garden city. Beyond and behind the wire enclosure, it is dust and stones as usual, cut by deep, sudden wadis rising to the naked cragged spurs of the Rift Valley wall. Nomads in pick-ups and veteran trucks pass the compound to their tents, hidden in folds of the wasteland. Sometimes their flocks of sheep and goats, led by the inevitable donkey, graze past under the watchful eye of a boy who pauses to sit on a boulder and practise his flute; little liquid, haunting flurries of melody from the shepherd on the rock, along with a strong pong of livestock, drift through the dense air.

Karameh town, approached through the narrow belt of horticulture under plastic cloche and of orchard, is a long sun-beaten street with mostly one-storey buildings, some of which are shops with sloping counters of goods projecting under fixed awnings. There is not much there except a baker's table with thin rounds of Arab bread piled in hot towers under a cloth. There are mosques, but no cinema, no library, no bowling alley or café, trays of tea or coffee being carried across the street from a take-away. But wait! Here is a grocer's shop sporting a soft drinks cold cabinet and a chest freezer of ice cream. Venture inside to find well-stacked shelves from floor to ceiling on a find-it-if-you-can basis of a little bit of everything. At the rear, in a mealy smell of dried chickpeas, lentils and beans are cold cabinets of milk and milk products and some chest freezers of imported meats including – oh bliss – legs of New Zealand lamb. The grocery merchant speaks English – hurrah!

"I came from Palestine in 1967" says Abu Hassan. "I am happy to help you people from Italy, Britain." He attends to an urgent customer needing to buy two cigarettes. "Any time, anything, you just ask me please." He is suddenly a busy man with an eye for the main chance of this influx of foreigners for a period of three years. His well-worn family car, loaded to the gunwales like a removals truck, is busy flying down the empty miles of the Peace Road from Amman fetching goodies and other essentials of the Europeans. He and a brother, Abu Rashid, contrive to keep the shop humming from eight in the morning until eight at night. Intelligent, industrious, they are characteristic of the Palestinian middle class that has contributed much to Jordan's artisan aptitude in recent decades. They, and a number of their local customers, family men mostly with bulging shopping bags buying their household needs, are full of curiosity about these Europeans suddenly arrived in their midst.

"Come over for tea" invites Kitty in her candid Canadian way to a portly lady in ankle-length gabardine coat and generously proportioned headscarf met in Abu Hassan's shop.

"Anne, I've gone and invited a Karameh family over for tea." Kitty is taken aback by the unknown factors in the invitation – will they come, how many will come, what would they eat?"

"We'll bake plenty of brownies and have tea and coffee ready."

In the event, three ladies traditionally dressed in long coat and headscarf, are delivered to Kitty's door where, divesting themselves of their street clothes, they are seen wearing expensive, fashionable dresses or designer trouser suits. Young David is an icebreaker, the brownies are much enjoyed but the coffee is not strong enough, they admit when asked. Punctually, their driver collects them and as they don their robes and headscarves, they press their suit for a return invitation next Friday afternoon.

Behind Karameh's main street are two-storey houses hidden by high, uncompromising walls, the homes of the Palestinian middle class. A lad opens tall metal gates to reveal a secret domain with vine-covered trellis over a marble patio; with a gleam of precious water tinkling down a concrete channel and citrus trees thick with white orange blossom. Here is a shock – a paradise in treeless, dust-clad Karameh.

On the shady patio among tubs of vivid geraniums in cool fragrance, are table and chairs where sit the family arranged as if for a formal group portrait. Abu Rashid is smoking a water pipe; his mother the matriarch, in an ankle-length white dress, her grey hair plaited, is smoking a cigarette, a packet of Marlboro at her hand. She is flanked by various sons, daughters and daughters-in-law, whose shy children hide behind skirts, to be pulled forth to shake hands. Names are difficult as are the relationships among the family. It is probable that they are indeed all closely related, marriage within the extended family being still a norm rather than an exception: it is not a social solecism but a feature of an ancient heritage. The Bible records that Sara, Abraham's wife, was also his half-sister and Lot's two daughters inveigled their father to lie with them begetting sons to continue the bloodline. The Jordan Government has been exercised by the deleterious effects of too frequent consanguine marriage to the point of recommending affianced couples undergo blood testing for consanguinity at their clinics.

Meanwhile, in a Karameh garden, it is a charming scene: the young ladies fetch more chairs and old Mama extends a smile and paper-wrapped sweeties to Kitty's two little boys. Strong coffee in tiny cups, cold fruit juice in a jug, a tray holding bunches of grapes, a big bowl of radishes and another of some sticky pastry balls is laid before them. Talk is general with only a fleeting interest in Anne's or Kitty's world: perhaps so much energy is expended on their world of Palestine West Bank and Israel that spare curiosity for other worlds is not available. At length, after many smiles and long pauses while everyone searches for a new topic to comment upon, to admire, Kitty and Anne take their leave.

It is not long before the Selini compound is humming with social activity, slowly assuming the appearance of a well-managed theme park. Autumn rains bring on the planted trees and grass, lawn mowing being organised by the head gardener. He has a roguish twinkle in his brown eyes and a snappy military salute with every communication. He is very much part of his surroundings; grey fatigues, grey vest beneath, both the colour of the Rift Valley dust, but for a red check *keffiyah*, head-cover which is a belisha beacon to reveal his whereabouts: he may be seen sometimes under the water tower doing cunning things with a network of tiny water channels from the overflow valve and ridged beds of radishes, tomatoes and beans. Keen to learn more Arabic, Anne asks him words for the plants and vegetables. "And what is the word for this?" indicating the embryo lawn. He bends down, fingers a wiry tuft, "Hashish," he says, in a tone one might use to instruct a child.

A winter deluge of rain in the valley brings reports of half a metre of snow in Amman on the plateau. Winter also brings numbers of young city dwellers down to the warmer climes of the Rift Valley to enjoy the hospitality of the Italian engineers; there are tennis parties, a Santa Barbara Festival, patron saint of miners and engineers, with a superb dinner at the Mess, of salamis and Parma ham, of delicious pastas, of barbecued king prawns and quails. They enjoy Christmas Dinner, New Year's Eve celebrations with unparalleled cuisine; and later on into the summer when day leaps suddenly into night, when sparklers of fireflies explode over the lawns, poolside parties and dancing attended by young, well-heeled Jordanian friends of Selini, professional party-goers many of them.

Winter also brings a letter from Linda to say she is unable to continue with travel to Karameh. What now? The merchant grocer, of course.

"Yes," says Abu Hassan. "We shall arrange that."

To Kitty comes Umm Djemal who is tall, elderly, stout, talks non-stop Arabic with great panache and smiles freely despite everything.

"My husband died. The Israelis, you know, they broke his ribs and later he died. I live in my husband's cousin's house in Karameh until I can go back to the farm in Palestine."

Children? "Of course. There are fourteen now, I think; perhaps sixteen." Anne later discovers that Umm Djemal has had twenty pregnancies, and is now fifty-seven years of age. And yet, in her sky-blue robe and capacious white headscarf, with her beatific expression and kindly eyes, Umm Djemal resembles a mature, middle-aged Virgin Mary. Sean and David adore her.

To Anne, comes the sister of the grocer's storekeeper. Mariam is just seventeen; slim, encased in long gabardine coatdress and generous headscarf, she disrobes on arrival to work in designer jeans and short-sleeved T-shirt. Travelling in on the morning staff bus, Mariam goes home at one o'clock, walking half a mile down to the main road and catching the public transport bus. She is a lovely girl; reliable, of good family, strong, willing to water the evolving garden, quick to learn English-style baking. But she rarely talks. She answers questions, yes, but seldom asks a question and never tosses a comment, an opinion or a hint of reaction to being plunged into a European household. Umm Djemal is full of talk; stage orations addressed to David on her hip; homilies to Kitty when she suffers from amoebic dysentery; humorous harangues to the gardener. But from Mariam, so little communication. Anne places the Gibb-supplied television set in the spare room where Mariam does the ironing and sometimes the girl slips next door for her tea break to bask in Umm Djemal's motherly comfort. Bear in mind, she has been trained from babyhood to say little, do all. The privilege of speech comes when she is a mother of five or fifteen, when she is a mother-in-law and matriarch. Arabs have perhaps attended to the generation dilemma more assiduously than their Western counterparts, who have successfully parked many of the older generation up a grassy siding by the time they are fifty.

Nevertheless, doubts about Mariam remain: she will suddenly be recalled by her family for marriage: the stress of loneliness will prevail and she will leave, although she seems to be more at ease with her situation, and has even offered to come in while Anne and John are on leave to clean the house and water the garden. The event, when it comes, is a mortar shell shock. Anne, idly watching Mariam, in her coverall headscarf and long gabardine, depart down the hill to the main road, notices a man friend walking with her. Silly girl; she knows the rules of her society but at seventeen, presumably thinks she can covertly bypass them. The young man she is meeting is trained from infancy to regard all women who are not his mother, his sister or his wife, as whores. For all Anne knows, they may have plans for assignations in John and Anne's house whilst it is empty. In Mariam's society, the penalties for not conforming are hard, cruel even, murders for family honour being commonplace in Jordan. Anne, determined not to be involved in Mariam's secret escapades, asks Umm Djemal to help her explain to Mariam's brother that it is not suitable for her to continue working on the Selini compound.

Now Anne has Umm Mahjid, a mature well-covered matron of about thirty-five with nine children ranging downwards from the eldest of twenty years, and with an ailing husband. "He was caught and beaten by the Israelis because he went back to see his farm on the West Bank. Now he cannot walk." She wears a comfortable cardigan of dolour, has a *triste* turn of the mouth, but she is willing and soon capable. Anne would like to ask her to do some Jordanian cooking but must wait until after Ramadhan. Both Umm Mahjid and Umm Djemal are observing their fast more strictly than some of the men folk employed by Selini, who slope off to the pool of shadow under the water tank for essential moments of respite found in a shared cigarette. Whether the ladies' devotion to duty depends on personal conviction born of illiteracy and of insulation in the home, or whether rigid adherence to the Moslem charter is upheld by the older women of the community because they have most to lose if their young do not conform, Anne does not know.

Spring comes suddenly to Jordan: it is as if the world's garden centres have tipped out their stock of anemones, irises, crocuses, lilies, hyacinths, tulips, poppies, brooms and mimosas. Behind Anne's house is a green bank of ragged weeds. "Good for salad" says Umm Mahjid, in the told-to-children Arabic she uses for Anne, picking a leaf and popping it in her mouth. It is wild rocket (Eruca Sativa) and makes a delicious accompaniment to a lunch of Umm

Mahjid's fried aubergine liberally sprinkled with spicy crimson, sumach powder (Rhus Coriaria) and served with *laban*, Arabic cream cheese, and rounds of unleavened bread.

Umm Mahjid, with a countrywoman's knowledge of local herbs and spices, introduces Anne to interesting culinary combinations, this rapport strengthened by Anne's obvious curiosity about Jordanian cuisine. When one of the Gibb engineers, who is actively interested in Jordan, Palestine, Christianity, Jerusalem, Israel and the Middle East as most of the Gibb staff are not, celebrates a significant sixtieth birthday, Anne and Kitty propose a local Arab dinner party cooked by Umm Djemal and Umm Mahjid instead of the usual barbeque.

"O.K.," say the other Gibb wives, "But don't expect our husbands to eat that sort of food. We can feed them early and they can push food around their plates at the party."

On the day of the event, Anne's kitchen is deep in excited Arab ladies who decide to cook *mansaf*, the traditional Jordan feast dish. *Mansaf* seems to be quantities of boiled lamb meat (New Zealand frozen) added into quantities of spiced and beaten yoghurt and *laban*, the Arab cream cheese. Interesting! The Jews have a taboo about meat and milk products together. Indeed, Orthodox Jews must have separate kitchens for meat preparation and for cooking with milk, and it would appear that this taboo dates from early Jewish history when their priests were trying to destroy the indigenous Baal worship. The most sacred dish to offer Baal, and his priests of course, was a dish of kid cooked in its mother's milk: a dish not dissimilar to the Jordanian Arab feast of *mansaf* which, tasting like a delicious rich Irish stew, is served with turmeric rice and a mutton broth of vegetables. And since some of the Gibb engineers cannot join the invited guests to enjoy the culinary experience, there is plenty to spare for the cooks and their families too.

"Today is Mothers' Day," observes Umm Mahjid, arriving for work with a presentation posy of herbs from her garden and a saintly smile. Anne shakes her hand offering congratulations on her blessing of children, asking after Majhid her eldest son who confers upon her the honorific of 'Umm Mahjid', mother of Mahjid.

"May your fortune continue," rejoices Umm Djemal at tea break, but the lady lacks her customary sanguine buoyancy. She mops a moist eye.

"My son fell off a roof, has broken his leg." Djemal, employed on a construction site, will be off work for weeks, unable to earn his living, then will have to look for a new job: unemployment being an ever looming threat to the unskilled in Jordan. An ugly witness of unemployment is a lorry park on the outskirts of Jordan's seaport, Aqaba, where rest several hundred rusting hulks of juggernauts, idle since the 1991 Gulf War put an end to trade with Iraq.

If an advantage of Karameh is the privilege of living in rural Jordan rather than in cosmopolitan, sophisticated Amman, it is comforting to know that the fleshpots of the city are not far away and easily achieved. Ancient Rabbath Ammon, capital city of the Bible's Ammonites, Hellenistic Amman, Roman Philadelphia, Byzantine Amman, Ommayed Amman, Ottoman Amman and modern Amman are all there to be explored, much restoration work having opened up the past to a flourishing tourist business. Entertainment includes a concert in the splendid Roman theatre able to seat five thousand, or a 'Night With the Met' in one of Amman's ultra-comfortable hotels which is playing host to New York's Metropolitan Opera Company; a plethora of excellent, international restaurants; charity fetes and fairs, balls to mark national days such as Saint Andrew's or Saint Patrick's, there being many British and Irish lasses married to Jordanians who make their home in Amman; and Churches of all persuasions, for Amman is liberally cosmopolitan in tolerating Christian worship in this city of magnificent mosques. The Anglican Church holds a Christmas carol service, its congregation a majority of Arab Christians with a few European Anglicans, each singing the favourite tunes to the familiar words of their own language. Anne, no songster, finds it hard to keep the key, the tune or the timing but the packed candlelit church is emotional in the circumstance of so many Arab Christians in and around the Holy Land.

Amman is the seat of the British Ladies Association, organised by well-disposed ladies for the benefit of all British nationals in Jordan; coffee mornings, charity garden bazaars, Christmas parties and outings being their forte. One outing buses members to a Bedouin tribal village on the desert fringe to behold rug-making that has been encouraged as a commercial enterprise for the womenfolk; washing, spinning, dyeing and weaving wool, being done in primitive but effective ways. The 'loom' is but the ground, with a short branch of wood propped across two breeze blocks, the warp being stretched over and under the branch and secured to the earth with pegs. The woven products, half a metre wide only, are then stitched together to form larger rugs, which are sold in the USA, Lebanon, France, the UK (Harvey Nichols and Harrods) and outlets in Amman. The tribal women of the Nabi Hamida get their share of the monies and save up to build a house or buy an orchard.

"What are you saving for? Asks the interpreter of a young woman seated on the ground at her loom.

"I am saving for a husband" she grins shyly. "If I have a property, I can have a man of my choice." Her flying fingers among the warp pause momentarily, her face clouds as she recognises the enormity of her revelation; a disclosure out of tribal context.

"And what do the men of your tribe think about the ladies' ambitions?" The interpreter cleverly lifts the dialogue out of the personal and back to the general.

"Ah!" the weaver considers, her piano hands stilled again, "They are not sure what to say. The older ones do not like it but the young ones are quite keen." One hopes this charming young woman will be happy with the object of her aspirations.

At the other end of the tribal spectrum, is a couple John and Anne meet while on holiday in an Aqaba hotel. He came from a Bedouin background, joined the army, did well and completed specialist studies in Britain. His wife, a teacher in Amman, bringing up six children with the help of a Sri Lankan nanny, is a modern young career woman, although only one generation from tribal life and constraints. Jordan is working hard to engender social change.

Another bus outing of the British Ladies Association goes to picnic at El Hammeh in the Jordan Valley where mineral springs cascade into a private garden belonging to a well-known Amman personality. The large pool is fed by a stream gushing down a series of rock pool steps, each step a mini-jacuzzi of warm swirling water. Tiny fish swim in the pool and Roman capitals and urns artistically positioned in the shallows or around the pool perimeter, provide an aura of antiquity, the whole being set about with species of eucalyptus, date, banana, bamboo and pink-blossomed oleander. Their host, Mamduh, is gracious, ever thoughtful for his guests' comfort, fresh cold juice and sweet Arab tea being served around, and in, the pool. Anne, gratefully taking her share of the welcome, falls under his spell.

Living in Amman, having property in the Jordan Valley, Mamduh is a frequent commuter through Karameh, stopping off unexpectedly, bearing a bouquet of garden blooms or of fresh carrots, a bundle of runner beans or a box of beetroot, for coffee and chat: Mamduh, sometimes accompanied by his sister Leila, perhaps recognises a cloister characteristic of the Karameh compound, alienating the inmates from another Jordan of culture and refined civilisation, of poets and painters, of literature and letters. Invitations to visit in Amman and El Hammeh are issued to all and sundry, for Mamduh is a convivial chap who revels in company, conversation and debate.

Anne drives her guest, Ann Powell, the friend of decades and now an eminent Professor of art history, to El Hammeh in the hot, little Renault Clio, heat radiating from the road, dust-laden verge and sun-struck car. High walls, a stout metal gate swinging open into blessed shade and there is Mamduh, prosperous, smiling, engagingly seigneurial; a rich merchant from Tales of the Arabian Nights, though he is in fact Christian, not Moslem. Leading his guests through the shrubberies scattered with sarcophagi and funerary urns, casually reclined among the trees, to a heavy stone door ajar under a low lintel, Mamduh tucks his hand under an elbow. "Mind your head," he warns, "This is the door of a tomb. Here you leave your hot, travel-weary selves behind and step through into paradise." An impish grin flicks across his face. There, suddenly, is the swimming pool of celestial blue fed by its silver cascade of rock pools; a magical place, an Elysian field beyond the ancient tomb door.

"And here are the changing rooms," says Mamduh indicating two small cabins each with a little metal replica of a skull and crossbones on the door. "You go inside in your earthly clothes, emerge in your heavenly garb, your swimming costume." His dark eyes twinkle with esoteric mirth. Ann, the Professor of art history, is intrigued by Mamduh's imagery: she has been researching eighteenth century theme gardens of Europe and sees his conceptual garden at El Hammeh as belonging to this genre.

There is much to explore in the small country of Jordan; Crusader castles, Ummayed fortresses, caravanserais, baths and palaces; a Dead Sea resort to swim, reclining comfortably in the warm dense water then shower, dine on the terrace and watch gilded ripples race across to the unhappy occupied West Bank as the sun sinks behind the Jerusalem hills. Mount Nebo, whence Moses gazed across the Jordan Valley to a Land promised by God to the Israelites regardless of any Canaanites, Moabites, Ammonites, Edomites, or other Gentiles who might be inhabiting the area, is a prime upstanding spur of the Amman plateau. The view is tremendous. Westwards across the Jordan Valley and Dead Sea, it encompasses the hills of Judah and Samaria; in fine weather, the towers and domes of Jerusalem, the oasis of Jericho and the scarp holding the Qumran Caves are visible. On the peak of the spur is a modern chapel, built on the ruins of a Byzantine monastery, and an exquisite metal sculpture of the Bronze Serpent of Moses by the Italian sculptor, Giovanni Fantoni.

The ancient acropolis of Nebo may be identified nearby by the ruins of at least five Byzantine churches with remnants of mosaics depicting rural and hunting scenes, by fragments of cisterns, streets and stairs now compressed concertina-like by the forces of geological movement. Another collapsed hilltop site is that of Machaerus not far from Nebo. On this hill, bare as an icecap now but formerly tree-covered, stood the fortified palace of Herod and his son Herod Antipas; he who had John the Baptist beheaded at the request of his wife, Herodias' dancing daughter, Salome.

The district centre for Mount Nebo and Machaerus is Madaba, ancient Moabite capital city. The modern city of Madaba is renowned for its mosaics, chief among them a map of the Holy Land. Discovered a hundred years ago beneath the floor of the Greek Orthodox Church of St. George, this remarkable mosaic was originally twenty-five metres long by five metres wide and once contained over two million tesserae. The sixth century map of Palestine, now far from complete of course, shows the main physical features of Dead Sea, Jordan River system, West Bank hills and East Bank plateau. In central position is the walled city of Jerusalem with its streets, domes and towers, other settlements and religious sanctuaries being shown by symbols. Natural resources are depicted by date palms, vines, hunted game, vessels plying the Dead Sea and fish in the Jordan River. It is a remarkable fact that fish reaching the toxic Dead Sea, turn and swim back upstream. This ancient map, both historic document and superlative monument, is set in natural stone, a Taj Mahal of Byzantine creative craftsmanship. In Madaba, Italian aid is equipping a craft school of modern mosaic making: it is hoped that ancient artistic skills, dormant in the genes of the Jordanian/Palestinian heritage, may be released.

Also in the Church of St. George is a vivid and compelling painting depicting the Prophet Elijah's departure from life in a fiery horse-drawn chariot, rocketing skywards through a cloudscape of sensational animation. The Bible's Second Book of Kings in chapter two, describes Elijah's final journey from Jericho on the West Bank across the Jordan River to the land of present day Jordan, so Madaba has historic claim to the spectacular event.

In the same church is a modern bronze relief showing St. George in medieval armour and chivalrous equestrian pose slaying a dragon. The Saint does not get a good character from Edward Gibbon. The eighteenth century historian describes George as a parasite who, by flattery and procurement, by fraud and corruption, became rich as purveyor of bacon to the Roman army. Compelled into exile, and devoting his many talents to Christian doctrinal study, he embraced Aryanism, then a heretic sect, to such good effect that he was invited to assume the archiepiscopal throne, displacing the Orthodox Archbishop, Athanasius. George, continuing his usurious dexterity, oppressed the clergy and congregations of his diocese until a successive Roman emperor announced his downfall. Whereupon his victims threw George into chains and dragged him to prison where a mob broke in and killed him, casting his remains into the sea lest he become a martyr. As indeed he did. Edward Gibbon does admit in a footnote that the calumnies heaped upon George may have been a smear campaign put about by the Athanasian sect. Churches dedicated to St.

George abound throughout the Byzantine Empire; his fame in Europe and connection with chivalry resulted from the Crusades.[28]

And Pella, beautiful Pella, some twenty-five miles north of Karameh on the lower slopes of the Rift Valley. If Petra is described as 'half as old as time', Pella must be twice as old as time, its Palaeolithic tools and weapons being dated at about twenty thousand years. The core city, around the wadi El Jirm, one of the Decapolis towns – that commercial league of wealthy Graeco-Roman trade centres – is now an enchanting mishmash of stone and marble masonry lying snug against a hillside, in springtime carpeted with sky-blue irises. Beside the springing waters of the wadi, stand the remnants of an Odeon in which water nymphs will have cavorted or mock sea battles been fought; the ruins of extravagant Byzantine basilicas built of recycled stone are evidence of Pella's changing fortunes; and there are fragments of Ommayed walls and forts all around.

In the same way that Pella re-invented itself as successive waves of Macedonians, Romans, refugee Christians from Roman Palestine, and Islamic people passed by, so did Gadara, another Decapolis city on the plateau to the north. Watered by permanent wadis, near the therapeutic warm springs of El Hammeh, ancient Gadara was a fashionable rich Roman spa resort. Its modern tourist Visitor Centre at Umm Qais, on a spectacular spur of hillside looking down over fertile olive groves and flower-filled fields to the Sea of Galilee, houses a small museum of beautiful mosaics, discovered locally. Intricately woven patterns, plaited convolutions, sinuously coiled compositions suggest Celtic art. It is unlikely that the Celts passed this way but the Roman rich and mighty who travelled with their entourage of slaves, servants and artisans, may have employed Celtic craftsmen. The visitor

---

[28] Gibbon, Edward, *The Decline and Fall of The Roman Empire*, Vol 2, Ch XXIII, pp 451-453

centre holds yet another surprise, a modern architectural gem. The door of the ladies' toilet leads directly into… the garden, set about with canna lilies and rambler roses. This cannot be right. But wait! This patio garden under glass porch contains the necessary porcelain, pipe work, paper products and mirrors, fully operational and clean. Thus one discovers Jordanian creativity expressed in contemporary function.

Jerash, yet another member of the Decapolis league, magnificent Roman city shouting wealth, is littered with monumental public buildings on a vast scale. Since Anne's visit in 1955 to Jerash, much reconstruction has been undertaken, not always to full height but enough to recreate a make-belief of Roman life. The Jerash Festival held over two weeks in June makes full use of the ancient city's sublime aesthetic ambiance.

Attending a Japanese opera production of 'Medea', during Japanese Week in Jordan, at the massive open-air South Theatre in Jerash, Anne carries in a cushion and appropriate evening refreshment to last through the marathon event. The five thousand seat auditorium contains an audience of barely a couple of hundred but the velvet night air is warmly euphoric, if redolent of popcorn. The opera is being sung in Japanese, but such is the dramatic skill of the producer and the body language of the performers that subtitles projected on stage would be both unnecessary and distracting.

The opera opens with the chorus, in silver-grey habits under huge grey Oriental coolie hats, genuflecting rhythmically, diagonally across the vast stage, declaiming in sonorous Japanese: it is slow-moving, sensational, sinister. Medea, daughter of a Magus and herself a sorceress, sings key sentences from a letter she carries; a letter from her husband Jason announcing his decision, for political reasons he says, to divorce Medea and wed the daughter of King Priam. Medea's shock, distress and horror registers with the chorus who, silently removing their coolie hats, expose close cauls of red or purple, the colours of passion and of violence. Euripides' famous ancient drama continues with Medea's confrontation with Jason and her plotting with her old nurse to destroy all that Jason holds dear, his bride-to-be, Medea herself and their two children. But the timeless fury of a woman scorned fails to engage the Jerash audience and by the time the spirit of Medea, still singing imprecations upon Jason, is raised skywards by a high lift-loader (borrowed from a reconstruction unit) disguised with silver tinsel and draperies and positioned behind the stage, most of the audience has gone home.

Petra is another landmark to have witnessed excavation, research, reconstruction, incomparable access and formidable tourist development since Anne last passed this way in 1955. At first glance, it is hardly the same place. Tarmac road from Wadi Musa downhill into a forest of hotels, guest houses, pensions, tour operators, visitors' centre, colourful bazaars of souvenirs and car parks holding forty tour coaches and a couple of hundred cars, visitor numbers being set at 2,500 per day. Gone are the Bedouins living in the rock-cut tombs and ancient monuments quarried in the cliffs: now the local families live in modern villas and apartments in a settlement just without the actual site, with tarmac road and vehicle access to business enterprises in Petra servicing the huge tourist trade. Now a symphony orchestra of seventy-five musicians, all their instruments and a grand piano can be transported into the rock-cut amphitheatre thought to be able to seat an audience of eight thousand in its heyday.

It is still possible to hire a pony and be led down the Siq, that great gorge carved by floods of water racing down the sun-cracked rocks, carrying chunks of stone, crashing round corners, finding weak strata, quarrying out massive boulders and hurling them along as tools of further destruction. However, arrangements for the return ride may be frustrating when, at the appointed hour, one spots one's mount and its attendant double booked and busy with other customers.

"Just a few minutes, lady. Please wait. Be with you soon" shouts the lad in charge of the horses, knowing that they can discharge their bonus clients and be back in half an hour. The dust raised in the narrow confines of the Siq and the manure deposited is unacceptable and in 1995, all horse traffic is banned in the Siq. The disabled have access through the residents' settlement; everyone else can walk the two miles to the ancient city centre. Petra's spacious site, hilly to the point of rock-cut steps to high places, is demanding, the return walk through the Siq becoming the last straw on the back of a long day's hike.

It is worth it. Anne scrambles, breathless, up the final gully to El Deir, known as the Monastery, to stare, stunned, at the size of the classical façade forty metres high and forty-six metres wide. She beholds nearby a black Bedouin tent offering souvenirs, canned drinks from a cold cabinet and, oh bliss, tables and benches. How did they get all that up the mountain?

"By donkey, of course" says an amused proprietor of the tent. Dakhilallah, a mine of information in fluent English, has worked with British archaeologists for many years. "Petra existed here on the trade route from southern Arabia to the Mediterranean Sea and Europe because the Nabataeans were good water engineers. They knew how to harvest run-off rainwater, collect it in chiselled grooves, channel it along the contour and into cisterns underground. They even had sand beds to filter out impurities before storage in the reservoirs." Dakhilallah, who lives in the new settlement, is justly proud of the skills of the ancient tribes whom he sees as his ancestors. "They cut a tunnel through the rock to divert water away from the Siq and into the citadel reservoirs." The narrows of the Siq affording guarded access to Petra, and the availability there of water, accounts for the Nabataeans' success as a trade centre, their obvious wealth appealing to successive influxes of builders and developers from Hellenistic through Roman to Byzantine and even crusader settlers. Nevertheless, the Siq has in modern times flooded heavily, in 1963 drowning twenty-three tourists and necessitating a barrier dam at the point where the Siq suddenly narrows.

In one of the rock-cut chambers is the Petra Bookshop, business outlet of Mohammed and his New Zealand-born wife Marguerite, where John and Anne, charged with the delivery of a message from a mutual friend in Amman, are invited to take tea. A low, octagonal table set about with stools covered with embroidered cushions, is indicated in the cosy recess of the cavern.

"I came here twenty years ago as a volunteer," Marguerite brews sweet tea on a brazier. "I was a trained nurse. The Volunteer Service posted me to Petra in the days when the families lived in caves, to oversee public health. I fell in love with Petra, and with Mohammed."

Now, with Petra in the mainstream of Jordan's development, Marguerite is waiting to hear whether her clever daughter will attend one of the World Colleges. "It is likely that she will be offered the chance of a place on the strength of her school grades but of course there are many applicants. Also, Mohammed and his brothers will have to decide whether to permit her to take up the offer of a place."

Marguerite's serenity is reassuring, her patience laudable; perhaps after twenty years she has acquired forbearance in this fascinating but challenging country of Jordan.

Looking back on the vexed question of a three-year posting to Jordan to live in a compound behind wire in the sun-drenched, dust-dominated Jordan Valley 300 metres below Sea Level, reality proves not to be the expected sojourn in limbo but an existential experience. It presents a landscape, not beautiful and picturesque except in the brief bloom of spring, but always magnificent; a landscape sculpted by great earth movements, polished by aeons of wind and weather, not yet all stained by Man's excesses. In a complex web of past and present, in a small country astride one of the world's great political problems, always challenged, caught between a rock and a hard place, living with a chip on the shoulder, anxious for its self-esteem, uncertain of the future, easily offended, not very motivated, Jordan presents a suspicious, brittle society to its expatriates.

As the region's troubled past has been exfoliated époque by époque by archaeologists and historians, there is an insight into the remarkable ability of these peoples to adapt and reinvent themselves. Anne cannot but wonder at the continuity of custom and culture, despite the hazards of history. Perhaps, in this age of information technology, the modernity that is manifesting itself in parts of Amman will appeal to and flow into the rural communities. Anne hopes so.

Chapter 18

Byzantium

What next after Jordan? It is 1997. John at sixty-two has a fine yacht, a Nicholson 32, and Anne now sixty-four has an apartment in a handsome old mansion house in the Borders of Scotland. Anne, in a home of her own at last, reviews over thirty-five years on the overseas circuit; no longer driftwood around Africa and Asia Minor, she is content to hang up her hard hat. She would not have swapped her travelling life but things have changed since John and Anne went to Pakistan in 1962. Gone are the plummy postings they enjoyed in the 1960s and 1970s. The overseas jobs are now in undesirable places such as Libya, Saudi Arabia with its ban on women driving cars, or the Popular Socialist Arab Republic of Syria. Contracts in Ghana, Istanbul and Kenya have been mentioned in the past few years but nothing has come of them.

"We have a job for John," beams a friend in the American consultant engineers head office that was once Sir Alexander Gibb and Partners. "It's Turkmenistan, an ex-Soviet State: needs its water supply rehabilitated. Not an easy place but the pay is good, very good." The Republic of Turkmenistan! It is mostly desert, its temperature ranging from -40°C in winter to +40°C in summer.

"No thanks," John responds, "I'd rather stay in Scotland." This denial is, however, a puffery, a bravado born of discontent, a reluctance to contemplate the blighted sands of Turkmenistan after three years of Arab intransigence in the diffusive dust of the Jordan Valley.

Anne, caught on the horns of a dilemma, recognises that John might need to burn off more energy before facing the mental trauma of retirement. Moving into life in Britain, into life in the Scottish Borders, into life as owner-occupiers of an apartment in a corporate mansion house after so many years cocooned in company housing existing socially as here-today-gone-tomorrow people, promises to be as challenging as setting up in any of the overseas contracts hitherto faced. Someone has to mend Turkmenistan: why not John! Perhaps they should view Turkmenistan as empire building for Britain (sorry, for Europe, nowadays). Anne's ancestors did their share of empire building in the old India from the eighteenth century onwards. Perhaps one more adventure in the world's wild places can be accommodated before retirement. It is said that Ashgabat, the capital of Turkmenistan, has an incomparable weekly carpet market and a passable chamber orchestra.

John remains frustrated; irritable as a bluebottle on a windowpane. "I'm not going to hang around waiting for this Turkmenistan job. I am going to the boat in Antalya (southern Turkey) and I'll get on with jobs on her. There's plenty to do on an old boat."

No sooner does he say this than the phone rings, Head Office on the line.

"John, we want you in Istanbul: it is the Yeşil Çay Contract that has been on the back burner for years. When can you leave? We can bundle quickly through the paper work. What about next week?"

So Istanbul it is. The project, supervision of the building of a water treatment works, appeals to John. But, but: Anne has hung up her hard hat, invested time and energy in the new home in the Scottish Borders. However, she cannot resist Istanbul. Byzantium calls. Anne has begun her travels in Salonika, part of Byzantium in days of yore. She has taken part in the students' *enosis* rally there in 1954, she has spent time in Istanbul helping to copy an ancient mosaic. It is, perhaps, destiny to return and see what changes have taken place: the wheel is coming full circle. Byzantium had such a bad press in the eighteenth century from Edward Gibbon, but John Julius Norwich finds otherwise.[29] It is a nice conundrum.

John flies to Istanbul in mid-December, spending a week on paperwork, provision of a Company car and site visits. It is bitterly cold with a knife wind direct from Siberia. Next morning, half a metre of snow shrouds the city. Undeterred, drivers dig out their vehicles, attempt to drive to work, get stuck, slither on the steep slopes, shout, swear, crunch into other vehicles, cause a log jam of traffic on all the residential roads until the following morning when, with most of the snow melted, drivers can retrieve their abandoned cars. Anne arrives on 20th December. Staying in a company apartment in an up-market residential suburb of the city while the incumbents are away on a month's leave, they tour the adjacent suburbs, orientating and flat hunting.

The Rough Guide to Turkey warns that: 'Flat-hunting for long-term residence can be a time-consuming business'. The first apartment to be viewed in a suitable location near a shopping centre is spacious, with good views from the balcony to the Marmora Sea beyond the city. It is bare of furniture, light fixtures stripped out, hanging wires and truncated pipes in the kitchen indicating where appliances have been positioned. 'Rented accommodation is rarely furnished' reports *The Rough Guide*, adding that 'Buying furniture in the flea markets can be fun.' This flat seems sepulchral and Anne is loath to start hunting for furniture and fittings.

---

[29] Norwich, John Julius, *A Short History of Byzantium,* Viking 1997.

Another flat in the prosperous suburb of Levent is viewed, fully furnished and fitted as though the landlord's family is still in residence.

"We lived here for twenty years" says Mr Aksoy, "But we have just bought an apartment further out of town. This area is becoming a bit commercial."

Tape recorder, sound system, colour television, curtains, china ornaments, pictures of Koranic calligraphy, telephone; all are there. Pots of amaryllis, African violets and cacti in magnificent flowering colour adorning the window sills and balconies suggest that Mrs Aksoy possesses a dominant cultivator gene.

"I have taken most of my plants to our new home," adds Oya Aksoy, "These are just a few left over. I am delighted for you to have them." Such is the rapport between prospective landlord and tenant that the deal seems a foregone conclusion. John glances askance at a pile of mail addressed to the Aksoys.

"Ah yes, you see we have only recently moved. We want to rent this apartment in good order to a good tenant and get a good price for it so that we can afford to send our two sons to university in USA. We will call in each week for mail."

John signs the contract on Christmas Day, moving in on December 27th. That afternoon, they receive their first visitors, Mr and Mrs Aksoy bearing a bottle of whiskey as a goodwill Christmas Present. Luckily, Anne has not yet taken down the framed Koranic texts on the walls.

The flat is on the fourth floor of a residential building with a small creaking lift, and a concierge known as 'Jimmy' living in the basement who collects rubbish, obtains demijohns of drinking water, changes gas bottles, pays their contribution into the electricity office when their bill is presented and will fetch hot loaves of bread on a Sunday morning. There is a pleasant Garden Square to the front and they can just see the Marmora Sea and Princes Islands between the high rise buildings and forest of construction cranes. To the rear, is a line of trees and more apartments, and just round the corners in either direction, are supermarkets. In situation, the district might compare with Richmond, Surrey; it certainly shares the same car parking problems in and around a maze of narrow one-way streets. Anne is not tempted to acquire another car; she can walk to the shops and take a bus to the city centre.

Once in residence, the apartment's various idiosyncrasies are manifested; John spends time fixing electrics, failing only with the tape recorder. As he sees it, the problem is that the interior of the apartment has been modernised since it was built thirty years ago, when furniture was smaller and expectations lower. Bathroom space is minimal since the room houses a massive marble-topped basin suite, a king-sized bath and a clothes washing machine, which works, so long as Anne remembers to place the outflow hose in the bath. A window opens onto the lift shaft and if left open by night, may admit a number of obese cockroaches.

The formal sitting/dining room, with heavy rococo furniture, upholstered Empress Josephine style in oyster brocade, is not as comfortable as the family living room to the rear of the apartment, but it is the only place for meals and has a pleasing balcony for summer living. Kitchen, like bathroom, is minimal having been designed for a sink, four gas rings and a gas bottle. Into the kitchen subsequently have been fitted wall cupboards and cabinets, worktops, an electric oven/grill unit with dishwasher in its lower half, a kitchen table and one chair.

The site and John's office are over on the other side of the Bospherus since the treatment works being built are for Anatolian water sources, which will be fed into greater Istanbul's water supply eventually via a pipeline under the Bospherus yet to be built. The Turkish contractor has a design-and-construct contract, John's position being that of observer on behalf of the funding agent, which is an Arab development bank.

Istanbul does not offer the easiest of living conditions. The city of over twelve million people, shoe-horned into a 1950s plan for a city of five million, is still growing, like Topsy, ad-lib in all directions. Road traffic is indescribable, gridlocked at rush hour, which appears to be much of the day. Anne walks in the suburb of Levent but pavements barely exist; construction, rubble, holes, parked vehicles and a forest of concrete mushrooms designed to prevent pavement parking, frustrate the pedestrian. Walking in the road is risky and worse, may deliver a dirty douche as vehicles whoosh through residual rainwater. Levent and other trendy suburbs, leaping to the twenty-first century aided and abetted by their young, vigorous, upwardly-mobile residents, sport modish boutiques, gimmick novelties, internet outlets, high technology equipment and services: a new branch of Pizza Express opens with the razzmatazz of a celebrity wedding; shopping malls with fast food, loud *musak* and smart bars vie for the well-heeled clientele.

Meanwhile, the elderly and bewildered, leaning on their walking sticks, towing a fat poodle on a lead and carrying a couple of baguettes and a bag of onions, struggle along the non-existent pavements. They might perhaps be more comfortable plucking up courage to move out to the country and grow radishes.

The apartment building houses some middle-class retired couples, most of whom have been in residence twenty years or more and also the rooms of a couple of specialist consultants in psychology or urology. Some are faintly curious about the 'guests' in the Askoys' flat but the language barrier is more than they care to struggle with. Anne's Turkish is too halting for them to understand easily so they give up. Not the concierge's wife though: she has agreed to come weekly and clean the apartment so she must persist. Jimmy Hanim (Mrs Jimmy) has given up long, fast sentences and uses slow, easy questions with plenty of body language. Alas, she has known the apartment in the

Aksoys' residence and automatically rearranges it as she sweeps and dusts.

"Where are the antimacassars?"

"In the cupboard here, clean and safe."

"Do you not like them on the chairs?"

"No, we do not use them in Britain."

"What is your apartment in Britain like?"

"Just like this one" Anne indicates the Aksoys' flat; which is not strictly true, but it serves. They exchange details of their families, remark on the pleasure of living in Levent, observe that Ramadhan is about to start and that the local shops are full of culinary delights and patisserie treats for '*iftar*', the daily evening feast that breaks the fast.

Jimmy Hanim is about forty years of age, has a comfortably ample figure, a Mary-Mother-of-God smile and an abundance of beautiful hair, shining faintly auburn, probably rinsed with henna. It is noticeable how many young women in Istanbul have lovely hair, mostly dark in colour, often long, always well-cut and silken. Stylishly dressed, high-heeled, confident, eye-catching, the ladies seen in and around Levent wear the livery of beauty. Lady Mary Wortley Montagu, whose husband went to Istanbul, the Sublime Porte as she called it, as Ambassador in 1716, remarked on the physical beauty of the young women.[30] In Byzantine times when ladies fell from grace, when an empress, a princess or a concubine needed to be discarded, she was shorn of her hair and immured in a nunnery, this being a fate worse than death, the ultimate humiliation and penalty. For an unwanted emperor, a rival prince or a maladroit vizier, the penalty was blinding or murder, usually strangling by bowstring.

Family come to visit: Marion with her husband Jeffrey and their five-month old daughter, Alice. Having London stock market connections with the travel business, Jeffrey takes up an invitation from Airtours to visit one of their

---

[30] Grundy, Isobel, *Lady Mary Montagu: Comet of the Enlightenment,* Oxford University Press, 1999.

cruise liners now in Istanbul. Built in 1996, accommodating two thousand passengers, this enormous ship is a floating luxury hotel catering for all sorts; teenagers, infants, senior citizens, intellectuals, honeymoon couples, history buffs.

"The Captain has three hundred and fifty for his honeymoon party on this cruise" informs a young, well-polished public relations officer. "Of course, everything is in five languages; Italian, Spanish, English, German and French."

The ship at this moment is an abandoned city; its shopping malls, theatres, gymnasiums, disco halls and restaurants empty and echoing, its cabined residential suburbs the domain of domestic staff.

"Our guests have gone ashore sightseeing. Up to sixty coaches are arranged. Istanbul has a big choice of sites to offer the tourists. We have some coaches for those on a day excursion with lunchboxes and others for those on half-day excursions, coming back to the ship for lunch. Each language has its own bus, naturally."

Later, in town, some of these coaches are seen navigating the threadneedle streets of the old city; numbers 17, 2, 56, 38 and 24 manoeuvre skilfully round congested corners to park at the Saint Sophia Museum. It is an education in logistics.

Saint Sophia, the Church of the Holy Wisdom, was built initially by Constantine the Great soon after he founded his city in AD 330, on the site of a village called Byzantium by the shores of a creek on the Bosphorus. He meant to call his foundation 'The New Rome' but 'Constantinople', city of Constantine, stuck; the name 'Byzantium' being applied to the Eastern Roman Empire to distinguish it from the Roman Empire of the West, ruled from Rome by a brother-in-law, Licinius. Together these two parcels of the Roman Empire extended from modern Iraq to the Scottish Borders, from modern North Africa to Bulgaria. The Empire of the East, Byzantium, gradually adopted the Greek language whilst the Roman Empire of the West, continued in Latin; thereafter there being little common ground and much confrontation between the two halves of the Empire.

Saint Sophia Church, damaged by earthquakes, periodically looted and fired, ruined by rioting in the fifth century, was rebuilt by the Emperor Justinian, much of his construction being there today. Justinian took as his model, King Solomon's temple in Jerusalem, the dimensions of which are found in the Bible's Old Testament in 1 Kings, Chapter 6; it gratifying Justinian's ego to be able to surpass the size of Solomon's masterpiece.[31] The measure of the interior of Saint Sophia is breathtaking, its consummate dome soaring to an apex of neck-stretching limit; the scale dwarfing huge plaques of Koranic calligraphy hung at the Church's conversion to Mosque after the Ottoman conquest in 1453; the whole vastness bringing to mind the turbine hall of a power station as in the Tate Modern in London.

Among excursions Anne and John make from Istanbul, is a *Bayram* holiday to Iznik and Bursa, *Bayram* being the Moslem Eid feast to commemorate Abraham's slaughter of a ram instead of his son Isaac. Passing through the ancient walls of Iznik by a massive gate of Roman origin, rebuilt several times by Byzantine defenders, there is an overpowering farmyard smell; dozens of sheep and some goats are being sold in preparation for the *Bayram* sacrifice on the morrow when devout Moslems the world over ritually kill the animals for the meat feast. Iznik high street is crowded with compulsive shoppers bargaining for shoes, shirts, children's gear, toys, jewellery, everything, this celebration comparing to the Christmas season of presents and treats.

Iznik, in lovely fertile farming country on the shore of a sizeable lake, became a popular Byzantine garden city called Nicaea. It was here in AD 325 that the Emperor Constantine called all the bishops of the Roman Empire to a council meeting. Deep divisions of dogma had arisen in

---

[31] Taylor, Jane, *Imperial Istanbul,* 1B Tauris Ltd, London 1998.

the Christian Church over the nature of Jesus Christ: was he God or Man; equal to or subordinate to God the Father?

The principal protagonists were the Arians, followers of Bishop Arius who claimed that the Son was similar but subordinate to God the Father, and the Athanasians, followers of Bishop Athanasius, who insisted that the Son was divine, a manifestation of God in human guise, as was the Holy Ghost, a manifestation of God in spirit or flame form. The argument, raging for months until mid-July, was only settled when Constantine, no doubt longing to get to his seaside palace at Nicomedia, modern Izmit, banged the table and ruled that Christ was consubstantial; it was God the Father, God the Son and God the Holy Spirit.

Constantine, a Christian since experiencing a moving spiritual incident which confirmed an instinctive sense of divine destiny, a man who saw himself as a monotheist possibly the son of the god Apollo, who had his head portrayed on coins in a multi-rayed halo and who ordained Sun-day as holy, was instrumental in establishing Christianity as the accepted religion of the Roman Empire: his council meeting in Nicaea and his final ruling, a milestone in the Christian Church as well as the basis for the Nicene Creed, was however more about unity in the Empire than doctrinal detail.

Unity within the Christian Church was to remain elusive; obstinate presumption and malice among the leaders dogged the early Church; fanaticism, prejudice and power struggles divided it in later years. The dogmatic divisions manifested at Nicaea in 325 were to continue over the centuries dividing the Western and Eastern Empires by more than miles on the map. The Western Roman Catholic Church, inheriting Constantine's dictum of the Holy Trinity, applied bureaucracy, law and order. The Eastern Orthodox church, regarding Constantine's dictum as deviant, turned to mysticism and ecstasy; spiritual contemplation assumed defence of the True Faith to a degree able to influence politics.[32] Western and Eastern Churches drifted further apart until in 1054, there occured a crisis: in Saint Sophia Church, Constantinople, visiting Catholic legates issued a Papal Bull of Excommunication on the Orthodox Patriarchs. Thereafter, Christianity was irrevocably split by a schism, a religious fault-line; to the West, the Roman Catholic Church and all the Reform and Protestant Churches devolving from it, to the East, all the various national Orthodox Churches.

In modern Iznik, Anne and John are booked in at the Hotel Şener, said to be the most prestigious and sited in the town centre. Shown to a spacious bedroom with private bathroom by a smiling hotelier, they soon discover its shortcomings. There is no hot water, no plug in bath or basin, no central heating for a chilly spring evening and no breakfast next morning. A reconnaissance of the empty hotel suggests that breakfast is normally served from a first floor kitchen; but not on *Bayram* morning. Having packed an electric kettle for emergencies and able to plug it into the shaver point in the bathroom, they are elated to find the electric point operational. A small grocer's shop, open early, supplies the necessities for an ad-lib breakfast.

Poor old Iznik; the sleepy hayseed town is a far cry from elegant, ecclesiastical Nicaea but it possesses a rustic gallantry. Everyone wants to proffer *Bayram* greetings to the foreign visitors walking the walls in the rain. It is impossible to avoid both the Eid butcher business and the constant demand for handshakes and exchange of courtesies.

'*Hoş geldiniz!*' The traditional Turkish welcome compels.

"Where are you from?" and "Are you tourists?" "Ah, you are working. Where? What work?" Anne and John's Turkish language ability can answer these questions in Turkish. Thereafter, floods of further questions defeat them and they must rely on shrugs, nods and grins.

---

[32] Clark, Victoria, ibid.

Next morning is Sunday, the day that clocks in Britain change to summer time. Has the hour changed in Turkey? In general, Turkey keeps in step with Europe but the hotel clock at the Reception desk stands at yesterday's time; the hour has not changed. So to Bursa which is as Paris, London, New York to the country hicks arriving from Iznik. Bustling, efficient, fast-lane city, Bursa is half a century away from Iznik and an hour ahead, having moved its clocks to summer time with the rest of Europe. Iznik is probably still on Greenwich Mean Time. Why change? Farmers and fishermen get up and go to bed by the sun.

Back in Istanbul a friend, Ann O'Neill, arrives from Amman, Jordan, to stay for Easter. They all go to the Anglican Christ Church in the Pera district of Istanbul just across the water of the Golden Horn from the ancient Byzantine and Ottoman city. It is a big, mid-Victorian, neo-gothic edifice, that serves to accentuate the scanty congregation. Hymn book, prayer leaflet and baptism sheet having been handed out, a pew is selected as a group of six VIPs are ushered into the two front rows. The service begins with an awesome procession led by the Anglican vicar, Canon Ian Sherwood, splendidly enveloped in dazzling silks, brocades and embroideries. He is followed by a black-gowned Orthodox Priest in stove-pipe hat; then a train of lace-trimmed and gowned servers, bearers of crosses, chalices and incense dispensers, a choir and what-nots.

This is interesting: Anglican Catholic priest and Eastern Orthodox priest in the same procession together for a service of worship! When one considers the calumnies exchanged between Catholic and Orthodox Churches in the middle ages after the schism of 1054; when one remembers the violence and bloodshed occurring between Christian and Christian at the time of the crusades, this juxtaposition of priests at Easter Eucharist in 1998 is significant.

To recollect for a moment a bit of medieval history, the leaders of the Fourth Crusade to free Jerusalem from the

Saracen decided to go by boat, to ship their armies to the eastern Mediterranean. Only the Venetians had ships enough for this purpose and the price was high, a price determined by the Doge of Venice, Enrico Dandolo, an eighty-plus years old blind but astute businessman and cunning politician, who set a price tag greater than the crusaders could afford. The Doge then accepted a plan to interfere in Byzantium's nefarious politics and agreed to divert the crusader armies to Constantinople for a bit of emperor juggling; Dandolo foreseeing that this would serve to emasculate rival Genoese influence in Byzantine commerce. The Crusade leaders were enticed by a substantial financial contribution to their coffers, and the bait of a promise that a new incumbent on the throne of Byzantium would submit the Orthodox Church of Constantinople to the authority of the Pope in Rome.[33]

Not loath to a bit of fighting and looting, the armies of the Fourth Crusade swept into Constantinople. West European Catholics perceived the Greek-speaking Byzantines who called themselves 'Romans' as heretics, more orientally devious than the Moslem Seljuks, more unscrupulous than the Turkoman tribes now in Anatolia, more threatening than the Saracen. Moreover, Constantinople, known to be the world's richest city, would be a treat to plunder. Nevertheless, the violence of the vandalism following the fall of Constantinople was excessive, the desecration inflicted on holy places and property, outrageous. Eyewitness reports describe looters bringing their horses and baggage mules into Saint Sophia in order to carry off its fittings and furnishings and when the animals slipped on the stone slabs, they were wantonly killed, covering the floor with their blood and excrement. A prostitute, seated on the Patriarch's throne, hurled insults at Jesus Christ and danced bawdily in the holy place. Meanwhile, the canny Venetians, recognising superb craftsmanship, carefully carried away their treasures and

---

[33] Norwich, John Julius, ibid.

shipped them to Venice, including the four bronze horses now on Saint Mark's.

In modern Istanbul in 1998, the Anglican Easter Eucharist starts with a traditional liturgy during which the six VIPs get up and exit through a side door of the nave, presumably a vestry. The congregation is invited to proceed to an aisle and gather around a font, which proves to be a sunken marble bath with marble steps under the surface of the water. The lace-gowned servers are now carrying towels and the six VIPs re-entering in procession, are in their underwear ready for baptism, Byzantine-style. Anne, having heard of adult baptism by total immersion in modern swimming pools, having seen baptistery pools in ancient basilicas either ruined or restored as tourist sights, views this baptism as doing in Byzantium as the Byzantines did; Ann O'Neill, a church warden and elder in the English-speaking Anglican Church in Amman, says she has never seen anything like it; and John thinks it is a lot of mumbo-jumbo. And yet, on 4 May 2001, Pope John Paul II, visiting Athens, apologises profoundly to the Eastern Orthodox Church for atrocities committed by the Western Catholic Church in the thirteenth century Crusade, so perhaps this Byzantine baptism at Easter 1998, can be seen as an element of a rapprochement between Western and Eastern Churches.

Chapter 19

Byzantium Revisited

Anne makes various holiday excursions with old friends who come and stay, visiting spectacular Greco-Roman ruins in Western Turkey. There is also a tour in eastern Turkey of ancient Byzantine churches and monasteries in the company of Ann Powell, the Art History friend of decades, and of Jill who likes remote places such as the so-named 'Georgian' Valleys. Described in *The Rough Guide* as 'bleak, inhospitable and melancholy', this mountainous and inaccessible region of Turkey is represented as Turkey's Siberia, the (Australian) Outback and the North Slope (of Everest) rolled into one. They fly to Erzurum, gateway to the mountainous Georgian region, spending a day there planning their onward journey by bus.

Erzurum, at 2,000 metres altitude, is worlds away from the smart residential suburbs of Levent in greater Istanbul. From the hotel roof terrace, enjoying beer in condensation cold glasses, the vista is panoramic; rolling, windswept steppe converging in waves upon green hills and distant blue mountains. Walking round the market, they admire the cornucopia of vegetables and fruit on offer.

"Are you English?" The voice is unmistakably English; the young woman who accosts them wears the cover-all coat and headscarf badge of Islam. She proffers a hand to shake and smiles warmly.

"My name is Filiz. That means spring tendril in English. I am twenty-three- years old and reading English at Erzurum University. I was born in West Germany and moved to my grandparents' home in Bolu, which is between Istanbul and Ankara, when I was ten. Grandfather speaks English and I want to perfect my English. My flat-mates and I like English conversation with English people."

Your English is excellent," Jill assures her. "We are admiring the lovely produce in your market. Why don't you walk with us and we can talk."

"No, no, I don't have time now. What I want is to invite you to supper in our flat tonight. Come at six o'clock."

"Thank you very much but three guests seems rather a lot at such short notice." It is now four o'clock.

"We feel it is too much to expect of you and your flat-mates," adds Ann.

"On the contrary, they want you to come. Yusuf, my boyfriend, and Arslan will be looking forward to have you spend the evening with us."

"This is unexpected. We have arranged to eat in the hotel tonight."

"Tell them you will be out for dinner," says this control freak adding, rather tartly, "I don't *have* to invite you, do I? I want you to come and eat with us."

In the face of such determination, the three tourists repair to their hotel, wondering what a young woman, who appears devoutly-scarfed and presumably chaste, modern, intelligent and obviously Western in manner, is doing sharing her flat with two males, one of them the current boyfriend to boot.

Ushered upstairs into a second floor student flat, hastily tidied by the look of the books and boots stuffed under the bed, which serves as a seat, Filiz introduces Arslan and her boyfriend, Yusef. As she and her two friends serve coco cola and lay the table, Filiz enlarges upon her hopes and fears.

"I was nineteen when I decided to become a deeply-committed Moslem and wear the long coat and headscarf." She pauses to order Yusef to bring in the food, "And the problem is that the Government has banned headscarves. I must give up my scarf next academic session or be barred from my final year, be denied my final exams."

She directs Yusef and Arslan to finish preparing the food and bring it in, she herself continuing to dwell upon her dilemma. "My parents are modern, you understand. They live in Germany. My mother does not wear a headscarf and my father is furious with me because I have adopted Islamic dress and he says I will waste his big investment in me if I drop out before finals and fail to get my degree. And what's more, I shall be banned from jobs if I wear the headscarf." Her eyes sparkle with elation as she contemplates a possible future martyrdom.

As the meal, of aubergines stuffed with spiced rice and herbs served with a mysteriously spiced macaroni in tomato sauce, all of it delicious, progresses, it become transparently clear that Filiz enjoys dominating her two flat-mates. When she says 'jump' they do so, as do more friends arriving for coffee, which Yusef prepares. She is a strong personality but is she perhaps using the moral high ground of her Islamic uniform, to impose her opinions on as many greenhorns as possible? She wants to change the world: now. She seems to be a little intoxicated by the obvious effect she can exercise upon her companions; appears to be suffering a moderate attack of crazy mixed-up adolescent who has glimpsed vistas of adrenalin-raising excitement in her confrontation with parental and government authority.

Later, back in Istanbul, Melahat, a Turkish friend, comments that people like Filiz are paid by the Mullahs and that the money probably comes from Iran, part of their crusade against the USA and the West. Noticeably, Erzurum is the only provincial Turkish city to have an Iranian Consulate.

Meanwhile, in eastern Turkey, the three tourists take to the local buses, making for the enchanting town of Yüsüfeli where the river Barhal joins the Çoruh river; where the Barhal *Otel* offers basic accommodation and superb cuisine, with cold beer on a balcony barely above the raging river Barhal, a turgid, tawny torrent with a voice like thunder, flung furiously down to the foaming river Çoruh. From Yüsüfeli, a taxi is arranged for the day to visit remote but significant early Byzantine ruins. A hard bargain being driven by the taxi driver, he then assumes an avuncular role, being determined to achieve the difficult destinations in spite of various setbacks arising. The road is blocked by rock-falls, thunderstorms roll ominously around the deep valleys and broken bridges necessitate searches for detours.

Artvin, further down the Çoruh River, is the next stop although the town itself is something of a mystery, being invisible from its bus station on the main road along the Çoruh valley floor. Puzzled and asking for Artvin, they are directed to a shuttle bus, which winds up the hairpin bends of the cliff to the city some 500 metres above. Here is a terraced town of rock and stone built into the valley side, topped by a gannet colony of modern high-rise glass and concrete. Rumour has it that there is not enough flat ground for a football pitch in Artvin, a privation which must be felt keenly by the football-loving Turks. Nevertheless, the town can offer a taxi to remote ruined churches.

No taxi in the region having a meter, the driver again demands an exorbitant price, again asserts patriarchal charge. He plans the route, removes boulders from the track, interrogates villagers about the way ahead, advises on photogenic spots and patiently waits for his flock of three middle-aged tourists. One group of villagers questioned are members of a funeral party, wending their way to a mosque to bury a farmer killed by lightning in yesterday's storm. The taxi driver eyes the sky anxiously and, being reassured, proceeds to a photo stop.

"This is a Georgian bridge." He points to a wooden trolley on a rope and wire pulley. "Does anyone want to go across?" Waving to a farming family all working on the far bank of the tawny torrent he adds, "Look! They are inviting you over. They are sending the trolley for you."

Anne, the sole volunteer, balanced carefully in the middle of the rickety wooden tray and clinging on for dear life, is hauled across and helped out by gallant rustics.

"Hoş geldinez?"

"Hoş buldok!"

"Nasil sinez?"

The exchange of greetings is voluble and sincere. Thereafter, their curiosity is palpable and Anne's limited Turkish language is tried to the hilt. Photographs are taken and this is followed by an exchange of postal address so that copies may be sent to the Turkish family. Pressing an armful of warm, honey-scented ripe apricots into Anne's lap, they haul the trolley and her back to civilisation.

Lunch is in Ardanuç, at a small bistro passed by the driver as usable in this one-horse town. A colossal bun-loaf bastion of red granite rears up behind the small settlement and on top of the hill, stands the silhouette of a massive castle, now the only evidence of a former Byzantine capital city.

The track from Ardanuç proceeds with difficulty, winding up and round and through successive gorge and intermontane plain, until at last the splendid Byzantine ruins are found. The sky, now heavy with pillows of cloud, worries the taxi driver and sightseeing must be limited. Not before time, they begin the return journey. Soon sparks of lightning stab the boiling cloud tops. Then comes the staccato, rifle fire sound that precedes an overhead explosion, a streak of lightning discharges to the heart of the gorge and ricochets around the ravine: the whole episode an epitome of this region's natural perversity. Farming here is not for the faint-hearted. These valleys, remote, high and fertile, accommodate an industrious and innovative people prepared to suffer cruel winters, to cultivate hard in the short, bounteous growing season and to trek far to market. Inaccessible montane pastures offer opportunities to outweigh the challenges. Modern Georgian farmers are vibrant, industrious, tolerant and masters of their rugged environment: who, at the turn of the twenty-first century, would habitually cross a raging river in a tiny trolley slung from a bit of wire? This is a far cry indeed from the safe, comfortable Europe that Anne knows.

Back in Istanbul again, a weekend pleasure is to drive down steep twisting roads from Levent to the Bosphorus shore, to walk along the front avoiding the singing lines of casting fishermen, to peer into their plastic pails of tiddlers and to enjoy a fish takeaway from a moored boat. Pan fried fish fillet in half a baguette garnished with tomato and onion slices, a sliver or two of pickled gherkin, all sprinkled with salt, is mouth-watering. Whatever the delights of a fish baguette, there are few summer treats in Istanbul more delightful than an alfresco fish luncheon in one of several posh and pricey restaurants along the Bosphorus. A favourite watering hole occupies a disused landing stage where one can watch the busy shipping in and out of the Black Sea as well as the local waterbuses, excursion boats and various private craft.

Onshore, across the road from the restaurant, stands the vast *Rumeli Hisar*, the 'Romei Castle', planned, designed and constructed by Sultan Mehmet II and his troops prior to his assault on Constantinople. Mehmet, a brilliant linguist and gifted engineer, an able scientist and historian with a talent for organisation and an eye for the main chance, completed the monstrous edifice of *Rumeli Hisar* in just twenty weeks: he was then nineteen years of age. His final onslaught on the Byzantine capital on Tuesday 29 March 1453 took only six hours before it was all over.[34] And to

---

[34] Crawley, Roger *Constantinople: The Last Great Siege 1453,* Faber and Faber 2005.

this day, many a Greek will shun Tuesdays for any significant action.

The Byzantine Empire lasted eleven hundred years. Given the historical facts, there is no denying that it occupied world centre stage as a commercial hub of wealth, stability, power and oriental splendour; a legend in its time. The testimony of magnificent buildings, churches and palaces all over the Empire, not just in Constantinople, bears witness to long periods of security, to master builders with patrons' money to spend: superb mosaics, painted icons, frescos and sculpture speak of consummate craftsmen and artists employed by seriously rich patrons. Such wealth is not the result of poor government.

On the other hand, Byzantium also acquired a reputation for intrigue, indolence, internecine rivalry, greed, corruption, scandal, sexual deviation, distrust and Machiavellian machination. The adjective 'byzantine' in modern usage, is applied to describe an administration of such complexity, of such rigid hierarchy and labyrinthine connection, that it fails to deliver.

A third strand in any contemplation of Byzantium must be religion. Constantine I was responsible for instituting Christianity as the state religion. Thereafter, state and Christianity were inextricably linked. Costumed in Byzantine court dress, its furnishings, decorations and art emblazoned with gold, with colours of ruby, sapphire and emerald, the Christian Church of the East flourished during the centuries of Goth and Hun invasion in Western Europe; unfolding in step with its Byzantine government. Oriental mysticism, convoluted bureaucracy and internecine sectarian intrigues, thriving in the basilica (the word from 'basil', king), nevertheless succeeded in keeping alive literacy, learning and the splendid heritage of ancient Greece and Rome. No mean achievement!

Upon capturing the city, Mehmet II, The Conqueror, rode into town, declared Saint Sophia Church to be a Mosque and forbade all looting and violence. Istanbul, a contraction of 'Islamopolis', came into being, capital of the Ottoman Empire, which was to continue until the end of World War I in Europe in 1918.

It was not sudden death to Byzantium. From the eleventh century onwards, the Byzantine Empire had been living with the Selçuk and Ottoman Turk Empires. Territory exchanged hands, yes, but culturally and socially, the two empires became entwined, embraced each other, giving occasion to an explosion of architectural creativity.

Islam tolerated Christianity. More specifically, Islam respected Orthodoxy as a monotheistic religion; the more so after Catholic Christianity's attack on Constantinople in the Fourth Crusade when the Christianity of the Three Gods, the Trinity, assaulted the Christianity of the one God, that is Orthodoxy. And Islam shared with Orthodoxy an interest in the esoteric; in mystery and ecstasy as expressed in Sufiism and the whirling Dervish Sect.

The Turks, conscripting and assimilating Christians into their administration, carried on with the tradition of palace and basilica-like mosque construction after the Fall of Constantinople. The Suleymaniye Mosque in Istanbul was built, a century before Christopher Wren designed Saint Paul's Cathedral in London, by a Christian engineer/architect called Mimar Sinan. Modelled on Saint Sophia, it inspires by its interior expanse soaring to splendid dome. And the Selimiye Mosque in Edirne, Sinan's crowning architectural masterpiece, possesses a fascinating interior which marries space and daylight under an immense dome, creating an aura of awe and sanctity. The *Topkapi Sarayi*, built like a Byzantine palace as an assembly of pavilions, courts, gardens and chambers and now a magnificent museum, houses wonderful ceramics, jewels, illuminated manuscripts, crafted ivory, gold and wood; all of which uphold the Byzantine tradition of outstanding artwork.

In Western Europe, the Fall of Constantinople was viewed as a disaster of the first order, a barbarous affront to all that was Romano-Greek; in other words, the civilised world. The Byzantine Empire was in fact geographically now no more than the city itself, a strip along the north shore of the Dardanelles, a few Aegean Islands and the Greek Peloponnesus. Thither the Greek-speaking Orthodox Christian refugees from the city fled, taking all they could carry; travelling also to Venice, of course, to the Balkans, to Russia, Rumania and Cyprus.

As mentioned earlier, in Chapter 1, Lawrence Durrell opines in his book, *Bitter Lemons of Cyprus*, that Byzantium 'is the true parent of Modern Greece' to which may be added, and of Cyprus too. It was also observed in Chapter 1 that Greece and Cyprus followed different paths to freedom from Ottoman rule; Greece gaining independence in the nineteenth century and taking a Hellenic moniker rather than a Byzantine one, while Cyprus, that true bastion of the Byzantine legacy, remained in Ottoman hands until the end of World War I when it was given to Britain. *Enosis,* unity with Greece, was to follow in the 1950s.

Anne had, as a member of the Edinburgh University Expedition to Salonika, taken part in light-hearted *Enosis* marches alongside Salonika University students. But by 1955, *Enosis* became violent under a gang of terrorists with the acronym EOKA; the *Ethnarch*, spiritual and political chief executive officer of the Cyprus Orthodox church, Archbishop Makarios backing their violence with unlimited Church funds. The Byzantine dream of restoration, cherished through five hundred long years, was making yet another attempt to reinstate Byzantium, to raise again the standard of the double-headed eagle.

In 1960, with Britain giving up its millstone colony of Cyprus and Makarios being elected President of the new Republic, the real struggle for Cyprus began, Makarios and the Byzantine diaspora in Russia and the Balkans still having an opportunist eye for the main chance. As Victoria